BUILDER'S APPRENTICE

BUILDER'S APPRENTICE

ANDREW J. HOFFMAN

a memoir

10 9 8 7 6 5 4 3 2 1

ISBN: 978-193239924-0

HURON RIVER PRESS
PO Box 7797
Ann Arbor, MI 48107-7797
www.huronriverpress.com

Printed in the United States of America.

LIBRARY OF CONGRESS CATALOGING-IN-PUBLICATION DATA

Hoffman, Andrew J., 1961-
  Builder's apprentice : a memoir / by Andrew J. Hoffman.
    p. cm.
  ISBN 1-932399-24-0
  1. Hoffman, Andrew J., 1961- 2. House construction--United
States--Biography. 3. Architects and builders--United States--Biography. 4.
Apprentices--United States--Biography. 5. House construction--United
States--Case studies. 6. House construction--Massachusetts--Nantucket
Island--History--20th century. 7. House
construction--Connecticut--Fairfield County--History--20th century. 8.
Creative ability--Case studies. 9. Vocation--Case studies. I. Title.
TH4809.U6H64 2010
  690.092--dc22
  [B]
                              2010002906

For my father

WHEN I WAS TWENTY-SIX, I fell in love. The object of my affection was not a woman, but a house, an extraordinary house that sits atop a gently sloping hill along a rural highway in southwestern Connecticut. It is a house that distracts drivers into averting their eyes from the road as they navigate the oncoming bend; a house that that lures guests to explore its many facets when invited inside; and a house that most builders would give their eye-teeth to have the chance to build, many waiting a life time for such a contract, and most never attaining it. That is why I was in love. Twenty years ago, *I was the builder of that extraordinary house.*

That love affair continues today. The house enchants me each time I see it. But it is not just the house itself that draws me. It is my intimate connection with it. When I look at the house, I see what everyone else sees, but I know much more, what people can't see. I know every leg of its structure and every square inch of its surfaces. I see both the beauty of the craftsmanship and recall the tradesmen that added their own particular skill to create it. I see the history of how it came to be; the plans as they were originally drawn, the alternatives that were considered, the changes that were made and the obstacles that had to be overcome. I see the anguished decisions of the clients and feel the frustration of helping them through that anguish. The memories pour over me each time I walk through its halls, rooms, porches, gardens, basements and attics; memories that present and future owners will never have.

This was the first of a series of houses that I can claim as my accomplishments as a builder, each one larger and more complex than the last. These were no ordinary homes. They were mansions, estates, whatever word you choose to define something so rare. They were on a scale and level of detail I had never imagined before. They ranged in size from five thousand square feet to almost thirty thousand, the latter able to swallow up the house of my youth more than ten times over. They sat on lots that ranged from two acres to nearly two hundred. They were custom-designed to the finest detail and to the owner's particular desires and tastes. Whatever the owner wanted, that was what the owner got. These homes were the standing product of what the owner wished, translated through architects and engineers and made real by the builder; *me.*

But what is most extraordinary about these accomplishments is not just that I was the builder, but that just two years prior, I had no credentials to claim such a title; that is, save one. I had a passionate and overwhelming belief that I had found my *calling* as a builder. I believed that this was what I was meant to be doing, and I threw myself into it completely. I quit everything that had been my short life thus far—a college degree, a suit and tie, an engineering job, graduate school acceptances, a close circle of friends—and set out on a new path, one that, for the first time, I had chosen for myself.

It was no easy transition. As I look back, I see the trials and challenges of how I grew from an enthusiastic novice, to a scared journeyman and finally, to a self-assured builder. The beginning of this path was a combination of wrenching soul-searching and extraordinary good fortune. I still marvel at how I stumbled into the mysterious world of fine, custom home building; a private world of extremely wealthy and demanding clients; a world where the best builders do not advertise. Such an act of self-promotion would betray the exclusivity of their service. In this world the most sought after builders are not hired; they are solicited. They are only found through private referral and a reputation built by years of satisfied clients. One cannot simply enter the world of custom building on this level. But I did. I unwittingly entered this world with one phone call to a custom builder named Jack Schneider.

As I look back at my life after that fateful phone call, I see a structure for retelling it. In a way, the journey resembled that of a monk entering the monastery. According to the rules of St. Benedict, there are six steps to becoming a monk, steps that can take as long as five years to complete. First, a man enters as an *Aspirant,* visiting the monastic community and sharing in prayer and work. After having lived the lifestyle, he is asked to leave the monastery and return to the world for consideration of a more serious commitment. This is called *Discernment*. If he determines that this is still the right choice for him, he then enters the community as a Postulant and starts training as a *Novice*. From there, he progresses through the stages of *Junior* and *Senior* monk.

It was not my intention to walk through these stages when I entered the world of fine home building, and in the midst of the process I did not see this progression taking place. But upon reflection after 20 years of distance, I see parallels between the commitment and conversion that I went through and that which a monk goes through. I was moving from white-collar to blue-collar work, from engineering calculations at a desk to physical labor in the field, from a job to a calling. And in this process of transition, I adopted a new identity, becoming something different than what my life thus far had taught me to be, by completely immersing myself in a new culture and adopting its rules and beliefs as my own. It was a journey that has left an indelible mark on me; one that I will never forget because it is part of who I am now. I am indebted to those who guided me through it all; some for altruistic reasons, others less so.

In the retelling of this story, the events and people I describe are all true. They are based on my personal experience building houses in Nantucket, Massachusetts and Fairfield County, Connecticut in the 1980s. The names and some of the locations have been changed, not for legal reasons, but to protect the privacy of the people I met, worked for, worked with and now write about. In the case of the Shaw House chapter, I have condensed experiences from two houses into the tale of one house for the sake of clarity and simplicity. But none of the details of the houses have been altered or exaggerated in any way. I would like to thank my editor, Gene Young, and my publishers, Steve and Shira Klein, for helping me bring this story to life.

Andrew J. Hoffman
Ann Arbor, Michigan

PROLOGUE

"**H**ELLO, S&S CONSTRUCTION." His greeting was simple, but sharp and abrupt. It made me feel like an unwelcome intruder and fueled my fear that I had no business making this phone call. On my desk, atop engineering reports awaiting my review, lay the help wanted section of the *Boston Globe,* a red circle highlighting one ad among many others that had already been "X"'d out. Next to the newspaper, lay two graduate school acceptance letters, one from Harvard and one from Berkeley, impatiently awaiting my answer. But my attention was on the newspaper ad that had prompted my call.

Carpenters needed on Nantucket, top pay,
housing provided, call Jack, 617-555-1212.

Timidly, I asked, "Is this Jack? I'm calling about the ad for carpenters."

"Yeah, this is Jack Schneider. How much experience you got?"

I squirmed. The other calls ended with the same question and the admission that I, in fact, had very little. Each time I was rejected I added another red "X" to the page, moved down the list and redialed the phone. This was looking to be another short conversation.

Careful to keep my voice low so as not to arouse the attention of those in the adjacent office cubicles, I began my pitch. "Well, I really don't have much, but I'm willing to learn. My father taught me some things and I just helped a friend build a deck. Her father is a contractor and says I have the skills to do this kind of work."

"Then why doesn't he hire you?" Jack asked.

Stung by the comment, I was at a loss for how to respond.

"Do you have a job now?" Jack continued.

"Yes, I'm an engineer in Boston." I answered, quickly adding, "But, I'm not happy with this job and want to learn how to build houses. Trust me, I work very hard and I'm a fast learner."

Silence hung. I worried that I sounded too pleading, too desperate. Doubt reentered my mind that this was a crazy idea; no one would hire a carpenter without tested carpentry skills.

Finally Jack said, "We'd have to meet to discuss this. I can't do it over the phone. You have to come to Nantucket."

My heart raced. Without hesitation, I blurted out, "Yes, I can do that. How do I get there?" and instantly felt foolish. It came out too quickly, too honestly. Who would trust someone who didn't even know how to find the job he was applying for?

"PBA has flights every hour from Boston. If you catch the flight tomorrow morning at nine, I'll pick you up at the airport."

"Okay, I can do that," I answered excitedly.

"What do you look like so I can find you?" Jack asked.

"I have light brown hair, blue eyes, medium build." I paused. "I'll wear khakis and a light blue oxford."

"Fine. I'll meet you at the gate. I have light brown hair. I'll be in a black blazer."

THOUGH THE YEAR WAS 1986, the PBA flight was an old DC-3, the kind of plane that Ingrid Bergman boarded at the end of *Casablanca*. As I stepped inside, I entered a new world. Once airborne, I studied the unfamiliar surroundings; the tiny cabin, the noisy propeller outside my window, a muddy trickle of oil streaming back along the wing, the blue sky beyond and the green ocean below. Before long, my mind drifted off to what had driven me to this illogical trip.

Recently, and for the first time, I had grown to wonder what I was doing with my life. Every life decision I had made to that point seemed automatic. I went to college because that is what was expected. It was merely a continuation of high school: grades thirteen through sixteen. In 1983, I graduated from college, ending four uneventful years in which I was taught by the faculty of chemical engineering. I dutifully studied thermodynamics, heat transfer and physical chemistry. Outside classes, when I might have been considering why I was studying these topics and what I hoped to accomplish, I instead spent my time drinking beer with my friends.

When I graduated, I was faced with a sudden recognition that I wasn't really sure what to do with my degree. Why did I pick chemical engineering? This decision got as much thought as my decision to go to college in the first place—very little. I knew that chemical engineering was considered the toughest major in the university so it had to be a worthy achievement in itself. This was hardly a thoughtful reason to pick a lifelong profession, but in truth, it was all I had. To satisfy anyone who asked, I said that my choice was based on my aptitude for math and chemistry.

But, I soon found that such trite reasoning held little sway when seeking a job. When I interviewed with recruiters from companies like Dow, DuPont and Monsanto, I fumbled through the conversations, unable to confidently answer questions about my goals and aspirations. As I didn't really know what it was supposed to mean to be a chemical engineer, I was at a loss to tell them what kind of engineer I was going to be. I had assumed that recruiters would tell me what I was supposed to do for them. I would simply turn myself over to them as I had to my professors and I would be guided on to the next step in life, continuing to do what I was expected to do; just following the path of least resistance; trying to fit in. But they were looking for me to tell them where I wanted to go. And I couldn't.

I found a job with the Environmental Protection Agency, an opportunity that energized me. In college, I had a minor in environmental sciences after a brief moment of inspiration from the horrific images of toxic waste at Love Canal. I decided that I wanted to clean up the environment and now with the EPA I was going to do it. I took an apartment in Boston and worked hard at my nine-to-five job. But after two years with the federal government, I grew restless. I didn't feel as if I fit as a federal employee and I didn't feel that I was cleaning up the environment. I felt that I was mostly generating paperwork.

So, in searching for satisfaction, I fell back on what had been ingrained in me from my upbringing. To grow and find new opportunities, the answer was a masters degree; grades seventeen and eighteen. I decided that if I got more schooling in public policy, I could move up the ranks of government and then find the satisfaction I sought. It would look great on my resume, and it would be a natural linear progression of what was expected of me. That I hadn't fully considered the foundation of that progression was irrelevant to my thinking at the time. In terms of what I then saw as a career, it fit. I applied to the best schools for public policy and got what I asked for when Harvard and Berkeley accepted me.

But then I froze. I looked at the offer letters and for the first time questioned what I was doing. I was not feeling better, but worse, and I panicked. What was going on? Where exactly was this going? I didn't know. Clearly a degree from one of the most prestigious schools in the world was what I was supposed to do, wasn't it? To everyone else, particularly those in my family, it seemed to be the right thing to do, and normally that would have been enough for me. But now I wasn't sure.

To work out my dilemma, I read career self-help books, but they were of little help. I talked it over with friends, but most seemed unable to articulate what their careers meant to them. My girlfriend, Diane, was one exception. A strong woman, she was clear in what she wanted and seemed to be free of any of the self-doubt or self-analysis that consumed me. While sympathetic to my plight, she laughingly viewed my consternation as a form of masochism, summing me up several times, "Andy, your problem is you think too much." One critical piece of advice she offered was that I should meet with a career counselor; a profession I did not even realize existed. And so I did. Finding one in the yellow pages, I arranged to meet him. But the meeting began badly when he outlined his fees, a sum that was far beyond my reach. Out of pity, he gave me twenty free minutes to discuss my predicament. And during the discussion, a strange thing happened. When he began suggesting ideas for fields of work, he stopped suddenly and smiled.

"You should see your face right now. It just lit up when I mentioned house building."

I blushed and said, "I always thought it would be cool to build houses. But I don't know how." I shrugged, "I have no experience."

"Then you'll have to figure out how to get that experience. And you'll have to take a chance. Chances are necessary to find any opportunity."

It sounded like a stock line as he smiled a self-satisfied grin, pleased with himself at having solved my problem. He ended the meeting with a cheery, "Nothing ventured nothing gained!"

Sure, I thought, he could be bright and cheery. He knew what he was doing with *his* life. I didn't and I wanted someone to tell me what to do with mine, not simply recite glib quotes and canned remarks. But an obstacle had been dislodged, even if only slightly. I had felt it. House building! I could feel something stir inside me, not in my head, but my gut. I had no data, no analysis, no reasoning to justify this as a profession. I just had a feeling that this is what I should be doing. And that was enough. I hoped it was a seed that might, if cultivated, grow into something strong enough to carry me forward.

Again, I fell back on what I still believed was the answer to all such challenges. I began to look for schools that taught carpentry. But those I found were expensive and none offered the training I wanted, focusing instead on specialized types of carpentry, like cabinet-making. It seemed I was finally asking the right questions, but I did not know how to answer them. And I couldn't find anyone to answer them for me. I, for the first time, knew that I had to answer them for myself. I had come to the sudden realization that unless I intervened in my own life now, it would follow the path set by what was expected of me by others and started for me by the naïve seventeen year old kid who thoughtlessly followed the path of least resistance seven years earlier.

WHILE I WAS EMBROILED in the angst of finding purpose in my life, Diane was busy having fun in hers. With some money she had saved, she bought a cabin in New Hampshire for weekend getaways. Resting on a hillside, it had a deck that hovered over the lake below. But the deck needed to be rebuilt. Diane's father, Jeff, was a contractor from New York and offered to do it. He recruited me and two other friends as his crew; a week was set aside, materials were ordered, and work began.

It was my first and only real taste of building. The four of us worked tirelessly for three days and throughout, the seed that had started with the career counselor's comment, continued to grow inside me. It was a feeling I did not fully understand and could not explain. It was simply a feeling of joy. When the deck was finished and the tools were packed away, I relished the feeling. I couldn't resist the desire to look at the deck, stand on it, smell it.

As I admired the deck, I was drawn in deeper. I scrutinized every nail head, every saw mark. I studied how each row of decking formed a straight line along its entire length, matching the plank on its right and left. I studied the gaps between the planks for uniformity, noticing even the slightest deviation. The grain of the wood possessed a beauty I had never noticed before. Although all of the planks were the blonde of fresh lumber, the waving grain of each was different and appealing in its own way. Knots marked random spots on the surface. Knots, I had learned from trial and error, were also too hard to drive a nail through and forced an alteration in the nailing pattern of two per board, one inch from either side.

I recalled the simple logic explained to me while we were building it. "The three most important things in carpentry" Jeff explained, "are *plumb, level and square.*" I could now see how all the individual parts of the deck worked together to fulfill that logic. I could see all these things because I felt what could best be described as an intimate connection with the deck.

I saw the process of how it came to be, and I could connect that process to the satisfying ache in my muscles. I knew the history of each piece and how it went from being part of a lumber pile to how it was cut, fit and connected to become part of the whole. I loved the tactile sensations of pulling a piece of wood from the pile, passing the saw through it, smelling the sawdust as it flew into the air, feeling the wood yield to my hammer as I drove nails into it. I could see hammer marks where I had missed a few. I could see rough edges where my sawing was not as precise as I would have liked. But regardless of the mistakes, despite the flaws, I was infatuated. I had built it! I had taken a random collection of lumber and given it a new life and purpose. I had been guided by Jeff and was part of a team of two others, but I felt a special ownership, a special connection, something I had never experienced before.

To celebrate the deck's completion, Diane threw a party, barbecuing corn and steaks on the grill. I joined in the celebration but was distracted by the excitement that had been growing within me through the week. In a moment alone with Jeff, I asked a question that I had not really formed until I articulated it. "Jeff, do you think I could be a carpenter?"

Jeff laughed. "Andy, you don't want to do that. They're a tough lot."

"Seriously Jeff, do you think I could do it?"

"Andy, from what I saw, you've got the aptitude and you could pick up the skills fairly quickly. It's not rocket science. But, carpentry's a hard life. It's not for you."

But while he was trying to dissuade me, I had heard enough to find encouragement. "Maybe you're right," I confessed outwardly and let the matter drop. But inside, the idea had taken root and to my surprise, the paralysis that had gripped me about graduate school was loosening. A decision was germinating. I decided to explore the help-wanted pages for carpentry openings. I rationalized the irrationality of such a decision by telling myself, "what harm could it do to just look?" And that was the beginning of a pleasantly slippery slope of searching all week for carpentry jobs that left me now seated on an airplane, traveling to an island I had never visited before, to interview for a job for which I had few qualifications, all while neglecting the job for which I had been trained and the graduate schools offers on my desk. It felt great.

THE HEAVY PLANE PULLED to a stop and the two engines quit their violent labor by exhausting one last gasp of smoke. I stepped out of the plane, breathed in the damp sea air mixed with the scent of pine and scrub brush, both of which bordered the airport. I took off my coat to reveal my pre-agreed attire, crossed the open tarmac and entered the small terminal, empty of life so early before the tourist season. On the other end, a lone man waited.

"Hi, I'm Jack," he said.

His full head of light brown hair was combed back in a casual wave, projecting a youthful appearance. I learned later that he was forty-three, but he looked younger. His weathered face was square and he had a strong jaw. He wore a chamois shirt, tight faded jeans and tan work boots, all impeccably clean and neat. His shirt-sleeves were rolled up, revealing a large tattoo on his right forearm. Above all, I could smell his cologne.

"Hi, I'm Andy. It's a pleasure to meet you."

We shook hands. Jack's grip was firm, sure, and deliberate. But he said nothing. He simply nodded and led me out of the terminal. I watched his walk, and felt his physical presence. He filled his space with a barrel-chested, six-foot frame. He took command of it. He was a strange mix of opposing impressions. He gave me the sense that he was capable of great ferocity if provoked, yet he carried his brute frame with ease; his appearance of physical power was softened by the understated way he dressed.

"I thought you were going to be in a black blazer?" I asked, trying to make small talk.

Jack just pointed to his truck, a black Chevy Blazer. I smiled but he didn't notice the humor of the misunderstanding. We got in and Jack started to drive. Like his clothes, the truck was immaculate, very little dirt outside and none that I could detect inside. And now, in these close quarters, the smell of cologne was overpowering.

"I'll take you to the jobsite. Show you around. You'll meet my son, Neil, the foreman. You'll also meet the other carpenters; Eric, one of my other sons, and Larry."

The sky was overcast and the air was damp. "Is it like this often?" I asked.

"Yeah, the planes get fogged in a lot. You shouldn't have any trouble today. But the airport is on the south side of the island and gets fog when other parts of the island stay clear. It was a dumb place to put it."

We drove east on Milestone Road, through the village of Sciasconset. "Sconset," as Jack pronounced it, is a small collection of former fishing shanties, now expensive vacation retreats, each one backed up against the next. All were adorned in the same way: tan cedar shingles with white trim. In fact, all the houses I had seen wore the same color scheme. The roads were empty of people and cars, the vacation season having not yet begun. The grey sky cast a pall over the town, completing the feeling of loneliness. Winding our way through the tiny streets of the village, we emerged on the other side and continued beyond town until we reached a small dirt driveway leading through thick, tall brush that hid the house within. Above, the Sankaty Head lighthouse loomed over the bluff and the ocean beyond.

The large house had the same signature markings of a Nantucket house: white trim along the corners and the edges of the roof and tan cedar shingles. The roof was already covered with the requisite cedar, not yet turned the weathered gray of the other houses. But the walls were not yet done. The windows interrupted a white plastic covering marked with the words "Tyvek." Several carpenters were at work to remedy that deficiency. I could smell the sweet aroma of cedar the instant I opened the truck door.

The yard was impeccably neat; an emerging pattern. A dumpster rested in the driveway and lumber was stacked in piles inside the two-car garage. I counted four decks from this side of the house and at least twice as many doors to the inside. A large white box truck with the words "S&S Custom Builders" emblazoned on the side was parked in front.

As we stepped inside the house, I was instantly caught by my ability to see clear through the unfinished space, a mass of geometrical shapes, angles and parallel lines created by the framing. I could walk from room to room without using doorways. My footsteps sounded hollow as I walked across the plywood floors. I slid my shoe and felt the soft scrape of sawdust that permeated the space. The air was thick with the sweet smell of wood. My pulse began to quicken. It was beautiful.

As we walked, I could hear the carpenters on the outside of the house, sounds of saws and hammers. And always the sound of talking, sometimes joking, sometimes giving instructions, "Cut that at four inches." "Where do ya wanna end the last course?" I was thrilled at the rawness of it all; the smell, the look, the feel, the sound.

Jack walked upstairs and I followed. He introduced me to someone who was unmistakably his son. Although twenty years younger, he had the same barrel frame, chiseled face, and light, wavy hair.

"Andy, this is my son Neil. He's running this job."

I extended my hand. "It's a pleasure to meet you."

Neil locked eyes with mine and responded with a firm grip like his father. Yet he carried himself in a more brooding way. His was not as self-assured. "Nice to meet you too," he said in a short and impersonal way. His curtness gave me an uneasy feeling. I worried that he may be unhappy about my being considered for a job. Did he have other ideas about picking his crew?

The three of us walked through the house with Jack doing all the talking. Pointing out the different features, he explained that the house had three floors with a total of five thousand square feet, and another five thousand square feet on its seven decks. He called it an "upside down house." The bedrooms were on the first floor. The living room, kitchen, dining room and master bedroom suite were on the second. The third floor was a small study with decks on either side. A spiral staircase that wasn't yet built would provide access. As we walked the job, I felt increasingly the foreigner. I had never been in a house project before, let alone one this big.

"We run a pretty tight ship here. Isn't that right Neil?" Jack proclaimed, nodding approvingly towards his son.

"That's right," he responded and nodded obediently back.

"Yeah, this is one strong mother-fuckin' house," Jack said forcefully. "When we built the first floor deck, we parked three pickup trucks on top. There's a picture of it in the building inspector's office." Turning to me, he beamed, "What do ya think of that?"

I felt uncomfortable at the unabashed cursing and boasting. I wasn't used to it. And I felt awkward about how I was supposed to reply. "Impressive" was the best I could muster.

"Impressive huh?" Jack said. Pausing for a moment, seeming to digest my answer, he walked out onto the nearby deck with Neil and me in tow. "This'll impress ya. See that salt marsh over there? The owner wanted to see that pond from this deck," he said, pointing out over the brush and then down to emphasize his point. "So before we started, we built a platform, placed a chair on top and told him to have a seat." Laughing, he said, "then we raised and lowered his ass with pump-jacks till he was satisfied with his view. When he said 'good', we shot the elevation and built the house to meet it." Pounding the railing, he concluded with no trace of modesty. "That's how ya build a goddamned custom house."

I smiled in appreciation, still awkward about whether I was showing proper admiration. It was clear that the deck was well positioned, offering a clear view of the blue marsh, followed by a stretch of sandy beach and the greenish blue of the Atlantic just beyond. But his boasts carried an urgent expectation that a specific response was required; and I didn't quite know what kind.

Jack explained that he had been involved in the actual building of the house only until it was framed. "That's when I turned it over to Neil. He's been in charge since then and doing a great job." He smiled and nodded at Neil.

Neil nodded in reply.

"Well, you seen enough?" Jack asked abruptly, signaling the end of the visit.

I nodded yes and he concluded, "Okay, let's go talk some business."

"I'd be glad to have you join the crew," said Neil. Shaking my hand, he added with forced gravity, "I appreciate a man who looks me in the eye when he shakes hands."

JACK DROVE ME TO A SMALL, modest house in the middle of the island; nothing like the one being built. Giving me a tour that involved no more than five steps, Jack showed me the two bedrooms for the carpenters, two twin beds per room, immaculately clean and neat, and pointed to a bedroom down the hall and explained that it was his. We turned around and sat at the kitchen table.

"That was some house, huh?" Jack asked proudly.

Until now I had remained relatively quiet, unsure what to say or what questions to ask. Worried that I may be making a bad impression, I forced a question. "Who's it being built for?"

Jack leaned confidently back in his chair. "That house is being built for a very important and powerful man. You ever heard of Amalgamated Products?"

"Of course, everyone's heard of AP." I thought the question a bit absurd.

"Well that house is for the CEO of AP, Alfred Rogers. What do ya think of that?" Jack smiled.

Again, I felt pressure for some appropriate level of approval. And, again I didn't know what to say, so I nervously nodded and replied, "Wow. That explains why it's so big."

"Andy, tell me why you're doin' this?" Jack asked, abruptly shifting to a serious tone. "What's a college educated engineer doing down here talking about a carpentry job?"

"Well, I'm not sure I can explain," I began honestly. "I'm not happy with the professional track I'm on. I've never stopped to ask what I want out of life and just went to college without knowing why." I paused, searching for how to say what I was feeling. "I don't know if this makes any sense. I guess I just need to do something I'm really excited about. I'm excited to learn about building, more excited than I've felt for anything else I've done so far in engineering, so here I am. It's as simple as that."

"Okay, I can respect that," Jack said, nodding with approval. "When I first looked at ya, I wondered if you were just another of them smart-ass college punks." He sneered and looked past me as he added, "a lot of kids today don't wanna make a name for themselves. They just wanna buy one. They wanna buy their way into the right school to get the right job. Then they buy the right car, the right clothes, the right house; all so someone else can tell them that they done good. It's all just bullshit."

He seemed angry, as if this had been inside him for years, pouring out at the slightest opportunity. But then he stopped, bottled his emotion, looked up at me in a more approving way and said, "But maybe you're different. I like ya. And I'm willing to take a chance. Here's why. I'm impressed that you wanna pick yourself up by your bootstraps and make something of yourself.

That takes a lot of guts and I respect that. We can give this a try and see how it works. I'll start you at ten dollars an hour. Whadaya think?"

A wave of conflicting emotions flooded over me. I felt a strange surge of pride at his endorsement and realized that I had become impressed by him through the afternoon. I admired his confidence. His tone, his gestures, his choice of words projected a sense of strength that, by my simply being in his presence, spilled over into me. His affect was so powerful and so immediate that his approval now mattered to me. When he railed against people who didn't want to earn a name for themselves, I felt like he was saying that I was not one of them. When he told me that he respected my desire to pick myself up by my bootstraps, I felt he was telling me that we were alike, and I felt strengthened by that association. But I was also startled at the speed with which his offer had come.

Before I could answer, he continued, "Now, keep in mind, I'm paying you as an independent contractor. I won't take any taxes out. That's your business." With a knowing smirk, he added, "That should help you decide what to do."

My mind raced. His decision to hire me was sudden. A lot of his words and actions were sudden, catching me off guard. Once again, I felt the now familiar pressure to conform to him. I had expected to have more time to think it over but rushed my mind to compute the offer. I had done a rough calculation of how much I'd like to be paid and this was within that range. I wasn't quite sure what the implications of being an independent contractor were, but with what he was offering, I could continue to pay off my school loans and have some left over. Jack waited expectantly for a reply.

"Yes, I'll take it," I said quickly, afraid I might change my mind if I hesitated to think about it too much. The answer came from my gut, as I was feeling swept along by the feelings that had begun when I arrived.

"Good, can you start next week?"

"Whoa, I have to give two week's notice and get myself down here. That'll take more time."

"Okay, how about if you start in three weeks?" Jack didn't skip a beat.

I nodded hesitantly.

"Okay then, let's make a list of the tools you'll need." He slid a piece of paper and pencil across the table. "Get a circular saw. I think Makita's the best but that's up to you."

I wrote down "Makita saw."

"Get a tool belt, hammer—at least a nineteen ounce, but a twenty-one would be good—utility knife, tape measure, chalk line, some nail sets, an extension cord and a framing square. That'll get you started." I wrote as quickly as I could while Jack waited for me to catch up. "You'll also need a truck. My son drives a Toyota and has no complaints. You should look at one of those."

I nodded and obediently added "Toyota truck" to the list like it was just another tool to pick up at the hardware store. But my mind was moving elsewhere. I was thinking about how I would tell people back in the office that I was leaving, tell my roommates that I wanted to break the lease, get these tools and truck, then move down here in three weeks.

"You should also make a reservation for the ferry right away. It's starting to book up. If you can't get one, you can go stand by and they'll bring your truck over when they can."

I added this to a list that was now absurdly beyond my control. I was numb. He could have told me to put anything on it and I would have dutifully complied.

He handed me a business card. "You already have my number in Nantucket. Here's my number in Connecticut where I live full time. If you need anything or if anything changes, call here. It's a pleasure to welcome you on board." He smiled, winked at me and extended his hand. We exchanged another firm handshake and he said, "Let's get you to the airport."

NOW OBLIVIOUS TO THE CHARMS of the DC-3, I flew back to Boston in quiet reflection. The reality of the decision I had just made started to wash over me. And with that reality came many questions. What did I just do? I was on the island no more than two hours and I had accepted a job for which I had few qualifications, leaving one that I had earned a college degree to do. It would seem completely crazy to anyone else and I wasn't sure they wouldn't be right. I was going to be a carpenter. The thought both terrified and thrilled me.

And what did I really know about Jack? His pushy boastfulness made me uncomfortable. I had never liked people who bragged before. Could I believe everything he said? Or was he just a blowhard? What did I know about house construction? He could have been making everything up and I wouldn't know the difference. His decision to hire me seemed as sudden as my decision to accept. How did this work? I was open and clear that I had few qualifications. And yet he still hired me at a wage I could accept; something other contractors were unwilling to do. But it seemed that I was taking the greater risk. He could just fire me on a moment's notice. Or could he? Was he desperate for help on the island?

Despite these questions, fears and suspicions, the undeniable admiration I felt for Jack and his seeming command of his world overpowered my doubts and drove them into the background of my mind; at least for the moment while his impression on me was still fresh.

In what seemed only an instant, the plane touched down in Boston and I prepared myself to share the news.

"WOW! YOU'RE DOING WHAT?" asked my boss, Howard. We were sitting in his office, one he had occupied for over fifteen years and one he would likely stay in for at least another fifteen. "Where did this come from?"

I cringed. "I know it sounds a little odd…"

"A little odd? Do you know what you're doing?" he interrupted with fatherly concern. "Andy, you just got your engineering degree and now have two good years under your belt here. You're twenty-four years old and just at the start of your career. Are you going to throw that all away?" Then he paused and smirked. "Or is this just a way to spend the summer on the beach checking out the girls?"

The question amused me as I hadn't yet realized that I was moving to a beach community and that it could be perceived that way. "Howard, maybe I need to sow some wild oats. I don't know. I just know I need to do this right now. I'm excited about something for the first time and I want to act on it. I know it doesn't make sense. But, it's still something I want to do." I was smiling as I said this, beaming really.

Howard softened, leaned back in his desk chair and pondered my words. "Andy, to tell you the truth, I wish I could do something like this. I have a wife and three kids. I could never just drop everything and go off on a whim. I envy your freedom. It doesn't need to make sense; at least not to me. If it makes sense to you, then it's the right thing. If it turns out to be a mistake, you're young enough to recover."

His casual comment hit me hard. I would have preferred he didn't use the word "mistake" and that he would have concluded with, "You'll always be able to find something here." A backup option would have made me feel safer. But in a way, that increased the excitement. It was now official; the tie had been cut. We talked more about carpentry and how to terminate my employment. Then we shook hands and I went back to my desk.

Looking at it, I suddenly came to realize how my desk had begun to feel like a cage. I didn't know it for certain before, but now it was clear. I had grown to feel a certain futility at this job. The paperwork would keep flowing, whether I handled it or somebody else did. I could spend weeks, months, even years doing it, and the result would be no different than if someone else had done it. Now, more than ever, I felt an overwhelming clarity that this was not where I was meant to be.

I cleared some of the more urgent work from my inbox and then began to seek out my unsuspecting friends and colleagues. I felt a guilty pleasure in making the announcement, like I was announcing that I was breaking the rules. All were surprised. A few were supportive. Most looked at me in disbelief.

One whose opinion I respected was Leslie. She and I started around the same time, but Leslie was rising quickly to the top. She had been assigned to some of the more high profile projects in the region. This brought lots of national media coverage as well as the attention of the senior administrators in the agency. I saw her as a model of success.

"Andy, why are you doing this? You're throwing everything away," she exclaimed. "What are you doing with your life? Don't you have any direction? You were supposed to get this out of your system in college. You were all set to go to Harvard. This was going to open everything up for you. Your future was looking fantastically bright. Now, you're just going to turn your back on an opportunity that most everyone else would die for?" She concluded firmly, "I think you're making a big mistake."

Leslie never minced words. And for her, there was only one true school—Harvard—and I had proven myself worthy of being accepted. While I'd been smiling all morning, this slowed me. Though I had encountered questions, no one had been so clearly negative about the decision. And to my surprise, I realized that I had given little thought to the Harvard or Berkeley acceptances. It was true. I had worked hard to get into these programs and it was an honor to be accepted. Several people within the agency had written great recommendation letters to help get me in. So I said, "Well, I'm not going to turn down Harvard. I'm going to defer for a year. If this doesn't work out, I'll go back. What difference does a year make?"

Leslie eyed me suspiciously. "Well, if that's the case, then get out there and get this over with. Do what you need to do. Harvard won't wait forever. And I guess if you have some reservations about going, it would be better to resolve them and then throw yourself forward."

I was relieved to have weathered this attack. If I could withstand Leslie, I figured, I could withstand anyone else at the office. The rest of the day went much the same way as the rest of the week. People were surprised, amused, incredulous. While some thought I was doing something foolish, my closest friends seemed to be, at the very least, accepting. And each time that I explained my decision, I felt a growing strength that this was a defensible idea. But always in the pit of my stomach was the dread over how to tell my parents. I called home and invited myself to dinner.

"MOM, DAD, THERE'S SOMETHING I'd like to tell you." Concern came over their faces. I had never used such a tone before. Or more to the point, I had never made such a momentous and independent decision before. I always did what was expected of me. On the drive to the house in my roommate's car, I had rehearsed several possible ways to announce the decision, but none seemed right. They knew of my consternation over feeling dissatisfied at work and with the question of whether to go to graduate school, but they didn't know about my discovery of carpentry. I had decided that the direct way was the best. Just get it out, deal with the shock all at once and then answer the questions that would surely come.

"I've decided not to go to Harvard or Berkeley. I've decided to take a job as a carpenter on Nantucket." It came out easier than I expected. The silence that followed was much harder.

They both just stared at whatever was in front of them, seemingly stunned. I waited patiently, studying the familiar living room as if it were the first time I had ever been there, deeply focusing on anything that would help me endure this endless moment. Each second that hung in the air was agony, shrinking my resolve.

Finally, my father began in a formal tone. "Well, that's quite a decision Andy. Why do you want to do this?" His voice was controlled, each word metered out carefully. But his tone was one that I was long familiar with. It had the overtone of honest inquiry but an undertone of a judgment already rendered—this was a mistake.

But be it this way or any other way, I thought, the discussion was now joined. We talked for hours. My parents asked the logical and rational questions that any concerned parents would ask. They wanted to know about my long-term future, health insurance, the pay, my debts, my living arrangements, the opportunity lost by not adding to my tenure in engineering or going to graduate school.

My father shook his head, "Andy I don't understand this. You had a good stable job and an opportunity to develop your career even further, one that will provide security for you and one day, your family. You've got one important piece of your life in place. Now the rest will get easier as you start to settle down. Why give that up?"

"But Dad, I'm not looking for security right now." The words surprised him. "And anyway, I'm not happy working there. I can't do that for the rest of my life."

He replied simply, "Andy, no job's perfect. You have to take the good with the bad." I felt a mild dose of condescension and didn't respond.

With the brief pause, my mother began. "Andy, carpentry's such a rough business. You won't have much in common with the men you'll be working with. No one'll be as educated as you. And what about their morals? They'll bring you down."

This was something that I'd worried about. I'd been around college-educated people all of my adult life—what little there was so far. Would I have anything in common with carpenters? Would I fit in? Would I become cruder by working with them? I decided that I couldn't think like that. I hadn't bought into the role of engineer, I reasoned, so how could I look down on a carpenter? Maybe I would fit better? To defend my decision, I just focused on my excitement and enthusiasm. I replied with genuine optimism, "Maybe I'll bring them up."

My mother was unimpressed and frowned.

I told them that this was something I needed to do. I explained my lack of direction since college and raised the idea that I might have been better served if I had taken a year off before going to college. And to my great surprise, my father agreed, saying that he had often wondered the same thing himself.

With this as a concession, I explained this as a temporary step, one through which I could sort out what I was doing with my life. Framing it as a sort of time out, I was able to begin to win more measures of understanding. And with the momentum building, the course of the following hour found them making more small concessions.

"Well, I guess Nantucket's a better place than most to be doing this kind of work…Even if you don't stay in this profession, it's a handy set of skills to have…Working with your hands is an honorable and honest profession." … And then they finally started to accept my decision with, "Jesus, after all, was a carpenter." and "If this is what you think will make you happy, then I guess you better find out."

By the end of the evening, I was sure that they didn't fully agree with my decision. That may have been too much to hope for. But I left the house having accomplished what I had intended. I survived.

As I was leaving, my father paused at the doorway, stood formally and squarely to face me and imparted some final wisdom. "Now remember Andy. This is a job, not a vacation. You're being hired to do some hard work. If you don't produce, Jack will fire you. That's the way it works in construction." I stiffened, and not with formality. Of course I knew it was a job and of course I would work hard. I had no doubts about that. He was looking at the downside rather than offering the encouragement I craved. But I tried not to take this as a sign of defeat and instead, tried to attribute it to a father's concern. I smiled and said I'd remember that. Inside, I was irritated. As I drove home, his comment dogged my thoughts. Starting as a small seed in the back of mind, it grew into a nagging concern that maybe he was right and that I was not seeing this situation completely correctly.

THE NEXT DAY I COMPOSED LETTERS to Harvard and Berkeley asking for a one-year deferral. On the phone, their admissions officers assured me that my request was not unusual and that they would consider it carefully. The woman at Harvard added jovially, "Well, it's not everyone that can say they turned down Harvard." Her comment, as did many other comments, made me question my decision once again.

And as I thought about it, I realized that I felt uncomfortable making the request for another reason. I wondered if I was just deferring a decision that

I was afraid to make. I thought about the story of Cortez when he reached the New World. He burned his ships to motivate his crew to look forward rather than back to the sea. Should I just get the decision over with and burn my ship? I looked at the deferral letters and thought hard. I tore them in half, dropped them in the waste basket and signed the decline space in the acceptance letter. I was committed.

WHILE EXPLAINING MY DECISION to my parents and friends challenged my resolve to become a carpenter, tool shopping reinforced it. Diane joined me in my revelry. She had been entirely supportive of my decision and was only too happy to accompany me to a hardware store near her cabin in New Hampshire to buy the tools of my new trade. I excitedly told the sales clerk that I was going to become a carpenter. I knew that my childlike enthusiasm must have appeared silly, and the unimpressed way the clerk looked at me confirmed this—but my emotion was irrepressible. The clerk pointed out the various grades of tools and I bought the best, or at least the most expensive ones. The clerk asked if I wanted some Carhartt pants, explaining that these were the best work pants you could buy. He handed me a pair. Made of thick cotton, they had loops and pockets for all types of tools. But they were also as stiff as a board and felt very uncomfortable.

"Not to worry," the clerk explained, "After about two weeks of good wash and wear, these'll break in and feel like a second skin." Then he added with a smirk, "But in those first two weeks, you'll feel like they're wearing off your first layer." I gleefully put two pairs and some work-boots in my cart. At the register, I handed over the money with equal glee. It was completely guilt-free spending.

Once back at Diane's cabin, I admired my new purchases. I put on the rigid pants and boots. I unpacked each of the tools, holding them, feeling them. I plugged in the saw and entertained Diane by deliriously cutting scraps of wood into smaller scraps.

While the tools were an easy purchase, the truck was not. I realized that I had been separating this overall decision into many small ones of varying impact. First, the job; then my parents; now the tools. These would always be useful and I paid cash for them. But, buying a truck came with a four-year loan; my first. And to make matters worse, I never dreamed of owning a truck. I always admired sports cars and had hopes of one day owning a slick black Porsche, and not the red Toyota 4x4 now being shown to me.

Again, I explained to the salesman that I was about to become a carpenter. "Oh in that case," he quickly replied, "I would strongly recommend you upgrade to the Extra-Cab Deluxe. It's an extra thousand dollars but you'll get this space behind the front seat where you can store your tools. In my experience, contractors have preferred this."

Being called a "contractor" excited me and created a steadying effect. While I was leery of assuming a twelve thousand-dollar debt when I was about to take an hourly job with an uncertain future, I had little choice. I had to be on Nantucket in two weeks and I would either buy this truck or buy a used one, if I could even find a good one. I bought the truck and dragged my heels through every step: paying the down payment, signing the purchase agreement and loan forms, and finally picking it up. I drove it home in silence, adjusting to yet another step in my progression.

WHEN MY LAST DAY in the office finally came, I said my good-byes, boxed up my possessions and carried them to the elevator. When I loaded them into my shiny new truck, I found myself suddenly confronted with the full gravity of what I was doing and it hit me hard. I was now painfully aware that my decision was real. And with that sense of reality came genuine fear. In just two short weeks, I had changed everything in my life. The only final change was to move to Nantucket. I was ready, at least physically. Emotionally, I needed to catch up. All I wanted to do was go someplace private and succumb to the fear that was gripping me. I felt alone and unsure of my decision; the momentum that had carried me along was waning and inertia was setting in. What lay behind me was certainty, security and a clear future. What lay ahead was the unknown and I was having trouble moving towards it. My body felt like lead. I prodded it into motion with a depression of the gas pedal.

ASPIRANT

THE ROGERS HOUSE

"Do not copy the behavior and customs of this world, but be an original and different person with a fresh newness in all you think and do. Then you will be truly satisfied in what is good, acceptable and perfect."

ROMANS, 12:2

T HE FERRY LEFT THE HYANNIS DOCKS at nine in the morning to begin its two-hour passage to Nantucket. Cars and trucks parked on the lower level while drivers and passengers rested above. There was an overcast sky and it was too raw to sit on the open deck. People huddled quietly around the tables and chairs on the passenger decks. I felt as though I were part of some pre-summer ritual, everyone sitting quietly, lost in their own thoughts.

I sat alone, staring out the window at the rolling waves, thinking about the transition I was making. When I had flown to the island before, it took only thirty minutes. Once in the air, I could see the island in the distance. But on the ferry, I lost all sight of land, creating a more vivid sense of the physical distance I was traveling, one that matched the psychological distance I had already gone. Most of my belongings were now in storage in Boston and I felt lightened by having so few possessions in the truck below. With each passing wave, I felt the thoughts of what lay behind disappear while the anticipation of what lay ahead grew. Yet, it was a somber trip, matched by the grayness of the sky.

The ferry arrived in Nantucket harbor, a small bay filled with empty docks and moorings that awaited the summer's occupants. I had called Jack to tell him that I would be arriving at eleven o'clock and he said that Eric, his youngest son and one of the crew, would meet me at the dock.

Pulling my truck off the ferry, I scanned the parking lot for his pickup truck. It wasn't hard to find by Jack's description; big tires, a raised frame and a shiny black body. It was clean, just like his father's. He drove up to meet me and leaned out the window.

"You Andy?"

"Yeah. Are you Eric?"

"Yeah, follow me."

Not much for words, is he? I thought.

I followed, working hard not to lose him in the mass of disembarking pedestrians. There was only one road to get from the ferry into town and everyone was using it. I was engulfed in a sea of walkers, bikers, passenger cars and freight trucks. I followed Eric past a row of bars and restaurants on Easy Street, past the shops on Main Street and the historic whaler's homes just beyond. I learned later that the cobblestones of Main Street were once the ballast of the whaling ships that made the island's fortunes in the days of Herman Melville and *Moby-Dick*. Once out of downtown, the island took on more of the sedate character that I had seen on my first visit with Jack; lots of low trees and brush, and small cottages with cedar shingles and white corner boards.

We drove down Old South Road and then turned left onto the unmarked dirt road where my new home would be. I pulled into the dirt driveway and Eric jumped out of his truck to inspect the contents in the bed of mine.

"Whataya got in there? You got a stereo? We need a stereo."

"Yeah, I do." I had always set up the stereo first when I moved into a new dorm room in college. But I wasn't sure about the rules in this house and I was hesitant to upset the neat order that had been arranged. Eric's endorsement relieved me of that hesitancy. "I also have a bike, clothes and tools. Can you show me where I'm supposed to put them?"

"Sure. Oh, by the way, I'm Eric." He thrust his hand toward me and we shook. It was a formal handshake, much the same as those of his brother and father. And, like his relations, Eric had the same strong features. But he was thinner and more boyish in his looks and manner. He was twenty years old and carried himself with the awkwardness of someone still trying to figure out his place in the order around him. He also seemed to be trying to decide where my place in that order would be. There was a guarded hesitancy to the way he addressed me.

"Let me show you where your room is. You'll be rooming with Larry. You'll meet him tonight when he comes back from the Cape."

As I remembered it, the room was compact and neat, with two single beds. "This one's Larry's. You can use that one by the window."

I carried my clothes into the bedroom, packed my stereo into the corner of the living room and parked my bike in the basement, next to a weight bench and assorted boxes, neatly stacked in one corner. I went upstairs, unpacked my clothes and settled down on the bed. I was feeling lethargic, trying to catch my breath from the day's transition. Before long, Eric was back, eager for a playmate.

"You ready to go riding?" he asked impatiently. "We have two ATV's out back."

Rather than slip into a mild depression, I jumped up, "Yeah sure, let's go."

Eric gave me a helmet, and explained how the ATV worked.

Noticing that they had no license plates, I asked "Are these legal to be driving on the streets?"

"Oh sure. These don't need to be licensed. Just follow me if anything happens."

Eric sped off and I followed. We drove down the dirt road that connected to Old South Road, crossed to a trail and headed into the woods. We drove for ten minutes and emerged on the other side with the ocean in view and a paved street that ran parallel to it. Eric sped off and I tried hard to catch up, nervous not to go beyond my limits. Eric pulled into a dirt road. I followed but was having trouble seeing through the dust he was kicking up. Finally, the dust cleared and Eric was waiting for me at the corner of another paved road. I pulled up next to him.

"Can you slow it down a bit? I'm not used to these and don't know my way around the island. I've only been here about two hours for cryin' out loud."

Eric was about to say something when I noticed his eyes widen. He was looking over my shoulder and I turned to see a police cruiser with its lights flashing. Eric bolted and the cruiser sped after him. I now found myself alone and cursed myself. I should have known better, this was not legal. And worse still, I wasn't sure of where I was. I tried to backtrack the way we had come. But since much of that was in a cloud of dust, I had trouble keeping track of landmarks and found myself at an intersection that I didn't recognize. I didn't know which way to go, but rather than just sitting still, sped off in one direction. A car was coming towards me and it soon became clear that whoever was driving it was not sticking to his side of the road. He was trying to force me to stop.

This guy was either connected with the police or was the one who called them. Either way, I didn't want to meet him. I side stepped the car and continued in the same direction. Soon, I found the entrance to the wooded path we had taken before and cut in. There was no way for the car to follow unless the driver knew where this let out. Speed was critical now and I went as fast as I dared. I emerged at Old South Road, crossed and sped down the dirt road. Dust lingered in the air telling me that either Eric made it back all right or the police car was now waiting for me. I would soon find out. As I pulled around the house, Eric frantically waved me into the garage.

"Boy, that was close. Where were you? I was afraid you weren't gonna make it and Neil's ATV would get impounded. He would've been pissed." And with that Eric let out a laugh. I sheepishly smiled, trying to hide how annoyed I really felt. I was on unfamiliar ground.

"HI, YOU MUST BE the new guy. I'm Larry." The last remaining crew member thrust out his hand. He had just taken the ferry from Hyannis to be ready for work on Monday morning. About my age, he stood about six feet tall, with a thin frame, dark hair and dark eyes. He lit up the room with his buoyant personality. He wore an infectious smile and seemed to joke with every word.

"Is that bad boy out there your rig? Toyota makes a nice truck. Neil drives one. He loves it." He fired the statements off in rapid succession.

I felt some strange momentary pride in my new purchase. Here, in this company, a truck was respected.

Larry quickly pushed the conversation, "Check out my beast."

Eric had timed his return with Larry's arrival and the three of us walked outside to admire his 1975 Ford pickup; in good condition and clearly a work truck.

"You wouldn't believe how many people've offered to buy it from me. I can't for the life of me figure out why."

I liked it. When I was looking for my Toyota, I saw a similar vintage Chevy for sale along a road in New Hampshire. The romantic in me considered buying it, admiring the styling and the seriousness it conveyed as a true work truck. But my rational side lost nerve at the risk of buying what could have been a host of mechanical problems on wheels.

After the proper amount of time admiring each other's trucks, we went back inside. Eric put on some hot water and cooked up a meal of boxed macaroni and cheese while we continued to talk.

I learned that Larry lived on—what he called—"the mainland." This was opposed to being "on-island" as he explained it. He was engaged to be married and only came over to Nantucket for work because the money was good. Otherwise, he would never have separated himself from his "honey." I also learned that Eric was the youngest of three boys. Willie, the oldest, lived in Florida and had no interest in the construction business. Neil, the second oldest, lived on another part of the island with his girlfriend. He was trying to follow in his father's footsteps and take over the business as soon as "the old man" decided to let him have it. Eric was indifferent to the trade. And for that reason, he could not fathom why I would leave an indoor, salaried job to do outdoor, manual labor.

"You're out of your fuckin' mind," he exclaimed.

"Easy boy," Larry interjected. "If he has some need to try this living on for size, let's see what he says after one of them bone chillin' Cape Cod winters workin' outside."

Both of them laughed knowingly. Working outdoors during the winter was something I had not even contemplated.

We talked into the night and I began to recognize that these guys were not the rough and tough kinds of personalities I had worried about. They were easy to get along with and there seemed little difference between them and the guys I met in college.

AT SIX O'CLOCK, Neil arrived to make sure everyone was up and ready to go. "Rise and shine, ladies. Another wonderful day is ahead of us," he bellowed.

My new presence added confusion to what must have been a predictable routine before I arrived. The shower order had to be renegotiated.

Within thirty minutes, everyone got into his own truck and we drove to the jobsite in a caravan. Once on the jobsite, Neil unlocked the box truck in front of the driveway and Eric and Larry collected their tools. Neil turned to me "You can store your tools in the box truck. It's safe." I lamented the tool space in the cab of my Extra-Cab Deluxe.

Work began precisely at seven o'clock with Neil giving instructions. "Larry, you start shingling on the west wall. Eric, take Andy and show him how to shingle on the master bedroom side." Then adding loudly, "Andy's the new guy…reeeeeaaaal new! Green! But we're gonna show him the ropes."

Everyone was already in motion and no one responded to Neil's teasing. While I still worried that Neil might resent his father picking his crew for him, I felt no embarrassment at being singled out as the rookie. I was thrilled that my training was about to begin.

Once on the second floor, Eric led me onto the master bedroom deck. The first thing he did was set up his boom box and turned on some music. "You and I'll side this wall here. We're puttin' shingles on with four inches to the weather." Reacting to my confused look, he quickly added, "That's just a fancy way of saying we're gonna leave four inches of shingle showing. Here on Nantucket, we have to plan for horizontal rain so we're keeping the shingles tight. We're also caulking the shingles into the corner boards and up against the window and corner trim." Showing me a calking gun, he added, "This is what we use. Good stuff."

He held up a "story pole" with lines marked every four inches to note where each course of shingles was to begin. He marked the height of the next course and nailed a board to run from one side to the other. "We'll lay the shingles on top of this board and nail them in place with these nails here." He pointed to a box of nails on the floor, grabbed a handful and put them in his leather tool belt. I did the same.

The shingling was easy to pick up. I nailed shingles on my side of the porch door while Eric worked on his side. We worked until nine o'clock when we took a fifteen-minute break and then continued through the rest of the morning.

"Be sure to have your courses match mine and whatever you do, don't line up the seam of two shingles. They always have to stagger or water'll get into the wall. The trick is to *think like a raindrop!*"

The line rolled off his tongue like a piece of carpentry wisdom that had been passed down through generations of tradesmen. And I was pleased to be the next recipient.

When I ran my first course into the corner, I began to apply some caulking for the last shingle. But it was getting stuck on my fingers. Eric looked over and said, "It's easier if you lick your finger when you're putting it on."

I put my finger in my mouth and gagged.

Eric roared, "No, dumb-ass, lick your finger before you put the caulking on so it won't stick. Man, that stuff must taste awful."

Feeling every bit the rookie, I wiped my finger on my tool belt, adding a streak to what was pristine that morning, and went back to my work, diligently siding my portion of the wall until lunch. At twelve o'clock, Neil emerged from inside the house and announced, "Ladies, it's lunch time."

Mimicking Eric, I dropped my tools where I stood, walked to my truck to grab my lunch and sat down with the others on the back porch. The air was still cool from a sea breeze but the afternoon sun felt warm on my face. The topics of conversation were new to me. We talked about who made the best saw. Milwaukee was Larry's favorite. Eric and Neil much preferred Makita. Beyond the color differences—Makita was blue, Milwaukee was red—I didn't know the difference. Larry immediately jumped up in feigned dismay and led me into the house in order to rectify my deficiency. He plugged in his red Milwaukee and ordered me to cut some scraps. When I said that I didn't like the way my hand felt so high on the handle, he made me cut more. When I couldn't be persuaded to change my opinion, he led me back onto the deck and jokingly labeled me a "cretin" just like the others.

Another topic was who made the best trucks. Larry liked his Ford, Eric liked his Chevy, and Neil and I defended our Toyotas. The conversation on all topics was equally light, and when everyone finished his lunch, we lay back to enjoy the few remaining moments until work resumed at twelve thirty.

As in the morning, the afternoon work began with instructions from Neil. "Larry, why don't you take Andy for the afternoon? See if you can teach him anything Eric missed."

"Okay rookie, come on with me," Larry squealed.

He led me to the opposite side of the house from Eric and directed me up to a plank that was suspended fifteen feet above the ground by two extension ladders. The wall below the plank was already sided with shingles. Once in position, he joined me and began his tutorial. "Okay, here's how I've perfected siding in my many years of experience." He nailed a long board onto the side of the house just as Eric did, but he also attached a string along the house six inches above it. Then he rapidly slid shingles in behind the string, frantically shuffling them around to make sure that no seams lined up with those below. It was instantly obvious that this process was designed for speed.

"With a nail gun, you should see how fast I can do this. But," he added with a roll of his eyes, "these guys wanna do it the old-fashioned way!" Then with a wide smile, "Well anyway, come on, greenhorn. Don't just stand there. Start nailing these off as I put 'em up. Let's go. Chop! Chop!"

I liked working with Larry. While Eric had his light moments, he was too formal. Larry joked his way through everything. Yet, he knew what he was doing and we were soon siding together as a team, covering ground at a faster pace than Eric and I had done separately. On one of the courses, Larry wrote his name and the date on the tops of the shingles that would be covered by the next course. "I sign all of my work…many times!"

We got to the corner and it was time to run a bead of caulking for the last shingle. Larry grabbed the caulking gun. "You know, we have to do this here on Nantucket. Just like the four inches to the weather, we have to prepare for horizontal rain. On the Cape it's not so bad. This'd be overkill." The caulking gun was empty. "Could you grab me another one from that box down there?"

I climbed down the ladder, grabbed a tube and brought it back up. Larry cut the tip, loaded it into the caulking gun, gave the trigger a couple of squeezes and then poked the end of the tube with a piece of hanger he kept in his belt. It took a couple of jabs, but he was able to pierce the seal as he continued pressing the trigger. The goo spurted out of the tube and he moaned in a deep voice, "Oh baby. That's soooo nice."

THE WEEK PASSED QUICKLY, each day organized around the same routine. Work began at seven and ended at four. We took a fifteen-minute break at nine and a thirty-minute lunch at noon. At the end of the day, we stopped work fifteen minutes before quitting time and cleaned the entire jobsite. Just like Jack's truck and the house we were living in, everything would be clean and orderly.

As the weeks passed, the days got drier and sunnier, having a direct effect on the tasks we chose. With rain, we focused on indoor work. With clear weather, we worked outside on the siding. On Larry's suggestion we rotated our siding operations around the house to follow the sun and get the best tan. It was ideas like these that left Eric and Neil at a loss. His easy-going manner was far different from their more formal way.

That difference became vivid one particularly hot afternoon. After lunch, the sun had reached its highest point and we took off our shirts to maximize our tan. Always prepared, Larry retrieved some suntan lotion from his truck, put some in his hand and passed the bottle. We each took some, passed it on and put it on our arms, chest, legs and face. When the bottle was returned to Larry, he asked me if I would put some on his back. I obliged and asked him to do the same. When we were done, we looked up to find Neil and Eric frozen in their gaze.

"Do you guys want some on your backs?" Larry asked innocently.

Neil responded in disgust, "You're not touchin' my back. What are you guys, fuckin' homos?"

Not put off in the slightest, Larry quickly replied, "Well, my fiancée don't think so. But if you guys wanna burn your backs, suit yourself." And he happily packed the lotion away and turned to go back to work.

EACH MORNING I AWOKE anxious to learn everything that I could. Neil, Larry and Eric were my teachers. If there was any kind of new job, I asked Neil if I could help; a skylight installation, hanging doors and windows, building beams, anything and everything, no matter how menial. I laid a plastic vapor barrier in the basement crawl space. I applied tar to the inside of the windows—another protection against the horizontal rain of Nantucket. I lugged lumber around the site. I drove to the lumberyard to pick up additional materials. I wanted to experience everything, not waste a single moment.

With everything I learned, I learned more about how much I didn't know. So I asked a steady stream of questions to fill the gap. Since I hadn't been part of the framing, this topic was a major subject of my inquiries. Why does this house have a block wall foundation? How do you pour foundation footings? How do you build the walls, floor and roof? What size lumber and what thickness plywood do you use for each? How long did it take to frame a house like this? How do you frame a circular window like that? I wrote down every answer in a journal. It became my notebook on how to build a house. Viewing the house as my classroom and knowing that it would be eventually finished, I saw every moment as precious and didn't want to forget a thing. Even my growing vocabulary required its own section in the journal: studs, jack-studs, headers, joists, rafters, valleys, the ridge. I spent every day consumed with building. And I spent each night in deep sleep, exhausted from working my body far harder than it had ever been worked before.

WHILE I LEARNED the technical skills of building a house, I also learned the physical skills of using my tools to do it. I was becoming seasoned. My Carhartt pants were breaking in and my tools were becoming more familiar in my now calloused hands. I was beginning to actually feel the tools as an extension of my body. The most important was the hammer, an easy tool to use, a hard one to master.

When I first started, I muscled the nail into the wood with each blow. I would swing hard, figuring the harder the better. But this did two things. It increased my fatigue, particularly if I was hammering over my head. And, it increased the likelihood of my missing the nail and hammering my thumb or finger instead. Nothing hurt more than a hammered finger. Even the momentary delay between the actual blow and the throbbing pain was agony because I knew it was coming. All I could do was wait.

But one day, when I was building a temporary step from the garage to the main house, I experienced a revelation. I was driving home some nails, and for the first time, I truly felt the weight and balance of the hammer as it hit the nail. I experienced what it felt like to swing with ease and let the combined snap of my wrist and the balanced weight of the tool do all the work. It drove the nail harder and it took less energy. I had no idea that this could happen and smiled. Of course, I thought, it was no different than a golfer or a tennis player finally learning to let the equipment do the work with the natural flow of the body. I was an athlete of woodworking and I was learning the full capabilities of my tools.

With these kinds of revelations, I found my confidence growing and I eased into the new identity I was assuming. I was becoming less an engineer and more a carpenter. I looked and felt stronger. I was also sporting the darkest tan I had had in years, much to the chagrin of my friends back in Boston.

FOR ALL THE CONFIDENCE I was developing, there was always something to bring me back down to earth—a mistake that would remind me of how much I didn't know, and a willing carpenter to point out my deficiency.

One morning, Neil called me over. Pointing to the peak of the house, he said, "Would you paint over that knot on the rake?"

I asked, "What's the rake?"

"Aren't you paying attention around here?" Neil snapped back, annoyed. "The rake board is the piece of trim that runs up the roof-line on either side of a gable end. The knot's too high for an extension ladder. You'll have to get it from the ridge. Climb out on the third floor balcony."

Although uncomfortable with heights, I dutifully grabbed a bucket of white paint and a brush and made my way to the third floor. It was mid-morning and the summer sun had yet to reach its zenith. I gingerly stepped onto the cedar roof shingles and found that my boots slid on their smooth surface. So I took my boots and socks off and found that my bare feet stuck to the roof. I stood upright and walked to the peak, across the ridge to the gable and the offending rake board. Proud of my solution, I reached over, painted the knot and then paused to enjoy the view.

I surveyed the landscape; the rolling beach in one direction, the salt marsh that was so important to Mr. Rogers in another and the perfectly manicured Sankaty Head golf course in yet another. It was a beautiful sunny day and I enjoyed the short break above the noise and clatter of the jobsite below.

After a few minutes I turned to return to the porch and quickly realized that the soles of my feet had dried during my brief time on the warming roof. I had been able to walk upright because they were tacky from the sweat of being inside my boots. But they were now as slippery as the boots had been. I had an uncovered bucket of white paint in one hand, a wet brush in the other and what amounted to ice skates on my feet. If I spilled the bucket of paint on the roof shingles, there would be hell to pay to replace them. I could try to throw the bucket off the roof. But, there was equipment all around the house and I couldn't be sure which way it would splatter. The last thing I wanted was for Neil to catch me in this predicament. I waited patiently for someone to show himself, hoping all along that it would be… yes! Larry appeared on a second floor porch.

"Hey Larry," I called out softy.

No response.

I tossed a nail from my tool belt, calling a little louder "Hey Larry."

Larry looked up and exclaimed, "Hey, what's up, Kemo Sabe?"

I signaled for him to be quiet and to come to the third floor balcony. When he arrived, I explained my predicament, at which he let out a hysterical laugh. "Well let's see what we can do about this?"

"If you take your shoes off, your feet will be sticky for about five minutes."

"You're crazy! I'm not joining you in your predicament!"

"Just try it. There'll be enough time for you to climb up here and get this bucket and brush. Then I can slide down to you."

Larry reluctantly took his shoes off and walked slowly up to my perch. "Dr. Livingston I presume?" I handed him the paint and brush. He carried them back to safety and then assumed the position of a baseball catcher as I slid my way to the deck.

"Thanks a lot, you really saved my ass. If Neil found me first, I wouldn't have heard the end of it."

And that was true. Neil loved to tease me. While I escaped this opportunity for mockery, I was not so lucky on others. One day I was working on some ceiling strapping, hammering over my head. I was feeling comfortable with my new swing but had still not fully mastered it. Pounding the nail with successive blows, I finally drew the hammer back too far and nicked myself on the cheek with the claw. It drew a minor amount of blood but left a visible two-pronged claw mark.

Later, Neil asked, "What's that?" pointing to my cheek.

I replied coyly, "Oh nothing, I walked into a nail that someone left sticking out of a stud."

"Oh those nails! I hate that," he smirked. "For a minute there, it looked like you hit yourself with the claw of your hammer. Good thing you didn't do something as stupid as that."

WHILE I WAS FEELING MORE COMFORTABLE as a carpenter, my relationship with Diane wasn't working. My weekend trips and phone calls to Boston were growing less frequent, and as a result, our emotional distance grew. She wanted me to visit her whenever I came to Boston, but I had given no thoughts about getting married. Reflecting a young and idealistic naiveté, it was a request that I did not fully understand. She was looking to settle down and I was looking to do the opposite. Moving to Nantucket was an adventure in exploring who I was and what I could become. Becoming a husband was not even remotely on my mind. We soon broke up.

As I worked to fill the void of her leaving my life and trying to make friends, I began to realize something curious about who I was becoming. My identity was changing, something I hadn't anticipated.

Life on a resort island like Nantucket is split into several communities. There are the full time residents, trying to go about their lives as their town gets overrun by throngs of tourists for three months every summer. Then there are the summer residents, on-island only for those three months and board up their homes for the rest of the year. And then there are the regular tourists, visitors—often professionals from New York, Boston and beyond—who are on-island for only a day or a week. While I would normally have considered myself part of this latter group, I began to realize that that decision was not up to me.

The standard greeting when meeting someone was, "What do you do?" When I answered that I was a "carpenter here on-island," people reacted differently from when I answered, "I'm an engineer from Boston." I was a physical laborer; a *local* physical laborer, with all the connotations that come with that label. What they saw was not exactly clear to me. What was clear was their reaction, a subtle downward assessment, a degree of condescension, a shift in the tone and subject of conversation. While I found it amusing at first, I grew to find it troubling. In particular, meeting women had become a challenge. Most of the women coming to the island for vacation were part of that group of professionals that I identified with, but now a group that no longer identified with me.

I began to see that I was part of a fourth group, a hidden group. I was part of the service sector, comprised of the painters, landscapers and others who maintained the valuable summer homes on the island. And because of that association, I was also an islander, dismissed by one group but accepted by another. I was someone who enjoyed local knowledge of the island and the way it worked. This, I learned, should never be confused with being a "real" permanent islander, someone who lived there all their lives. This group was very selective and generally accepted only those that were at least born on-island and sometimes that wasn't enough.

There were certain conventional wisdoms shared by my group of islanders. We disdained the most popular tourist bars, preferring the more secluded places. We knew about where to get the best coffee, best breakfast, best beaches, best sunsets and, vitally, the types of women on-island and where to find them. One day over lunch, I received my first education on the topic.

"If you wanna pick up off-island women real easily, go to the Rose & Crown on Friday night," said Glen, one of the painters. "The women that stop there are just hittin' the first bar they find off the boat. By nine, they're half in the bag and ready for anything."

Neil teased him, "Yeah, that's the only way *you're* getting any action."

"Hey, whatever works," was his quick comeback. "I'm not particular as long as she's warm and willing."

Another continued, "Yeah, and if you want a weekender who's more laid back, head to the Atlantic Cafe. Then, for women who are staying for the summer, go to the Muse or the Chicken Box. Since those place's aren't downtown, the weekend women don't usually find them."

Neil was quick to add, seemingly from experience, "But be careful, don't get involved with those women unless you wanna spend a lot of time with 'em, especially at the end of the season. In September and October, those bars'll be filled with women asking if you're staying the winter. Remember, the only way to get through the winter here is *with either a bottle or a mate*."

I spent many nights in the bars with my new cohort. We lived a life separate of those from the "mainland," or "the United States" as the more extreme islanders called it. Over time, I began to see familiar faces, expanding my world of friends. Beyond our profession, one thing we had in common was that we were hard drinkers.

Weeknight drinking would often lead to slow mornings on the jobsite. On those mornings, the first scream of the saws caused groans among the crew. My mother might have seen this as sliding into the lifestyle of those "rough" carpenters. But it felt in no way different from my life as a college student.

Given my age, one night's drinking never left its effect beyond the nine o'clock coffee break. But on one particularly bad morning, I told Neil that I wouldn't be able to come to work until noon. Neil accepted the answer and left me to nurse my hangover. Around ten o'clock, I got up to shower and was surprised to be confronted by Jack emerging from his bedroom. I hadn't seen Jack since he interviewed me and didn't even know he was on-island.

"What're you doing here? " he asked angrily. "You're supposed to be at work."

"Sorry Jack. I'm not feeling so well," I replied.

He spied me closely, "Yeah I've seen that kind of 'illness' before." Then with some irritation, he warned me. "Let me know when you're here. I'm doing my work in there, making important phone calls. I want to know who may be hearing me. You understand?"

I was rattled by the sudden confrontation, especially in my hung-over state. "Yes Jack. Sorry. I'll just get showered and head to the jobsite right away."

"Good. Don't let it happen again." And he went back into his room.

LIKE FATHER, LIKE SON; Neil could also be hard to read, prone to sudden shifts in emotion. One day, I was helping him frame the opening for the spiral staircase between the second and third floors. The hole in the floor was initially framed square but now had to be turned into a circle. Neil gave me the list of necessary tools and materials and I lined them up for the job. He bent over the floor taking measurements of the square and then wrote numbers on the floor, trying to figure out how long to make the piece of plywood that would form the circumference of the circular opening.

I was good at geometry and offered to help. "You know Neil, there's a formula for the circumference of a circle."

"You can keep your fancy equations to yourself, college boy," Neil snapped. "If you're so smart, let's see who can come up with the better answer."

I was puzzled. There was only one possible answer and it was calculated as two times pi times the radius. But Neil did his own calculations on the floor, erasing numbers, adding others. When he was done, he didn't wait for my answer and cut a piece of quarter-inch plywood to be bent around the opening and wrapped it into a circle. "How's that Einstein? What did you come up with?"

I had written out the equation, calculated it on the floor and gave a number that was accurate to two decimal places. It was half an inch different from Neil's.

"Well, I'd say I got that one right, wouldn't you?" And he continued with the construction of the opening with an air of annoying superiority.

"That's ridiculous." I said. "There's only one right answer," Looking at his hen-scratching on floor, I was puzzled how he had gotten so close without using the equation. But I was also alert to the fact that he was still half an inch off.

Neil replied confidently, "I'd say that my *right* answer is just as good as yours. And I didn't need no expensive college degree to get it."

I began to suspect that Neil competed with me. Whereas my new identity changed how other people saw me, Neil still saw me as the college educated engineer, perhaps something that he resented.

BY JUNE, THE OUTER SHELL was completed—windows, doors, roof, siding. Neil announced this major milestone in the job. "We're *dried-in!*" The house now provided full protection from the elements and we could devote nearly all of our attention inside.

With this step came a transition. First, despite occasional reminders from Neil of my lack of experience, I was feeling very much one of the crew. I had helped us reach this milestone. Second, being dried-in meant that many other trades could now begin their work and, a new spate of subcontractors joined our crew. Electricians, plumbers, painters, plasterers, they all had their time and place on the job, and they all had their own personalities, their own cultures. I enjoyed learning not only what they did, but also how they fit into the flow of the jobsite.

I learned that painters were a flaky bunch. They would drift into a crew and disappear with just as little effort. "It doesn't take much skill to push a paint brush badly," Neil snarled. "It's a hell of a lot harder to do it well." The painting contractor was always looking for help. If he couldn't get skilled labor, he'd take whatever he could get and the burden would fall on the painting foreman to turn good work out of inexperienced painters. I learned that plumbers drove carpenters crazy because they came to the jobsite with powerful drills fitted with large bits to make room for their pipes. They would cut holes without regard to the work that had come before. I learned that the electricians, security team, and data system installers had the more technically complex jobs, having to run miles of wires for various uses in the house. At regular intervals, the building inspector made his appearance to perform his regular certifications: framing, plumbing, electrical.

Then, before I knew it, the trades were done and insulation was brought in to fill the outside walls. To keep us out of their way, Neil had us installing mahogany on the decks outside. After just a few visits inside during this toxic process, I understood the logic of saving this last outdoor task. The insulation filled the air with fine dust that left me hacking each time I breathed in its presence.

By mid-July, plasterers covered all the preceding months of work. I felt a mix of emotions at the change this brought. I liked the clean geometry of the framing, the stud walls, the framed windows and doors, the roof rafters and floor joists. Now the sheetrock and plaster simply covered it all over with a smooth flat surface that lacked the personality of what stood beneath, and the sanding of the joint compound left behind a layer of fine dust and a dry smell to replace the rich, sweet smell of lumber.

But on the other hand, the house was now turning into a home. The sheetrock turned an open collection of stud walls into rooms. Gone was the echoing expanse through which sounds and voices would carry. Now, you could no longer call out to anyone who was inside the house and get a response. Instead, you had to ask questions like "Where's Neil?" and hear answers like "I *think* he's in the master bedroom bathroom." There used to be no need for such questions, let alone such specificity in an answer.

MARINE LUMBER DELIVERED the first load of clear, sugar-pine flooring; blonde and smooth with gentle wide grains running lengthwise down each board. There was not a single knot to disrupt the patterns and each board carried its own uniquely beautiful design. The driver explained that this wood was very expensive and very hard to get. It had been sitting in the warehouse for two months and in that time, three people had offered to buy it.

"Yeah," Neil was quick to reply. "I wish they sold it. This is a big mistake. Look at this stuff. It's so soft. One woman with high heels and it's ruined." To make his point, he dragged his fingernail across the top of one board and very clearly left his initials in the surface.

Despite his reservations, Neil got down to business and took charge of the first step in laying the second floor. After careful measurements, I helped him snap one long straight chalk line through the full length of the house, from the master bedroom through the stair landing, across the living room and into the dining room. It was the only place where such a continuous line was possible. Then he chose the straightest, longest planks and glued and nailed them along that line.

Neil explained, "I want two 'face' nails every twelve inches to line up with the joists below. Put 'em precisely two inches from each side. When we're done, I want perfectly straight nail lines running perpendicular from the line of the planks. I want the holes to look like rivets."

I was impressed with the logical clarity of this important first step. Without knowing, I might have started on one side of the room and tried to work across the house. But I could see now that this first board was critical and how one chose it decided the outcome of the entire floor before it even started. In his measurements, Neil had planned for a nearly full sized final plank to end against each wall. As was the case so many times before, the carpentry skills I was learning made perfect sense, but only after the fact. The real key to carpentry was learning certain tricks so as not to commit to a mistake before the project was even begun.

Neil sent me to retrieve Larry so that the two of us could finish up. I found him on the third floor with a window trim workshop completely assembled; a plank on two horses, his chop saw positioned on top, a stack of pre-primed pine trim neatly stacked against the wall, a glue bottle on the sill, a pencil behind his ear and a tape measure in his hand.

"Larry, Neil wants us to do the floor now."

"Oh man! I'm just getting into my groove here." He groaned. "I'll be right with ya. Do you have what we need?"

"Well, Neil laid out the first board already. We just need to run more planks next to it."

"Did he get out the blind nailer?"

I gave him a puzzled look and he quickly added, "Ask Neil for the blind nailer and ..." He stopped what he was saying and, with an exaggerated strain on his face, he farted. Then, looking bewildered, he searched the floor for something that was only a figment of his imagination. Shrugging his shoulders, he gave up his futile hunt. "Hmmm. It's those damned barking spiders again."

I laughed. Larry resumed his instructions.

"Right now, get the blind nailer from Neil. And also, get some flooring from the garage; good long, straight lengths. Got it?"

I nodded and turned to leave. Larry stopped me and added, "Now watch out for them barkin' spiders!"

LARRY AND I SET ABOUT laying the pine flooring and I was never happier. The sugar pine was a sensual pleasure, unlike any other wood we'd used on the job so far. The surface was like felt, smooth and soft on my hands. The grain of each board possessed a unique beauty, the dark strands bending and swirling like waves of smoke drifting in a gentle breeze. The sound of the boards slapping and sliding against each other proclaimed a delicacy unlike the framing lumber. The scent it released dispelled the dusty smell of sheetrock and returned the house to its former aromatic self. In fact, it was infinitely better. Far sweeter than the Douglas fir studs, the pine was fresh and pure. It was very easy to work with. The saws, now fitted with finer blades and more teeth for finish work, cut through the wood with no resistance at all. The lightest grip was all that was necessary as the saw slid through each plank.

I felt a sense of completion with this task. I knew that this was one of the final steps. Other parts of the project were always in preparation for another step. We built stud walls. Electricians and plumbers installed wires and pipes. Then it was filled with insulation and covered over with sheetrock. The floor joists carried the plywood subfloor that was finally covered by this pine floor. But once sanded and sealed, this was the last step. This was work that the owner would see. It took on new importance.

Larry showed me how to pick boards. "Look here," he pointed to the stack of boards. "They're all ten inch planks but check out these two. These guys are different." Putting his tape on each, he measured one as nine and an eighth inches wide while the other was nine and three eighths. "If we were dumb enough to butt these two end to end, they wouldn't match. We'd have a gap. And we don't want no gaps." Then he eyed down the length of several boards until he picked one and measured each end with his tape. "And look at this bad boy, it varies within its length, nine and a half on this end, nine and a quarter on that end; variable shrinkage."

He looked at me to drive his lesson home. "Now put it all together.

We've got to make sure that we keep the planks parallel as we go. Too many wide dimensions on this side of the run and too many thin dimensions on that side, and our floor pattern will turn. We won't know it until we finish and our final row is no longer parallel with the wall. That's when we'll see it, that's when the owner'll see it, that's when it'll be too late to fix, and that's when we'd be," he paused. "What's the technical word for it? Oh yeah, that's when we'd be *fucked*!" He chuckled, "And we don't wanna be fucked; especially on flooring this expensive. I can't afford to pay for that mistake, and then my honey won't be able to afford to marry me!"

Again, more tricks for *not* making a mistake.

We laid board after board, working our way across the floor, constantly checking our distance to the far wall so as not to turn our plank pattern. Oftentimes a board would have a bend in it and would need to be pushed against its adjacent neighbor. With a minor bend, the blind nailer would push it over; a contraption that drove a nail diagonally into the edge of the board where it would be covered by the next plank, hence "blind" nailed. It was a clunky device, triggered with a blow from a large mallet. The blow, creating a loud pop like gun fire, both forced the nail into the wood and forced the board to slide over, securing it to the floor in the proper spot with one impact.

But sometimes, a board would have a severe bend. "Look at this baby," Larry exclaimed. "It's a regular banana!" He showed me how to identify the irregular grain pattern that caused the board to bend. To make it useful, we would nail another board to the floor and drive a wedge between it and the offending board, forcing it into its place. After nailing it permanently down, Larry would gleefully exclaim, "All right, that one's goin' nowhere *and likin' it!*"

When the second floor was done, we moved to the first floor. As I gathered another load of planks from the garage, I realized what Neil had done. He had started on the second floor because this was the prominent living space, assuring that it would get the first and best pick of the pine. This time, Larry laid out the first plank as Neil had done upstairs. But this floor had a lot of shorter runs as walls interrupted the full length of the house. So, the choicest lumber was not necessary.

One other feature this floor had was a trap door to the basement.

Larry turned to face me with faux seriousness. "Andy, I've got a big project for you. Are you ready?"

I nodded, smiling.

"You'll need to picture frame that trap door and put flooring on top of it. Make the frame six inches wide and wait on the flooring until we get there and can line up the seams. Remember, the frame has to be dead-nuts square." Looking at me seriously again, "Do you accept this mission, Mr. Phelps?"

I answered, "yes," smiling both for his joke and for the chance to do this on my own. As I walked away, he sang the theme to *Mission Impossible*.

I picked my stock from the pile and set up the table saw and chop saw. I ripped six-inch wide planks, sanded the edges and cut forty-five degree miters on each end. I glued the backs and ends, and nailed them to the floor, checking the corner to corner dimensions for square, both with itself and with the rest of the hallway and the flooring that was coming to meet it. Then I admired it. It was my first completely independent project on the house. Like the deck I built months before, I felt pride at having created this.

Larry looked over my shoulder, "Not bad, not bad, grasshopper."

We continued the flooring and when we reached the trap door, I filled it in, aligning the boards inside with those outside. In the days and weeks to come, I would admire "my" trap door at every chance I got. I was trusted enough to do it on my own and I had built it.

THE HOUSE WAS BECOMING a home that someone could live in. We could see it and feel it. And so could the owner. Mr. Rogers started to come to the jobsite to inspect the work. His visits—what were called "walk-throughs"— were treated with great seriousness. Sometimes he would swoop over the house in his corporate helicopter before landing at the airport and driving out. Neil told me that once he even landed on the private golf course next door, much to the ire of the club manager.

I felt sorry for Neil during these visits because Jack always came to the job to escort Mr. Rogers around, pointing out all the developments that Neil had supervised for the past months. It was Neil's site every other day, except when Mr. Rogers needed to be shown the progress. Then it was Jack's.

Everyone on the crew was informed well in advance of these visits and instructed to be on our best behavior, whatever that meant. None of us would ever speak directly to Mr. Rogers. We would see and hear him if he came near us but his wishes were communicated through Jack and Neil.

On one visit, Mr. Rogers just stared at an outdoor shower that I had spent the previous two days building. It hadn't made much sense to me in the first place. There was a window right above it so there was no privacy. But it was in the plans and Neil instructed me to build it. After five minutes of review, Mr. Rogers barked out, "Rip it out. I don't like it," and marched off. There was no discussion, no debate. Neil walked up to me, put his hand on my shoulder and finished Mr. Rogers' command, lacing it with his own frustration. "You heard the word, buddy. The man says rip it out, so riiiiiip it out!"

On another visit, Mr. Rogers stared at the window over the kitchen sink. "I don't like it. It needs to be wider and it has to have less mullions." Neil ordered a new one according to new instructions from the architect. We replaced it and put the old one in the crawl space with two others that Mr. Rogers had previously rejected.

Neil mused, "For a powerful CEO, he sure has trouble making up his mind! He's gonna have quite the collection of windows down there when we're through."

In the walk-throughs, I would catch glimpses of the unlimited confidence that Jack embodied. It was a trait that he projected before all others. And I could see that it was part of what Mr. Rogers was buying. Beyond the house, he was buying the confidence that he was getting the best and this was provided by Jack. I was reminded of the man I warmed to in my first interview, and I studied him again as he came to the site with more frequency.

On each visit, I watched him inspire everyone around him to follow his lead. It seemed that all of the people who met him felt his presence immediately. He spoke with a strength and bravado that commanded attention and drew people to him. He laughed easily, spoke intensely, and could switch between the two rapidly. He could cajole and joke one moment, putting people at ease with a charming manner. The next moment, he could focus on an issue with intense gravity, compelling people to share his sense of what was important. In this way, he exerted a personal control that kept people on their toes. To talk with Jack, you followed his tone shifts and emphases. He was the dominant, the alpha male in every conversation. I could see that Neil admired that trait as one that he did not yet possess. And I also sensed a frustration in him for that deficiency.

WHILE ON-ISLAND, Jack would have dinner with the entire crew. When no one else was around, he invited just me. He always paid. I always offered. He always declined. At first, I thought our private dinners were random, but I soon began to wonder if he was timing the invitations for this particular outcome. More and more, he had a purpose. While I would ask questions about construction in general, he would ask questions about the job in particular. His questions would be general at first—"How are things going out there?"—and then get more specific—"Is Neil doing a good job?" I would explain the day's events, trying my best to answer the questions objectively.

In response to my questions, he was an attentive listener and an unhesitant talker. I told him about a particular subcontractor who bragged about jobs he had done and looked at the Rogers job as "chump change." Jack leaned back and said, "Oh, Greg's just a loud mouthed asshole." Then, he looked at me with great seriousness and said, "Andy, *listen to what I'm about to tell you*"—he liked to emphasize serious statements with lines like this—"Never trust anyone who toots his own horn. Let me ask you something. If you walk up to two trash cans and kick 'em. Which one makes the most noise?"

I waited for his answer as I was certain I wasn't really supposed to give one.

"The empty one," he said. "The empty one makes the most noise. And it's the same with people. *Believe me when I tell you*"—another of his favorite lines for emphasis—"those who make the most noise have the least to say." And with that, Jack concluded with a wink and a nod and sat back in satisfaction at having imparted such important wisdom to me, his pupil.

ONE DAY ON THE JOB, I accidentally dropped the construction vacuum cleaner off the second floor. It hit the first floor hard, sending a crack up its side. It was very important that the jobsite be kept clean so I was concerned about the ramifications of this accident and made an attempt at gluing the crack with epoxy.

The next evening, I confessed the accident to Jack, explained my remedy and offered my willingness to replace it. Jack extended his hand, locked eyes with mine, and said, "I appreciate your honesty. I think the epoxy'll be stronger than the original plastic. Don't you?" He jabbed at me, laughing, "Huh? Huh?" He was cajoling me into a smiling affirmative. When I gave it, he added, "Stuff, you're a good man."

"Stuff?" I asked perplexed.

"Yeah, that's what I'm gonna call ya, Stuff. Is that okay with you?"

"I guess." What choice did I really have? I never found out why he chose that name.

Turning serious, he said, "You know, Stuff, when I first met you, I saw the oxford shirt and thought 'college boy.' I wondered if this was a mistake, a waste of my time. When you told me on the phone you had no experience, I decided that I'd test your commitment by having you fly out. When you did, I knew you were serious. You weren't afraid to take a chance. It was refreshing. And now look at you! You're a carpenter!" I stood straighter with each ounce of his praise.

Later, when he found out that I was a golfer, he began to take me to play. Sometimes we just grabbed three irons each and snuck onto the Sankaty Head golf course next to the jobsite. It was a private course, and got very little use, particularly towards the end of the day. So we would play the three holes closest to the jobsite, both frontward and backward. At other times, we played a full eighteen on the public course. We were evenly matched and played close games.

Eric didn't seem to mind my growing connection with his father. But Neil was different. While our dinners would make him uneasy, it was these golf outings that really bothered him. He played at first but couldn't match our game and soon stopped.

When it was becoming clear to Neil that I was spending a lot of time with "the old man," he would sarcastically ask questions like, "How was your dinner date last night?" "Did you kick his ass on the golf course?" I tried to give him answers that might put him at ease, but I suspected that the only answer he would have liked would have been that these dinners and outings with his father were not happening at all.

I began to see that something was happening between father and son, and I was finding myself in between. They were talking less to each other and more through me. And with that shifting dynamic, there was no way that the relationships could stay the same.

WHEN THE FLOORING on the first floor was complete, Neil asked me to run it on the third floor. A modest task, a small room that would become the office; it was the last area without flooring. He gave me no instructions. He didn't come up and lay it out. He simply said, "Andy, do the flooring on the third floor today."

I nodded and excitedly gathered the materials for the job. I was on my own for a second time. I took copious measurements and then laid the first board as I had seen both Larry and Neil do before. Then I began to run the planks off that board, blind and face nailing as I went. But I ran into a problem. Rather than one joist running the entire length of the room, this floor had two joists that crossed in the middle over a single carrying beam. I remembered Neil's earliest instructions that the nailing pattern was to follow the twelve inch pattern of the floor joists. So I ran my nailing pattern up one side of the room at twelve inch spacing and then shifted it by one and a half inches to follow the joist pattern on the other side of the room. I laid down three planks in the shifted pattern when Neil stuck his head through the round spiral stair hole to see how it was going. Climbing onto the floor, he saw the shifted pattern immediately.

"What's the matter with you? You're supposed to do a steady twelve-inch nailing pattern through the entire floor."

"Yeah, but the joists shifted and I shifted with them so the nails would bite."

"Can't you add, you fuckin' idiot. Twelve inches! Twelve inches!" Neil was livid. I could see now that perhaps the joists didn't really matter and that the plywood subfloor provided enough backing for the floor to be nailed to. "I thought you said..."

He cut me off. "My mistake; shouldn't have trusted you. Finish up the floor. The mistake's made; can't reverse it now." He shook his head, "College educated boy and he can't even measure fuckin' twelve inches."

I was cowed but infuriated. I had followed instructions. And while I could see the error now, there was no way for me to know. And besides, the shift didn't look that bad.

I finished the floor and wrapped up my tools to look for my next project. I feared that Neil would make good on his threat not to trust me to work on my own. And I was sore over the tongue-lashing. I found Neil in the kitchen, walked up to him and put a tape measure at his feet, marking two lines at twelve inches precisely.

"Twelve inches. That's twelve inches. Just in case you still had doubts that I could do it, there it is."

Neil looked surprised.

I angrily continued, "When you first told me how to do the floors, you said that I should follow the joists and I did. I'm sorry if that wasn't what I was supposed to do, but that's what you said. Next time, why don't you think more carefully about the instructions you give? Because you *can* trust that I will listen and carry them out."

"Don't take it so seriously Andy," he said calmly. "Let's wrap up. The day's almost over and we need to do a big cleanup. This place is a pit." And he walked off, leaving me standing in a dazed fury. I grabbed a broom and began to sweep.

THE FLOORS WERE GIVEN their first rough sanding and interior work began. Interior doors were delivered and Neil showed me how to hang them.

"Check the floor for level first and foremost. Make sure that there's a half-inch undercut from the higher side. Cut the jambs based on the level, not the floor. Nail off the hinged jamb first and then the strike jamb. No need to nail off the head. The trim'll tie it all together."

I was thrilled. Neil had given me instructions in the language of a carpenter and I had understood every word!

Between the four of us, we had all twelve interior doors hung in one day. Then, a new load of pine arrived for the baseboard, window and door trim and the closet poles and shelves. These were nearly the last steps for the carpenters in the house.

Neil explained the trick for "scribing" the baseboard to fit the floor. "Put the baseboard on the floor, slide your pencil along the floor to trace a line that matches the curves of the floor and then trim it to fit. Even though we built this house 'dead nuts' on, there're variations in the final thickness of the floor and it's no longer perfectly flat. And when the baseboard doesn't meet the floor, even for a sixteenth of the inch, there'll be a dark shadow. We can't have that." Then he showed me how to cut the outside and inside baseboard corners differently. The former were mitered at forty-five degree angles. For the latter, he handed me a "coping saw" and taught me a technique called "back cutting."

When he finished his explanation, I set up my workshop: baseboard stock, eight penny and four penny nails, glue, a coping saw, a chop saw, a circular saw and a square. I decided to start on a short outside corner first to get the hang of it. I cut my pieces and fit them together. Either the miter or the wall wasn't perfect, and I had a small gap opening on the outside. So I tried again. This time, there was an equally small gap opening on the inside. I still felt tentative over the floor-nailing encounter and wanted to make sure I didn't make any mistakes.

"Neil, can you look at these and tell me if they're okay?"

I set up my first miter and then my second. "If I have to err, where would it be better? A gap on the outside or the inside?"

"Andy, the correct answer is not to have a gap on either side."

He paused, waiting for my reaction. But since I earnestly accepted his answer, he amended it. "But, we don't want you takin' all day on this one corner. In truth, this baseboard's gonna be painted so we can tolerate a little more slop than if it was stained. So, err with the gap on the inside. Then we can still have a sharp outside edge."

I again accepted the answer earnestly.

Neil walked away chanting, "*A little putty, a little paint, makes a carpenter what he ain't.*"

THE SOUNDS OF HAMMERS and saws echoed from different locations through the house as we all worked on trim in different rooms. There were also sounds of conversation among the painters who were working in the house that day. Outside, the lawn sprinklers were being installed and the crew was creating their own particular noises. Every trade had its own sounds; each had become familiar to me.

Then, I noticed a new sound. It was a set of voices I didn't recognize and the tone was growing angrier. I looked out the front window. There on a second floor porch was Neil yelling down at a woman and a man in a pickup truck.

"Get the fuck off this property," he yelled.

"You owe us money, asshole," the strangers replied.

"You were paid what you were owed, now get the fuck off this property or I'm callin' the cops."

"Go ahead. We'll explain to them why we're here."

"Give it up, this is over."

"Yeah, tell your father it's not."

Neil turned around and emerged suddenly into the house, catching me by the window, twenty feet from my tools. "Okay, the show's over. Get back to work." He tried to sound relaxed but the redness of his face, the furrows on his brow and the bulging veins on his neck gave away the truth. Looking out the window, I saw the truck driving away, leaving a cloud of dust in its wake. Neil didn't even stop to see if I went back to work. He was on the phone.

"Dad, yeah it's me…Craig Painting was just here…They say you haven't paid 'em…Uh huh…They were pretty angry. They say this isn't over…Uh huh…yeah, okay." He hung up the phone.

At lunch, the fight was the first topic of conversation.

"Neil, what was that all about?" asked Larry.

"Aw, just some assholes that think they've got a right to be paid for work they didn't do."

"I remember those guys," said Eric. "They were real dickheads. They did lousy work and thought they were God's gift."

Neil explained, "We had to fire them after a week on another job. They weren't giving the windows a proper seal. That's what they were paid for and we had to harass them for everything. They complained whenever we asked them to touch up." He shook his head. "They did real condo-quality work. We paid them in full for the week and sent them packing. And they've been complaining ever since."

Tony, one of the painters added, "I've heard about them. They get a lot of expensive contracts on-island."

"Well maybe some of them are good. But the crew we got was shit," said Neil.

"When did this happen?" I asked. "They seem like they're still pretty raw."

"Man, it's been about six months. They must be short on work to still be looking for money," answered Neil. "But Dad will take care of this." There was pride and certainty in his comment.

"What's Jack like when he gets pissed?" I asked. "I'll bet he's fierce."

"He's tough. You don't wanna cross him." Neil paused for a moment. I couldn't tell if he was thinking about Jack's dealings with contractors or perhaps his dealings with his own sons. "Did you know that he used to own a garage and built race cars and race bikes back in the old days?"

"I can picture it," I said, smiling. "I can see him as a greaser."

"Yeah, you should see the old pictures. His hair slicked back, a white t-shirt with the sleeves rolled up, a pack of cigarettes in one sleeve. He was tough. Do you know anything about how he treated my mom?"

"No, she lives in Connecticut?" I asked.

"No, that's my stepmom. My..."

"And mine," Eric interjected.

"*Our* mom," Neil nodded to Eric, "lives in Maryland. Dad and she were married till Eric was about two. The way Dad tells it, she was crazy. Things got really bad and they were moving towards divorce. She wanted the kids and there was no way he was gonna let that happen. He sold the garage without her knowing, packed us up in the middle of the night and drove us to Connecticut. He says that the next day he walked into a lawyers office, gave him the entire check from the garage and told him that he was to make sure the kids stayed with him."

"I guess he succeeded," I said.

"Yeah, but I think it cost him a lot."

"Have you ever spent time with your mom after that?" I asked.

"Oh some. But Dad wasn't really interested in keeping in touch with her and so we didn't really either. A lot of bad blood between them. We talk every now and then, send cards at holidays, that kind of stuff."

Suddenly Jack emerged at the doorway. "What's going on gentlemen? How's the day's work going?" He had a bounce and an enthusiasm that was the mirror opposite of the mood of his son. And, as always, his mood raised that of the crew.

"The day's going well Dad, except for the little commotion this morning," said Neil.

"Yeah, well I'll take care of that shit. You can count on that. No one talks to my foreman like that and gets away with it. Believe me when I tell you. I'll have my lawyer working on them so fast their heads'll be spinning."

Jack started to laugh. "Then they'll be begging me to take back the money I already paid them just to stop." He nodded with an enthusiastic grin, "Don't ya think?"

We all nodded and Jack asked to speak to Neil alone. The rest of us returned to small talk; the fight, the work ahead, the girl that Tony had met the previous night, the party that was coming up the following weekend.

After lunch, work resumed. I could still see Neil and Jack outside. Jack appeared to be doing most of the talking. Neil looked down, listening and nodding.

I focused on my work. I had to run baseboard along a long stretch of the dining room and went to the stock pile for one of the pieces of long stock. The pile had many different lengths in roughly one foot intervals. In picking stock, I learned that the rules were to minimize waste and put the best wood in the most visible spots. So, if I needed an eight-foot piece, I tried to find one as close as possible. Nevertheless, the extremely long stock was in short supply and highly desirable. No one liked to put a joint in the middle of a stretch of baseboard. It was hard to make and ruined the look of the baseboard. So if someone took a piece of long stock and cut it into smaller pieces, there would come a reckoning with the other carpenters. Likewise, if someone needed a piece of long stock and it wasn't there, he had a right to claim it from another carpenter if he could show that the plank was either more closely matched to his needed length or if it was in a more prominent location. An informal hierarchy of rooms existed. The living room, dining room and master bedroom got top priority. Hallways got next priority and guest bedrooms were last. Closets and bathrooms could be filled in with scraps from the other rooms.

I found a piece that closely matched my needs and, given that it was in the dining room, felt no need to check with the other carpenters and took it. My piece would run from one inside corner to another and I cut it to length. I laid it on the floor, traced the curve of the floor and began to trim it.

"Hey Stuff, how's it going?" Jack emerged from behind me.

I felt instantly self-conscious at his observing me ply my new trade. I knew that I was doing the steps as I was instructed and hoped that I was doing them right.

"I think I'm on top of it," I said.

"You having fun?" asked Jack.

I smiled, "Yeah, I love this pine."

"Good, but don't have too much fun. We've gotta finish this house some time this year." Jack smiled and winked at me.

I responded with a smile.

"Hey, let me show you something." He picked up two scraps and placed them in the corner. "You should always cope the inside corner so as to turn the joint away from oncoming eyes. You should never see it straight on."

Then he shifted, becoming more stern. "Stuff, what did you think of our little event this morning?"

"Well, they were pretty angry. It wasn't very professional," I said.

His eyes narrowed. "Not professional on their part or not professional on Neil's part?"

I was uncomfortable having this conversation on the jobsite. Jack had never done this before. He directed me outside and closed the door behind us. "Tell me what happened."

"Jack, I didn't see the whole thing but from what I saw, Neil had little choice. They were pretty abusive and he got dragged into it. He just told them to get off the property and they just said they wanted their money. It ended with them telling Neil to tell you that it wasn't over. I guess I'd say it was pretty childish."

"Yeah, you can be sure I'll end this thing. Have no doubts about that," Jack replied firmly. "Do you think we need a restraining order?"

"Boy Jack, I don't know. They were pretty angry but I couldn't tell if they'd resort to violence. Don't you think a restraining order would make 'em madder?"

"Well maybe. It's hard to say with people like that." Jack paused for a moment. "Andy, I need you to think about the question I'm gonna ask very carefully. Will you do that?" His eyes burned into me.

"Yes, of course Jack."

"Okay here it is. How did Neil do in handling this situation? I need to know. Don't hold back. I really need to know."

"That's really hard for me to say," I felt put on the spot. "He got pretty agitated with them. He swore. He pretty much just told them to get the fuck off the job." I was trying to remain objective. But Jack wanted an assessment.

"Hmmm. Was he professional? Did he provoke the fight?"

"There was swearing going in both directions. And I don't know how he could have remained professional when they were so hostile. His staying on the porch was probably a good thing. There was no chance of any kind of physical fight."

Jack nodded, but I felt uncomfortable, not sure what message was being received.

"Would you have handled it differently?" asked Jack.

I sighed. "I couldn't say."

He shot back quickly, "Try."

"I don't know the pressures Neil's under or the history of this fight."

Jack became impatient and raised his voice. "Let me tell you something. When Neil finds himself under pressure, I take it away. That kid has nothing to worry about. I wish I had that luxury when I was in his shoes. And as for the history, that's between them and me. Neil only needs to worry about what goes on here and now. The real headaches are mine." He paused, then continued, his voice still raised. "So, would you have handled it differently?"

"Well Jack, it's not my nature to swear quite so much. So, yes. I would have handled it differently." I hoped that this would be enough, not sure how far Jack would push me.

Jack stopped, smiled and softened his tone. "Thanks Stuff, that's helpful."

I didn't like this. I didn't want Jack to evaluate his son based on my assessment. And I didn't want to be complicit in the rift between them. But I was coming into Jack's confidence while Neil was falling out. Jack seemed to have made a choice, heading in a direction that included me more and Neil less. And, if that seemed clear to me, it must also have seemed clear to Neil.

After Jack left the jobsite and work returned to its previous routine, Neil and I would pass each other, but now with a palpable tension. It was quite likely that he had heard my conversation with Jack. And even if he hadn't, knowing the conversation even took place must have been unnerving. We never spoke of it directly.

BY SEPTEMBER, THE SUMMER was coming to an end and vacationers were leaving the island. But our work continued. Larry, Eric, Neil and I worked our way through the house, finishing the wood trim and installing the finish hardware: door handles, towel bars, window latches, door stops. The painters were finishing the walls, windows and doors. Cabinet-makers were completing the kitchen, bathrooms and built-in window seats and dressers. Tile was being laid in the bathrooms. And the electricians were putting in the switch and plug plates, wiring the appliances, hanging interior light fixtures and trenching wires to install accent lighting around the grounds.

As the list of last remaining items was growing shorter, the "punch-list" was growing longer. A piece of trim that chipped had to be replaced. A dent in the wall from the appliance delivery had to be filled in, primed and painted. The house was in its most fragile state and we had to do everything with a mind towards being very careful. When the floor had received its final coat of urethane, we began working in stocking feet.

While replacing a piece of decking that had warped, I accidentally put the saw down with the blade still spinning, not noticing that the guard had stuck open. The saw ran across three planks, tearing into them. Larry nearby, quickly went into his Sergeant Shultz imitation, "I see nothing! Nothing!" I quickly and quietly replaced the damaged pieces.

But despite the punch-list and these occasional mistakes, it was clear that the job was coming to an end and the idea of completion filled me with satisfaction. I enjoyed closing the door to a finished room, listening to the echo of the latch catching the strike in the empty space, and knowing that no one needed to go in there again. The room was done. It was like an internal checklist and I was ticking off the rooms until there would be none left to tick off. I had to begin to decide what to do when the house was done.

Jack made it clear that he had no other work after this house. So, the crew began to talk openly about their next project and pressure Neil for an answer on when they could leave. Larry was the first to announce that he had indoor work that would take him through the winter. I learned quickly that this was the first and best option for all of the crew as the subs talked enviously of Larry's not having work outside in the cold winter months.

I weighed my options and decided that I had experienced enough of carpentry. My "how to build a house journal" was fifty pages of notes and drawings. Some recorded personal experiences, others described what Neil, Larry, Eric, Jack and other subcontractors taught me. I had sowed my wild oats and, I figured, it was time to get back to the "real world." I added "independent contractor" to my resume and sent it to consultants who

would appreciate my engineering background. A consulting firm north of
Boston expressed interest in hiring me, I took a day off to fly back for an
interview and was soon offered a job. I announced my "indoor work" to the
crew but they teased me about being a pansy for sitting at a desk.

As did the others, I asked Neil for a timeline on when I could go and he
promised we would be done in three to four weeks. When I asked for more
precision, he snapped and said "You're done when I say you're done. Unless,
of course, you wanna fuck me over and leave me short handed when I need
you most."

"Neil, come on," I replied. "I won't do that. I just need to plan."

But Neil was changing, becoming more tense at a time when everyone
else was feeling more buoyant. I wondered if the delivery of a finished house
was weighing heavily on him. I knew that there was a date that the house
was promised to be finished, but I didn't know what the date was, whether
we would actually meet it and whether there was any penalty of it being
late. Neil was always very closed with matters like this. He never even let
anyone see the plans to the house. But I also wondered if the straining
relationship with his father was also taking its toll. Whatever it was, it was
eating him up.

One day a request came in from Mr. Rogers. He wanted yet another
kitchen window, this time larger. Neil was livid. "This goddamned
kitchen is never gonna be done," he fumed as we removed the trim,
pulled out the old window and cut back the sheetrock. The entire task
was done with violent aggression. We literally ripped the window out
of the wall in complete violation of the care he demanded of our finish
work. We framed a new and larger opening and put the new window
and trim back in. Then he told me simply to, "clean up this fuckin' shit
and get the painters in here to make it look right." He stormed off and
I finished the job.

I WAS ON THE FIRST FLOOR, trimming the last closet, when I heard a
commotion on the second floor. I walked to the edge of the stairs and stood
silently trying to pick up what was going on. Jack's Blazer was out front and
he was arguing with Neil above me. While I missed the beginning of the
fight, I could tell by their tone that this was serious.

"Neil, that box truck is mine," said Jack, his voice raised. "It has my name on it. It's not yours."

"I painted and restored that truck," Neil answered. "And anyway, it was just sitting here over the weekend. No one was using it,"

"So you think you can just take it anytime you want?" Jack's voice was getting louder.

"Why not, it's no loss to you."

"No loss? That's my name on the side. On Saturday, I get a call from someone saying he doesn't appreciate my truck parked on his grass. I say, 'I'm sorry. You must be mistaken. My truck's parked in Sconset.' Then this guy says 'No, *you're* mistaken, I'm looking at your truck right now.'" He paused, pressure building in the hanging silence. "So now I'm a liar." Jack was now fully shouting. "And my company name is doing jobs I don't even know about. What if you make a mistake or there's an accident? What if you get sued? Who's gonna pick up the fuckin' pieces then? Answer me that!"

Neil was indignant. "I don't need your help. You don't need to pick up the pieces. I do first class work and I'm careful."

"That's irrelevant. It's my company name, not yours. And you *will not* use it, or my equipment, or you *will be* sorry. Believe me when I fuckin' tell you." Jack sounded ready to explode.

But Neil taunted back, "What're you gonna do, fire me?"

There was a heavy silence. I was shocked that Neil would so openly defy his father, someone who by his own admission was fierce when provoked. Only then did I notice Larry listening grimly right behind me. The tension mounted and we waited anxiously for what would happen next.

"You're fired!" Jack yelled. "If that's what you think, then get your fuckin' tools and get your fuckin' ass off my job. You're fired." There was a controlled fury in Jack's words that chilled me. I could sense that this fight had years of tension behind it, the tension that could only be created between a father and son. This ran much deeper than a single misunderstanding. Something was tearing here.

"Yeah, and who's gonna finish this job?" Neil sounded close to becoming hysterical, his words pouring out. "You never come to the job. I did everything. And now you have nobody. Good fuckin' luck." The job was silent except for the heavy steps of Neil as he stormed out of the house, slamming the door behind him. He started his truck and sped away in a cloud from the dusty driveway.

With the fight over, Larry and I felt suddenly exposed, huddled at the bottom of the stairs. Anyone would notice that all sounds of construction activity had ceased. We tip-toed back to our respective tasks, but I hesitated to break the still hanging silence with a hammer blow or a saw cut. Thankfully, Larry started first.

Jack walked into my room first, "Stuff, I need to talk to you, Larry and Eric for a minute." His voice was now calm, his fury fully expelled. We walked into the guest room where Larry was working.

"Guys, as I'm sure you just heard, I've let Neil go. This's been brewing for a while and it finally came. It had to come. Now, I'm relying on you. Can I count on you to finish this job up?" His question was not the plea of a man in a jam. It was a statement that he was placing his trust in us. While I felt sad for the rift that had just formed between him and Neil, his was a trust that I was proud to accept.

Larry replied optimistically, "No problem, Jack. Your job's in good hands. We know everything that's happened so far. And we know everything that still needs to be done. All the materials are here already, so we just need to button this baby up!"

I nodded in agreement, "Yeah, we can do this." I wasn't sure but felt confident in Larry's assessment.

"Okay guys," he reached to shake our hands. "I'll take care of both of you for this. If there's ever anything you need or any questions you have, you pick up that phone and call me. Anything! Do you understand? Anything!"

LARRY AND I DIVIDED UP the remaining tasks and listed them on a piece of scrap wood for the three of us. With the scope of the work clearly laid out, I could see now that the house would wrap up by mid-October.

And it did. With little fanfare and one last walk through of the completed home, Jack handed us our last paychecks and shook our hands warmly. "There's a little somethin' extra in there for stickin' it out until the end. I don't forget people who stand by their word. If you ever need a reference, don't hesitate to contact me. I'll give you the best goddamned reference anyone has ever gotten."

And with that, the summer ended. We all parted without sentimentality or ceremony. Eric left on a trip with his girlfriend. Larry and I packed up our belongings to move, me to Boston and he to Hyannis.

I packed away my Carhartt pants, now faded with the summer sun, softened from repeated use, dabbed with paint, caulking and joint compound and worn at the knees, hammer loop, and utility knife pocket. Next to the pants, I packed my tool belt. What started the summer as a stiff strap of leather folds had become a softened series of pockets. On the outside, the tanned leather bore streaks where, like my pants, I had wiped caulking, glue or paint off my fingers. Each marking reminded me of the task that caused it. The leather itself was worn from carrying the many varieties of nails and screws that were used to build the house. For each job, I had emptied the old set of nails and replaced them with new ones. The purging was never thorough and by the end of the job, each pocket contained a variety of nails that marked the progression of my carpentry experience. I liked the history that the tool belt told. It was a tangible sign to me that I had learned how to build a house.

Larry and I had one last beer with Neil who was pragmatic about getting fired. "Dad wasn't gonna be able to carry me through the winter anyway. This way I have work and I'll build my own company just like he built his." There was still defiance and bravado in his voice. He was much like his father.

I watched as Larry and Neil talked. I could see the makings of a ritual being played out, much like the one that had taken place among the subs as the job progressed. They had been through this process of parting often enough that they were used to the comings and goings of people into and out of their lives. There were many houses being built and many carpenters building them. In each case, new connections were made and old ones were broken. It was a never-ending cycle of crisscrossing paths. Carpenters came, met, lived and parted and no one lamented this course of events. They took pride in the jobs they had done and referred to them often; "I did a house once..." or "I worked with a guy on a house once..." The house was always the unifying factor.

DISCERNMENT

"People in the West are always getting ready to live."

I MOVED BACK TO BOSTON and began working for EEC Corporation, an engineering consulting firm north of the city. The job was interesting for its novelty and paid me about thirty percent more than I had earned in my old desk job.

I decided to shed the pickup truck and buy the expensive sports car I always dreamt of. But my dreams and reality did not mesh. I placed ads in the paper, feeling foolish at selling an eight month old truck. But, the only interest came from car dealers who wanted it for their used car lots. My pride and frugality forced me to reject their low offers and accept that I wouldn't shed this artifact of my carpenter identity quite so quickly.

In fact, the identity of carpenter had sunk in deeper than I had expected. I had changed. I now saw things differently, noticing things that I had never noticed before. My eyes would instantly scrutinize any carpentry that I passed. When I walked into the EEC headquarters, all I saw was the woodwork in the beautifully renovated historic warehouse. I admired the size and form of the sandblasted oak beams that ran the length of the exposed ceilings. I wondered how large a tree created them and whether any such trees still remained in New England. I wondered how they were cut and lifted into place when the building was originally built at the turn of the 20th century. I enjoyed the benefit of power tools but the original carpenters of this building did most of their work by hand. I felt a newfound appreciation for these early craftsmen.

I was tolerant of deviations from *plumb, level and square* in the early massive structure that had settled with age. But, I was critical of any deviations in the contemporary woodwork of the polished doors, cabinets, baseboard and window trim. Seams that weren't perfectly smooth or doors that didn't precisely fit their jambs bothered me. I found myself sighting along banks of windowsills and rows of cabinetry for any offending dips and rises. I assessed and graded the quality of the joinery at the corner of windows, door jambs or baseboard. If a cabinet drawer or door didn't slide or close easily, I noted it. It was involuntary. I saw it as almost a curse, distracting me from the overall beauty of the building that everyone else saw. I was now more aware and there was no way I could go back to making myself unaware.

MY DESK WAS IN THE CENTER of the building with no views outside. But as the winter progressed and the air got colder, I would steal glimpses out the office windows of more senior executives and think of the carpenters and subcontractors that I had met over the summer. How many had found indoor work? I shivered at the prospect of pounding nails in sub zero temperatures. I imagined hitting a thumbnail of an already frozen hand and counted my blessings that I was working safe and warm in a beautiful office building.

But after four months, I began to tire of the work and began to feel the same dissatisfaction I had felt with my old engineering job. I wanted to see some tangible results. My boss told me that I was doing well and had a bright future. But, I didn't feel satisfied with the work. It was again becoming merely a job and I wanted something more personal. There was none of *me* in the work.

My mind returned to the pure and honest joy I had felt while building the Rogers' house. I could watch it grow before my eyes. There were results that I could see, touch and measure every day. While I doubted that anyone else would see the difference between my contribution to the job and that of someone else, I could see it. When I looked at the trap door or the baseboard joints, I saw a part of myself. I saw my contribution.

I began to worry that I had walked out of the path that was going to make me happy. But always my own worst devil's advocate, I also questioned whether I could possibly make the jump back in again. My resume would surely suffer from my returning to construction, wouldn't it? And how would it look if I stayed at a job with a major consulting firm for only six months? I worried that I was ruining my career by entertaining such notions.

BUT, I BEGAN TO SCAN the help-wanted ads for carpentry jobs again, at first out of curiosity and then with more intent. I decided that if I found something local that looked appealing, I would make the call. I also wanted to move up the ranks into some kind of a foreman role and not be talked down to by another version of Neil. I made a few calls but all I could find were large companies building housing developments or condo projects. The dialogue was generally the same.

"How many years experience do you have?" "What tools do you own?" "Do you have your own transportation?"

Out of this series of questions, each discussion ended with an offer of an hourly wage and responsibilities far lower than what Jack had given me. Each time, it was explained that with less than one year's experience, I could not possibly start anywhere but at the lowest level of the crew. I realized that I had been very lucky with my first foray into carpentry and had to remain patient to find such an unusual opportunity again, if that was even possible. But the answers from continued calls did not change; I was too inexperienced.

I began to think of contracting on my own. If I couldn't get the right opportunity, I would make it. A friend told me about his uncle, Greg, who built custom homes in Lexington, an affluent suburb west of Boston. "Perhaps you'd like to meet him. I'd be glad to arrange for an introduction. Maybe he could hire you or maybe he could explain to you what it's like to contract on your own." Then he added sarcastically, "Or maybe he can rid you of this destructive fantasy."

I ignored his final remark and arranged with Greg to meet at his jobsite. We met on an unseasonably warm February day. He greeted me in neatly pressed khaki's and a button down oxford. By the feel of his uncallused handshake, I could tell that he did no labor at all. He walked me around the seven "spec houses" of his development. He had no clients when he started and was building them on speculation. He already had buyers for two.

"No need to worry yet," he explained. "I'll have the rest sold before the interest costs start to kill me. We began about a year ago and our total running time will be eighteen months. In that time, we expect to make between twelve and fourteen percent return on investment."

While he talked finance, I admired the architectural details. The seven houses were beautifully designed, each different, lining either side of a cul-de-sac. One house flared at the bottom giving it a sense of mass as it rested on its foundation. I made a mental note to add that to my house building journal from the summer. Another displayed a beautiful array of windows in the living room that allowed sunlight to fill the entire space.

"Did you hire the architect for this project or did you buy the plans?" I asked.

"The architect is an equity partner. He, some friends and I have each invested various percentages of money to get this off the ground. And our return will be paid accordingly. But it's my job to bring it to completion. For that, I get an extra percentage."

A young carpenter interrupted us. "Greg, when are your roofers ready for unit three? I wanna finish the interior framing. The electrician is anxious to get inside too."

"I'll push him to be over there tomorrow. But you can see he's falling behind on unit two." Turning to me he said, "Carl's my foreman. He's doing the heavy lifting here."

"Nice to meet you," I said.

"Same here," Carl replied and rushed off.

"What was I talking about before?" Greg asked absent-mindedly. "Oh yeah, the whole key to this business is financing. Keep things moving, turn over quickly and keep more of your return by giving less to the bank. The market is good right now. The real challenge is keeping your head above water when the market gets tight. I prefer these higher-end jobs. They're more recession proof."

As he was speaking, I started to smell alcohol on his breath. It was ten o'clock in the morning! I began to notice that he looked tired, worn. He lacked the energy and pride that I saw in Jack or that I felt at seeing the Rogers house go up. As he spoke, he also made me realize that I had not even thought about the business of construction. I was excited at building, not financing. But if I was going to go into business for myself, I would have to learn.

Carl returned, handing Greg a piece of paper, "Here's the punch-list for unit one."

"Godammit! This is the worst part of this job," Greg exclaimed, holding up the piece of paper. "Look at this. The dishwasher is missing a knob. It's going to take me two hours to track down a piece that some fucking plumber broke off or threw away!"

I thought about how I enjoyed the punch-list. It meant the house was almost done and I remembered how I loved the finishing touches and that feeling of completion.

"Greg, last question," I said. "How hard is it to speculate like this?"

"Look at me Andy, I've never swung a hammer in my life." My opinion of him dropped further. "I've done a lot of different kinds of jobs; real estate, writing. But I'll tell you, there's a lot more money in this than any of the other jobs I've done. All you need to do to start is start. That's the best advice I can give you."

I drove back to work with those words in my mind. Did I simply need to try? Is that all that was standing in my way? And did I want to build homes on spec? My mind was filled with more new questions than answers.

That evening I called Jack for his opinion. "Andy, this is serious business. If you wanna talk about it, come down to Connecticut so we can talk face to face," he said. When I agreed, he added one final thought before hanging up. "This is a big decision. But, I'll tell you this. If you get one crooked subcontractor, one asshole, he'll put you in the red so deep and so fast, it'll take you years to dig yourself out." And with that last bit of discouragement, I made plans to visit Jack at his home in Connecticut the following weekend.

MY DRIVE TO JACK'S HOUSE took me to the western edge of Connecticut. Getting off interstate 84, I drove down a winding country road, passed an old church nestled among the trees, a golf course set back from the road, houses separated by large wooded areas and, surprisingly, past the corporate headquarters of the Union Carbide Corporation, a guarded iron gate blocking entry into the beautiful grounds.

Jack's house was modest, one story with a small porch adorning the entry and a circular gravel driveway. Jack emerged at the doorway to greet me. As usual, he was wearing a chamois shirt, jeans and tan work boots. He greeted me warmly.

"Hey Stuff. Welcome to my home. Come inside, take a load off. My wife, Jane, is out right now. Were the directions okay?"

I smiled and answered in the affirmative, we shook hands and I walked in. The inside of the house was as simple as the outside. It was clean both in its lines and in its appearance. No, "immaculate" was the more appropriate word, I thought. Nothing was out of place and no dirt could be seen.

Jack looked me over, "Well, what a surprise! Stuff is here in Connecticut. I never would have guessed it last summer. And now, here you are, in my home."

It was true, I really didn't expect our paths to cross again. And now, here I was, in Jack's home, in Jack's world. It felt safe. Jack made it feel safe. I sensed that Jack's world had a neatness, an order, that he defined. I felt strangely out of place within it.

"I built this house five years ago," Jack said proudly as he led me on a narrated tour. But the narration was not about the house's visible aesthetics; it was about how it was built. "I put the walls up in three days. I had Freddie Carlucci, my plumber, help me with the rafters which I got up in another two days. I had the whole thing framed and dry in less than three weeks. I had some friends do the utilities and then I finished up the sheetrock, trim, doors and cabinets myself. I went from a hole in the ground to move in condition in roughly three months." A large grin enveloped his face as he prodded me, "Whadaya think of that? Not too shabby huh?" He looked at me, waiting for the appropriate appreciation at what must have been a superhuman feat.

I had forgotten about his intensity, how he could put me on the spot. "That's a big difference from the Rogers House," I said. "Who designed it?"

"I did, of course. I started with a simple idea in my head and then finished as I went. My original idea was to put the entry there, and the bathroom over there." He was pointing around the house. "But when I poured the foundation, I decided that I could get much better room and traffic patterns putting them where they are now."

Again, I took his cue and nodded in approval. I was staring at the fireplace as I nodded. It was about six feet wide.

Jack laughed, "You like that? Big, isn't it?"

"You must get monstrous fires in there."

Jack laughed harder. What he did, and what gave him pleasure revolved around being the most impressive, whether that be size, speed of construction, or test of his own abilities. Jack led me out onto the porch where we surveyed his land.

"I bought this whole lot," Jack said as he pointed beyond the neighbor's house. "I sold the other half to a friend and cleared enough to cover a major portion of this house."

This time I let silence hang, staring off into the distance. Again, as with Greg, the talk turned to matters of finance, and I felt nervous at the idea that I should know these things if I was serious about going into business for myself. And, I knew that I had nowhere near the financial stake necessary to start a project like this.

Jack broke my trance by leading me into the kitchen. Without asking, he poured two glasses of water and handed one to me, first placing a neatly folded paper towel underneath it.

"Okay Andy, tell me what's up? " He sat down and waited patiently.

"Well Jack, I'm thinking about building houses. I'm not happy at this new job and want to get back into the business."

"Andy I'm sorry. I would've been glad to keep you on after the Rogers job but I had nothin' goin' on then," Jack said apologetically.

"No Jack, it's not that. I understood where you were coming from. And to be honest, I'm not sure I would've stayed, even if you had offered. At the end of last summer, I thought I'd satisfied my urge for construction and would go back to where I was before. But, now I'm not so sure I can do that. I think I needed to find that out. But, now I know."

"Well Andy," Jack sighed, "why do you wanna go into construction?" With a furrowed brow, he added, "What're you looking for?"

His concern made me self-conscious. Was I coming across as being lost, looking for something that I couldn't find? "I just love it, Jack. I love building. I love seeing the house go together. I love the materials. I love the tools. I love everything about it. When I do a project at work now, I produce a pile of paper. It's not satisfying, not like building. When I take an idea and make it real, that feels good. And I felt that every day in Nantucket." I added with extra emphasis, "Every day!"

Jack smiled with a warmth beyond what I had seen before. "Do you wanna know why I love it?" he asked. "I love making a promise to someone and then keeping it. When someone comes to me, they're putting their trust in me to make their dream come true. In many ways, they don't even know what's involved to do that. Even the architects don't fully understand about building. But, I take all their worries away when I shake their hand. And I deliver what they had only envisioned in their mind and on paper. I promise it and I deliver it!"

He stared at me in a kind, fatherly way. "Andy, when I look at you, I see someone who's willing to take a chance and move away from what others expect him to be. Is that accurate?"

"Well, I'm not sure about that Jack. I guess I'm trying to do that." While still feeling insecure about what I was looking for, I could feel myself respond to his praise. He could still do that; make me feel taller, more confident. And now, it was happening again. My insecurities were melting away. And with them receding, I recognized an admiration for him that I had not seen so clearly before. He was giving me individual encouragement and praise that I longed for.

"It's not easy," he continued. "When I was growing up, my father wanted me to be in the military. But I wanted to build things; first cars, then houses. Did you know that?"

I sheepishly replied "yes," admitting that he had been a subject of conversation on the jobsite.

He paused, his eyes narrowed but he continued. "Well the point is that that's what I decided to do. *I* decided! And I built this company with my own two hands. I built some houses here in Connecticut and then got talked into a helping a friend with his house on Nantucket. That house led to another, which led to the Rogers house. They saw the quality in my work and they came to me. I've never advertised a day in my life and never will. In each case, I delivered what I promised. Each one of those houses is the best money could buy. And I built my reputation, *house by house* so that people who wanted the best knew to come to me."

I admired him more for what he was telling me. While he was often boasting to me about his work, I liked the notion that, with his clients, his work spoke for itself. But I also had an idea that, while the houses may have drawn in the clients, it was his bravado, self-confidence and boasting that hooked them. I couldn't separate what Jack did from who he was.

He looked directly at me and asked. "Do you see why I'm telling you this? Do you see what I'm trying to tell you?"

I replied, "Yes," and in that one word, I acknowledged the crux of my dilemma. I was afraid to do what I wanted to do and was doing instead what I was expected to do.

"Andy, I know how hard it is to change your life. You're a college educated guy. I know the expectations that can place on you. I'll bet you got some strange looks when you came down to Nantucket. And I'm sure you're feeling some self-doubt about being here right now."

Jack was reading me perfectly. It made me uncomfortable feeling so exposed.

Jack continued, "But if this is what you want, then I want to help you do it." Then he got up from the table and announced, "Grab your coat. I wanna show you something."

I dutifully followed him into the garage. It looked as I would expect— immaculate. The floor was painted and spotless; no dust, no dirt, no oil. Along one wall were three professional mechanic's tool boxes, neatly arranged. No tools were lying on top, the drawers were all closed. Attached to the wall next to the driver's side door was a carpet remnant to protect either the car door from the wall or vice-versa. It didn't matter. Damage to either would have been contrary to the neatness in Jack's world. His truck was, again, spotless. And once in the cab, I was again engulfed by his familiar cologne.

We pulled out of the driveway and returned to the main road, turning deeper into the countryside than the way I had come. Along the road, expensive homes were comfortably nestled on hill-sides and among the trees. After several miles, Jack pulled the truck into a dirt driveway that led up a gently rising slope of open field.

"This fifteen acre parcel is owned by Randy and Maura Winslow. I'm building their house up there at the top."

The announcement startled me. I thought that he didn't have any other jobs since Nantucket. Jack saw my surprised look and sought to calm me. "I know what you're thinking. Just hear me out."

Up the hill, I could see excavating equipment and several piles of dirt; the only disturbances in the large field. As we approached, I could see the true proportions of the hole that created the piles. About two-hundred and fifty feet along its center axis, it had three wings that jutted out at perpendicular angles on the ends. Both the shape of the house and the work that would create it were very large and complex. The foundation would turn left and right, sometimes for long distances, sometimes for distances as short as two feet.

As I scanned the whole site, I could see each stage in the concrete foundation process. Some walls were complete and standing without forms.

Next to them, walls were poured and still contained by the forms and dark black blankets to keep them from freezing. Diagonal braces held everything in place. Next, I could see foundation forms standing, but there was no concrete inside them. Beyond that, I could see walls where only half the form was up and green "rebar" was suspended like a cage next to it.

Jack explained that rebar, short for reinforcing bar, were steel rods—in this case, half inch thick—that were embedded inside the concrete walls to give them strength. Next, there were walls without the rebar and finally forms and rebar were lying next to the foundations footings, waiting to be assembled.

"Not bad huh?" Jack added to the silence that accompanied my efforts to take it all in. The site was muddy from the warm sun. Beyond the site, I could see that one of the dirt piles was dark, rich, topsoil. The other six were the lighter soil from the deeper levels. Among the excavating equipment that created them were several flatbed trucks that carried concrete forms from one end of the house to the other.

"This is one hell of a foundation," Jack pronounced. "I've got the best concrete company in the area working on it. There aren't a lot of guys that could pull this one off. Take a close look at how many times this thing jogs. This is somethin' else."

I was unambiguously impressed. I could see the scale of this house; this was the kind of project I had wanted to find back in Boston. To get a better vantage-point, I climbed on top of a finished wall and walked along its erratic course. Every six feet I stepped over a threaded bolt that would eventually attach to the wooden frame of the house. I had seen these in the basement in the Rogers house but never had the chance to see how they were put together. While I was not experienced in the intricacies of concrete work, I could appreciate that this was the beginning of a complex house, something special and out of the ordinary.

But it also sobered me. If I started my own company, had my eight months in Nantucket really prepared me to run a project like this? Was Greg really right in saying that I should just do it? I began to feel that this whole idea was harebrained.

"Andy, let's go get a cup of coffee and talk some business."

We walked back to the truck. Before entering, each of us made a special effort to remove as much of the mud as possible from our shoes. I knew without asking that this was expected. We both found sticks to remove the particularly sticky clumps of mud and then wiped the rest on nearby grass. I hadn't noticed it when we arrived, but I could see now that Jack had chosen where to park the truck so that such cleaning amenities were nearby.

He drove to nearby Ridgefield center, past the bucolic homes that dotted the wooded country-side and pulled into Nina's, a coffee shop with rows of pickup trucks parked outside.

"This is where all the contractors come for morning coffee. It may look like a lot of trucks now, but you should see this place at six in the morning. They have good breakfast. Their lunch is good too. Hope you're hungry."

I was ravenous.

"ORDER UP. MY TREAT," Jack announced,

The waitress took our orders, and once she walked away, Jack said, "I'll cut right to the chase." His demeanor was serious and his eyes were fixed on mine. "I'd like you to oversee the project I just showed you." He leaned back and waited, letting his words hang in the air with the importance they deserved.

I was stunned. This wasn't what I had come here for. Then I was skeptical. "Why me Jack? There must be more qualified people around here."

"Andy, I'll tell ya. I know you're green. But, you've got the intelligence and with a little bit of the right support, you could gain the confidence and the skills to run a job like this. But what's more important, I think I can trust you." Then he added after a pause, "I'm willing to take a chance here, can I trust you?"

"Yeah Jack, you can trust me," I replied with measured sobriety.

"Andy, this is a hard business, and I hesitate to trust anyone. I tell anyone I know to do the same. I've learned that, in the end, allegiances are fragile. They last as long as people's interests are the same. But, if they diverge, the other guy'll put himself first, and it'll be at your expense. And worse yet, you won't even know it happened until it's too late, until you're fucked. Believe me when I tell ya. Integrity is rare in this business."

I was still incredulous. "And what does it mean to *oversee* the project?"

"The subcontractors are all lined up. I want you to manage them."

I waited, needing more explanation to understand.

"I'll be honest with you, Andy. I didn't want this job when Randy and Maura first came to me. But they pressed and I agreed. I'm not interested in swingin' a hammer anymore. I planned to run things from my house using subs to do the work. As you saw, the excavator and the concrete crew are hard at it. It's gone reasonably well, but I've had to be more involved than I wanted. The framer is lined up to start next month and he'll need even more oversight."

Again he waited, allowing the words to sink in and to gauge my response. Then he began again, deliberately and slowly. "Andy, I want you to be my eyes and ears on the job."

I felt deflated. I wanted to run jobs, not oversee them. But was I kidding myself, expecting too much? I wasn't quite sure how this arrangement was supposed to work, but sensed that this meant that I would not be in the center of the activity. This overseer role was still confusing to me. I couldn't grasp what it meant.

Reacting to the disappointment on my face, Jack said, "Andy, you haven't got the experience to be running a job like this by yourself."

While I knew them to be true, his words slowed my enthusiasm even more.

"Don't be disappointed. Look, this's no small job. And you'll get to see and do everything from beginning to end. You can learn concrete work, framing, electrical, plumbing, anything you want. I need someone I trust to be there and act as my representative. You said you wanted to learn how to build houses. This is the best way I can think of for you to learn. You'll be responsible for the job but be fully protected. You'll be me and if anyone gives you shit, they'll have me to deal with. I'll give you my full authority to do whatever you think is right."

Overseer was starting to sound better.

"Whadaya say Andy? I need you. Do you want the job?"

My mind was working fast to put everything together. This wasn't exactly what I thought was going to happen this weekend. I thought I was going to talk about contracting in Boston on my own. But through the course of the morning, my confidence that I could do that had been eroded and I was being offered a job whose role was unclear.

"I need a day or two to think about it." I said, staring back at Jack with the same intensity with which he had offered the job. We shook hands; a firm and solid grasp that, for me, conveyed a deeper bond than merely boss and employee. I hoped Jack felt the same. For me, this was a continuation of the bond that I hoped had begun on Nantucket. Jack could still make me nervous with his sudden shifts and intensity. I felt a need to navigate carefully around him. But, paradoxically, I felt an ever-growing admiration for him. I appreciated that Jack was bestowing on me a great trust and faith. He was opening a door that I had begun to believe would not be opened for me by anyone else. I was slowly beginning to understand that an extraordinary gift had just fallen into my lap. I was being given exactly what I wanted.

"I'll give you fifteen dollars an hour to start and we'll revisit your salary as we proceed."

"Can my title be superintendent or project manager?" I felt sheepish at the request, but I knew that project manager was a title of some note in the consulting world, and this would look better on my resume. I still couldn't get past evaluating myself by my resume.

"That sounds fine to me."

We shook hands once more, agreeing that I would call in two days.

ALONG THE ENTIRE DRIVE from Route 84 to the Massachusetts Turnpike I tried to get used to the idea of quitting my traditional career path once again. This time, I would really be taking the leap into construction whereas my earlier experience had been more of an exploration. I had been a visitor, a tourist in house building. Now I would be making a real commitment.

When I got back to Boston, I picked up the phone and called my best friend, Paul, to talk it over. Paul went into business for himself after college, opening a shoe store in his hometown. I had always admired him for that and thought he'd have the best advice at the moment.

That evening we met in a bar where I explained the offer and the decision I had to make. Paul listened patiently, nodding at regular intervals. We kicked ideas back and forth, trying to find different perspectives to help me make my decision. Much of it was familiar terrain for me, ideas I had struggled with over the past year. After about an hour, I was beginning to test his patience when I finally said something that hit a nerve. "But Paul, what if I decide to get back into a professional life later in my career? How will this look on a resume?"

"Fuck the resume!" Paul said angrily. "Do you leave the clear plastic on your furniture when you buy it?"

"Well, I don't buy new furniture."

"Cut the shit. You know what I mean. Are you more concerned about the next person who might use it, or are you going to use it yourself?" When I didn't answer, he continued, "Think about it. Live your life for yourself. Not for someone else, at least not for some potential recruiter." He paused from his outburst and then continued in a more controlled tone. "I think that if you're doing what you really love, others'll respect you, no matter what. And if they don't, fuck 'em! Look at me. I own a shoe store. Part of my job is to scrub the toilet. You might think I should be embarrassed about that. But I'm not. I like scrubbing that toilet because it's *my* toilet. It's *my* shoe store, it's *my* business, and it's *my* fuckin' toilet. I'm choosing what I want to do, not someone else."

I sat quietly, stalling while Paul's words sunk in. Then I responded. "I guess deep down inside, I want my life to have meaning more than just making money and taking a job without thinking. Sometimes, I look around me and see a pattern that bothers me; tell me if you think this is crazy." I paused for a moment, searching for the best way to articulate what I was thinking. "I see people who grow up with big dreams about what they're gonna do with their lives; they're gonna cure cancer or become a great politician. They start on that path but then realize that those dreams take more commitment, persistence and hard work than they expected. So, they give up. Then they have kids and they project those dreams onto them. Then they die. And the kids grow up and live the same cycle. They have dreams, give up on them, pass them on to their kids and then die. I don't want to do that. I want the world to be different because I was here."

Paul laughed, "That's not crazy. But it's damned pessimistic. Shouldn't we just go out and shoot those poor bastards and put them out of their misery?"

"Maybe you should just shoot me!" I said. Then more seriously, I continued, "If I do this again, I'm gonna really commit to it. I'd move everything to Connecticut. I'd put nothing in storage." It was time, I thought to myself, to just get on with my life.

Paul nodded. "That makes sense. You'll never know if this is the right thing for you if you go at it half-heartedly. So go ahead and immerse yourself.

Make sure you have no regrets." He added with a roaring belly laugh, "And if it doesn't work out, don't come scratching on my door for food scraps."

"JACK," I SAID, "I'll take the job." While I spoke confidently and held the phone firmly, I was anything but confident.

My announcement was met with great praise. "Good Andy. I'm proud of ya. You're doin' the right thing."

We agreed that I would start in two weeks. Jack knew someone with a vacant room for rent and I took it sight unseen. Making the announcement that I was leaving EEC was relatively easy. I was glad to go and had developed few friendships. Even my parents had little opposition to my decision. My sister was especially supportive, saying that I was behaving like a "free spirit." I felt both flattered and wrongly labeled. To me, a free spirit was someone who was free from the expectations of others. However, I felt that I was, in fact, struggling to break free of those expectations. I felt them strongly, perhaps more so than others, and found it extremely difficult to be moved by my own spirit.

I finished my two weeks at the office, found someone to take over my lease, packed up all my things, loaded my pickup truck and with a trailer in tow hit the road for Connecticut.

NOVICE

THE WINSLOW HOUSE

"Each man has his own vocation; his talent is his call. There is one direction in which all is open to him."

RALPH WALDO EMERSON, *Series I. Spiritual Laws*

J ACK LEFT ME TO SETTLE into my new apartment with my belongings and, most importantly, a clean set of blueprints. I anxiously stacked my things in the garage, put my clothes, stereo and books in my room, and then sat alone with the drawings. Having never seen blueprints before, I devoured them. Each of the fifteen sheets of the plan measured two and half feet by two feet. The smooth, off-white paper was covered with lines and words in a deep fuzzy blue, and gave off a chemical scent from the reproduction process. The drawings were divided into four parts and described thirteen thousand square feet of living space.

The first part was the floor plans, detailing the foundation, basement, first floor and roof-line, each drawing marked with every measurable distance. Every door and window was numbered to describe its shape and size listed on another page. Each door had a quarter circle showing the way it swung. The main part of the house ran east to west for two hundred and twelve feet. At the east end, a four-car garage extended fifty-five feet to the south while opposite it, a bedroom wing extended thirty-five feet to the north. On the west end, a third wing extended forty feet to the south. This and the garage formed two sides of a large courtyard around the front door. Inside the courtyard was to be a Japanese garden.

As I studied each page, I imagined what the final building would look and feel like. My mind walked through the yet to be built space, envisioning a composite whole of the final structure. The entry room was in the center of the house. To the east was the dining room with the kitchen beyond. To the west was the living room followed by the study. These five large rooms comprised the central core with bedrooms located to the east and west. Large glass doors turned the north and south walls into almost complete glass.

Japanese shoji screens on tracks slid just inside them. You could traverse this core either through the rooms themselves or through a dramatic hallway of repeating archways that ran the length of the house.

One of the notable features of the layout was a small interior courtyard, accessible only from the house. A tree would grow out of its center. Another feature was the house's five fireplaces, one of them unusually located in the kitchen. The master bedroom suite also had a fireplace as well as a separate walk-in closet, bathroom, shower, and Jacuzzi tub. Each of the seven other bedrooms had private bathrooms as well. Two spiral stairs led to the lower level that was also accessible from the outside through even more glass doors. A verandah with a large semi-circular central deck ran the entire length of the upper floor on the north side of the house.

The second set of drawings detailed the four elevations of the house's exterior walls—east, west, north and south. They showed the roof-line sloping from the ridge at a nine/twelve pitch (nine vertical inches for every twelve horizontal inches) and then shifting to a four/twelve pitch, creating an angle in the roof-line for, what I was told, would be an Oriental effect. The overhang of the roof was a dramatic four feet around the entire perimeter. On the bottom of each page, the drawings showed the final grade of the landscape. The house was entered from the south side on the first floor, but the ground sloped away, allowing entry into the basement floor from the north side.

A third set of drawings showed cross-sections of the house—floor, wall elevations, ceiling patterns and roof-lines in whatever portion they were bisecting. Many of the ceilings sloped upwards into an inverted tray or a pyramid.

A fourth and final set of drawings provided greater detail of some sections of the house's floor plans such as the kitchen and bathrooms.

It was evening by the time I rolled the plans back into their plastic tube for safe-keeping. I was thrilled to be starting on the house in two days. I found a local restaurant to eat dinner and turned in for an early evening.

MONDAY COULD NOT come soon enough. I spent Sunday exploring the area, slept soundly that night and awoke to my alarm at five thirty in the morning. Normally, I would have had trouble waking at this hour, but I sprang out of bed, showered, dressed in my worn Carhartt pants, boots and T-shirt, threw the blueprints in the cab of my pickup and drove to meet Jack at Nina's for breakfast. The sunny morning matched my mood and anticipation.

"Hey Stuff, you ready to do some work today?" Jack was smiling as he waited outside.

"Ready as I'll ever be," I said with chipper excitement.

The parking lot was filled with pickup trucks, the contractors who owned them parked inside. Each looked as though they were wearing a similar uniform; T-shirts with different colors and logos, jeans or tan Carhartt pants. Many had hats. Conversation was loud. Everyone was drinking coffee and many were smoking. I was thrilled to be among them. We found a table in the corner. The waitress took our orders the moment we sat down and two unsolicited coffees replaced the menus in front of us.

"Welcome to Nina's," Jack said, as though he owned the place. "Barry Sutton, my excavator, and Shawn McTiernan, my concrete man, will be on the job today. You'll meet both of them. I've known Barry for a long time. You'll like him. Everyone calls Shawn by his nickname 'Red.' He's a good guy, but be aware he's got a temper. He got a bad rap on another job some months back and I think he's using this job to prove himself again. I have to say, he's doing first rate work."

"What happened on the other job?" I was pleased that our conversation had an air of partnership to it.

"Oh, he got accused of getting hostile with the general contractor. I'm really not sure of the details. All I know is the gossip flying around and I don't put much stock in that. What I do know is that he was eager to take this job and gave me a good price. I think I'll be happy with his work."

Jack paused to shift the subject. "Today, I'll introduce you around. There's power and a phone on the job. I'll want you to stay there and get a feel for the place. I also want you to do me a little favor. When we drive in, you'll see a road sign right next to the driveway. Can you have it moved? It's too close. You'll see what I mean."

"Sure." I felt the first pang of uncertainty in my role. "Do Barry and Red know I'm coming?"

"No. But that doesn't matter. When I introduce you, they'll snap to attention." He laughed.

We finished our breakfast, Jack paid the bill, and we drove separately to the jobsite. Pulling into the driveway, I noted the offending road sign warning of an approaching curve in the road. Up the driveway, the job was full of activity. Along one side of the house were seven pickup trucks. One was the biggest I ever saw. It was hard to miss as it was also the shiniest, with chrome wheels and the words "Barry Sutton, Excavation and Construction" emblazoned on the door. In back of the house, a bulldozer was scraping the top-soil off the ground. A backhoe sat quietly nearby.

We parked and walked up to the side of the foundation. Below us, six men were moving concrete forms or tying rebar into place. We climbed down the bank and Jack led me over to meet Red. He was short, about five foot seven, bald on top, but the hair on the sides of his head was a deep auburn. His face was round, freckled and worn from being in the sun. He wore a T-shirt that was faded, though clean. I was impressed by his Carhartt pants; they were completely broken in, looking soft and supple. He was barking orders to the crew in a loud but joking way, using expletives in just about every other word. I noticed his hands as he was pointing. They looked like leather. I thought of my own hands and how much hard labor it would take for them to look like that. The callused toughness I had developed in Nantucket was gone from my time in an office. But even at the end of the summer, they hadn't looked like that.

"Red, this is my new superintendent, Andy. He'll be here full time now to answer any questions and coordinate the subs."

"Welcome to the job Andy," Red replied. "This is one motherfucker of a foundation, isn't it?"

I blushed and then felt stupid at my reaction. "It's fantastic," I said in genuine admiration. It seemed to please Red. "Do you mind if I jump in with your crew if I get a chance?"

Red was amused. "Not at all. Although I can't imagine why the fuck anyone would voluntarily set forms. The fun is the pour. Stick around for that and jump in if you have the balls. That's where we earn our money."

"Come on Andy, let me introduce you to Barry," said Jack.

"It's a pleasure meeting you," I said, extending my hand to shake.

Red hesitated at what must have been an unusual jobsite formality but then grasped my hand firmly. His hands were strong and even rougher than they looked. "Same here, Andy," he replied and then turned his attention back to the crew, cursing out more orders.

Up the hill, Barry saw us coming and idled his excavator, waiting for us to approach. He was dressed more neatly than Red; a collared shirt with his logo on the pocket, jeans and work boots. But more importantly, no signs of dirt or sweat. Smoking a cigar, he sat regally in the cushioned chair of his cab.

"Hey, Jack, how's it goin?" His voice was gravelly and he had to yell over the din of the motor.

Jack yelled back, "Turn that thing off and step down here. I want to introduce you to someone."

Barry leaned over, turned off the motor and climbed down from the cab.

"Barry, this is Andy. He'll be overseeing the job from here on."

Then turning to me, "Barry's a good guy. He does his thing out here away from all the action. Look at the way he's removing the topsoil. He's like a surgeon."

Barry nodded but quickly changed the subject. "Jack, have you made a decision on that screener yet? I think it'd be a really good idea to screen this topsoil. You'll have some of the finest loam in the State."

"Barry, this is already some of the finest loam in the State. It's been farm field for the last hundred years. Show me where the rocks are."

Barry leaned over and picked up a rock about four inches in diameter. "These potatoes are everywhere."

"Well, I'd agree with you if we were gonna plant a lawn or build some gardens. But, near as I can tell, the Winslows will just turn it back into fields when we're done. Screening would be a waste of money." Then Jack smiled and added, "You're just gonna have to find some other way to pad your bill."

They both laughed, but I was puzzled at what seemed a rebuff. I thought that maybe I hadn't read it correctly. Maybe they were old friends and this was the way they talked. But as we returned to the cars, and Barry returned to his task of blading off the topsoil, Jack clarified. "Barry's a good guy. But keep an eye on him. He's trying to squeeze a few extra pennies out of this job. His work is first rate, but if he can, he'll overcharge us."

Again, my spirit rose at the sense that he was really letting me into his world. And while I wasn't sure how to "keep an eye" on him, I nodded my agreement.

"Okay, you all set?" he asked.

I nodded again and he turned to leave.

"You'll do good out here," he said. "We'll talk tonight."

ONCE ALONE ON THE JOB, I felt awkward and invisible. The concrete crew was hard at work, Red was barking out orders. Barry was driving his bulldozer behind the house. I decided to busy myself with my small list of tasks. The first was to get the road sign moved at the end of the driveway. Next to the hole for the foundation was a wooden post with the temporary source of power and the temporary phone, both inside a padlocked plywood box for which I held a key. The box was open and I called the highway department. The matter was resolved easily with a promise to move the offending sign by the end of the week. My first task was complete.

Next, Jack had given me a professionally painted metal sign and wanted it mounted on wood and installed at the beginning of the driveway. It would direct contractors into the site and warn trespassers away. I backed my truck to the temporary power, got out my tools and found some scrap plywood and two-by-fours lying on the ground. I cut the plywood to fit the shape of the sign, screwed them together and cut two pieces of two-by-four as posts.

The entire time that I was taking care of these small tasks, I was distracted by the concrete crew's activities. They worked methodically, assembling and dismantling concrete forms. I could understand the general theme of what they were doing, but I wasn't sure about the specifics.

I finished making the sign, drove to the end of the driveway, drove the posts into the ground and attached the sign. My second task was complete.

When I returned to the site, I studied the concrete crew, trying to figure out their process.

Seeing me, Red yelled, "Hey Andy, come down here."

I sprang to attention, climbed down the embankment wall, and walked briskly to where he was standing.

"I saw you watchin'. You understand what's going on?"

"I get the general idea, but I'm not sure about the mechanics. Can I jump in?"

"Fuck yeah. I never turn away free help." Then he paused with a disclaimer. "But if you start fuckin' up, I won't give you a second chance."

I looked appropriately grim and nodded my understanding of this warning. "I'm free now, can I give it a try?"

"Sure, tell Jimmy over there that you'll be helping out."

I introduced myself to a young man with red hair, just like his father's. He smiled and told me that they were setting up the forms for a pour in two days. They were a little behind and he was glad for the extra pair of hands. "You can start over there. Let me show you what to do."

The forms were already standing, but only intermittently attached to each other. At twelve-inch intervals, there were holes into which I began attaching "dogs"—small plates of steel with slots in them. The first dog passed through the slot aligning the two forms, the second dog passed through the first as a wedge to hold it in place. I worked quickly, starting low and climbing up the eight-foot forms to get to the top. I was quickly catching up to the crew standing them, so Jimmy told me to help stand the rebar "cages" that had been assembled on the ground. The half inch metal bar was wired into a grid that Jimmy said was "spec'd at twelve inches on center, horizontal and vertical."

The next step was to stand the second set of forms and attach them to the first with the form ties, metal strips that kept the forms exactly twelve inches apart. We worked together, Jimmy feeding them through gapped spaces between the attached forms while I used another dog to clip them into place. I worked silently, anxious to do it right.

When we stopped for a coffee break, Jimmy explained that, "This is one Cadillac of a foundation. They don't need all this steel or for it to be this thick, but if that's what they want." He shrugged his shoulders. "It's only money!"

While the engineering specifications were lost on me, the shape of the foundation was not. Where a standard house was shaped in a rectangle and therefore had only four corners in the walls, I counted thirty-four corners in this foundation. One of them was only twelve inches before the next turn.

"Isn't that the stupidest fuckin' thing you ever saw," Red said, shaking his head. "These goddamned architects. That's gonna cost plenty and for what? For a stupid little detail that could've easily been gained by running the foundation straight through and letting the carpenters work in the jog." Then he added what I had heard from other subcontractors on the Rogers house, "Architects should work in the trades before they design anything. Then they'd know when they're doing something unnecessarily expensive like this."

Each time I heard this, it was accompanied with a kind of bravado as if to say, "If only we could teach these architects how to build, then the world of construction would be a much better place."

For the rest of the day, I climbed around the foundation forms, dogging, spacing and standing rebar cages. When four o'clock came, the job stopped abruptly. Everyone just secured their work, put down what they were holding, packed up their tools and walked off. What caught my attention most was the discontinuation of the bulldozer's groan. It was a blessed relief. As I locked the temporary power box, the concrete crew drove out in single file, six in a row.

Barry locked up his bulldozer. His hair was still neat. His boots weren't as mud-caked and his clothes did not share the same sweat and dirt stains as the rest of the crew on the job, including me. He walked casually to his truck, waved and drove away.

I basked in the silence of the job and admired what had been accomplished in my first day. I felt satisfied that the ache in my muscles was well earned. I cleaned off my boots, got in my truck and drove home.

That evening Jack called. "How'd things go today?" His tone was gruff and he got right to the point. I gave him a detailed accounting. All he said was "good," which he repeated several times for effect, "good, good, good." He asked how I was settling in at home and how I was feeling about my first day on the job. I gave positive reviews to both and Jack repeated himself again, "good, good, good," and hung up. All business.

MY SECOND DAY was spent entirely with the crew standing concrete forms. Once they were all in place, temporary diagonal braces were attached to hold them perfectly plumb. Then Red set up his builder's level. A device that looked like a small telescope on a tripod, the level allowed him to sight a level line over long distances. Along the forms, he aimed it at a tape measure that Jimmy held vertically, instructing him to move it up or down until it noted the intended height of the concrete on the inside of the forms for the next day's pour. This was repeated every ten feet, Jimmy marking the spots with a pencil. Then a chalk line was snapped connecting them all to outline the top of the finished wall. Small finish nails were tacked into the forms along the line.

Several others attached brackets to the side of the form and laid planks on top of them to stand on. And finally, one of them sprayed the forms with oil. Jimmy explained, "to make sure that the concrete doesn't stick to the forms and we can strip 'em easier."

Red proclaimed the foundation ready and told everyone to call it a day. It was two hours before quitting time and they couldn't do any more to get ready for tomorrow. "Go get a good night's sleep and come ready for a hard day tomorrow."

I finished my day studying the plans and walking the site.

ON WEDNESDAY MORNING the crew came to work with a notable energy. They had coffee cups in their hands as they always did, but this morning the caffeine was unnecessary. Everyone was wide awake, talking, joking and laughing in anticipation of what was about to happen. Their movements were rapid as they donned rubber boots and rubber gloves. They seemed more alive, more alert. They were a different crew and I felt very much an outsider as I watched their preparations.

Red was at the center of it all, barking out orders as if he was some kind of an army general preparing for battle. "Okay boys, we've got forty yards of concrete comin' this mornin'. Jimmy, you lead. Al, Marc and Ian, you shovel. Henry, you're on the vibrator." The crew laughed and teased Henry, who did not look particularly pleased at his assignment.

Soon, the first cement truck was rumbling up the driveway. Everyone jumped into action, all knowing their place. Red walked out to greet the driver and directed him to a spot that allowed him the closest access to the waiting forms. Chutes were assembled that extended the reach of the concrete mixer about twenty feet. The driver could turn the chute left and right as well as up and down from inside the cab. Red took his spot over the crew. Jimmy stood ready to direct the chute. Three stood ready with shovels. And Henry was holding a large hose with a metal cylinder at the end of it—the vibrator.

The pour began. Concrete flowed with a deafening roar down the chute and everyone moved at a feverish but choreographed pace. Shovelers pushed it around as it piled up over the chalk-lined height. Henry buried the vibrator into the mix, lifting it up and down with great effort. It made a loud buzzing sound as it shook the wet concrete. Seeming to liquefy the concrete, it was driving out any air pockets that might be forming inside.

After about twenty minutes of hard work, the first truck was empty and another pulled forward to take its place.

"Let's go. Hurry it up. We don't want any seams or honeycomb," Red yelled.

The second truck was soon pouring and the crew was hard at it again. Now Red was no longer directing the pour. He left that to Jimmy as he troweled the top of the concrete, bringing it to the exact height they had marked and giving it a smooth finish. When he had too much concrete over the line, he threw it to a low spot. When there was no low spot to throw it, he threw it to the ground. No time was wasted.

The pour took three trucks in all, each coming right after the one before it. It lasted about an hour and after another hour and a half of finishing they were done. Everyone was marked with splatters of concrete. Their faces, gloves and clothes showed the markings of a battle well fought.

"A good day lads," Red bellowed. "Let's break at Nina's. The coffee's on me."

They left for an hour and returned in even better spirits. Jimmy explained that coffee after a pour was usually spiced with Irish whiskey as a reward for a good day's work. The afternoon moved at a slower pace. The crew had an air of satisfaction, having completed the most important part of their work before ten.

SO IT WENT for the first two weeks on the job. I was part of the concrete crew, eventually working on the pours as well. Two days after the pours, stripping the forms was like unwrapping a present. There was always anticipation, hoping to see a nice smooth surface, no "honeycomb" where air pockets left a rough finish.

We dismantled the braces, pulled off the forms and stacked them on a flatbed truck that carried them to another part of the site. Dogs were collected and placed in bags. Form ties, protruding from the walls, were broken off to leave a smooth foundation wall. This step required a precisely aimed smack with a hammer and they would break off just beneath the concrete surface. A missed hit bent the tie and made it more difficult to break. I soon mastered the technique and was able to break off ties in rapid succession.

Each night, Jack called for updates and I debriefed him of my work with the concrete crew. One night Jack explained how to waterproof the foundation and told me to take charge of the task. I dutifully obeyed.

Beginning the next day I split my time between the concrete crew and waterproofing. I filled the holes from the ties with waterproof mortar and snapped a chalk line twelve inches below final grade as designated by the blueprints. I then began the messy task of applying tar over the entire concrete surface below that line. I laid a cant strip—a triangular strip of hardened tar—at the base of the wall to deflect water away from the seam between the foundation wall and the footing. I nailed a furring strip of wood along the top of the tar line and attached sheets of plastic that was pressed against the still-wet tar. And finally, I laid mesh drainage sheets against the wall to direct water down to footing drains that would wrap around the house. Jack explained that this house was so long and perpendicular to the grade that it would act as a giant dam unless measures were taken to direct the water around. "No house of mine is gonna have a wet basement," he pronounced with certain finality.

Though it was not a pleasant job, I threw myself into it. If a watertight foundation was the sign of a high quality house, then I was going to make this one watertight. I was developing a sense of ownership of the house. Just by looking at the foundation, I knew it would be the biggest house I had ever been in. But now I was taking a personal responsibility to do all I could to make this the *best* house I would ever be in.

AS CONCRETE CURED in one section of wall, forms were stripped from the solid walls that preceded it and carried to set up for the next pour after it. Waterproofing followed, and the foundation-building process continued in an orderly and smooth wave, leapfrogging from one end of the house to the other.

As part of this choreographed routine, the foundation had to be reviewed by the building inspector, first for the rebar placement before a pour and then for an assessment of the quality of the mix after. Sometimes the inspector walked the job with Red and me but he usually talked about baseball and the Yankees. At the end of the requisite time, he initialed the inspection sheet and handed it to me for my files. Other times, he didn't even get out of his truck but simply drove around the site, looked at the finished walls, handed me his approval and drove off.

"He must have some hot babe to inspect next," Red sarcastically remarked. I had learned that contractors saw inspectors as contractors who couldn't cut it. While some were seen as competent and necessary for "keeping the hackers out of the business," as Jack explained it, many of them were also seen as incompetent or even corrupt.

Red described a friend who did renovation work in New York City. "When the electrical inspector came to do the inspection, he said that everything looked great but there was one problem. He said that all the wires were going like this." Red took out a piece of paper and drew an S. "But then he said they're supposed to go like this." He drew two lines down the center of the S turning it into a dollar sign. "Asshole," he said to conclude his story.

AS THE JOB SETTLED INTO its own routine, I settled into my place within it. I felt comfortable with the guys, no longer needing to be told what to do. I liked working with them but it was different from working with Neil on the Rogers house. They were tougher; the work was harder; it felt more professional.

Every evening, I came home exhausted. After eating, I would relax with a book or the TV. Every night, Jack's calls for a progress report became a regular part of my day. "Hey Stuff," he would ask, "how'd things go today?" I would respond with a detailed account of the activities. I would also use the calls to ask about certain things I didn't understand or about what would happen next. Sometimes, Jack would ask very detailed questions about what Red or Barry were doing. "Did Barry get that back lot bladed off yet?" "Is Red gonna get that foundation finished by his deadline?"

I always took these questions seriously, but at times, felt I lacked the knowledge to assess such things. I tried nonetheless and Jack always seemed satisfied when he finished his inquiry and told me to "keep it up." I felt proud when Jack was pleased with my work. But in the back of my mind there was a nagging fear about whether I really was meeting his expectations.

ON THURSDAY EVENINGS of each week, I drove to Jack's house to give him my time sheet. The following morning, an envelope was always taped to his front door with my paycheck in it. Sometimes we would talk when I dropped off the time sheet; sometimes not. One Thursday, he began the conversation as usual. "How'd everything go today?"

"The concrete's moving along. Red's about sixty percent done. I'm waterproofing right behind him."

Jack shot back sternly, "You're waiting a few days before you put the tar on that fresh concrete."

I already knew that fresh concrete needed time to cure. Red had told me that twenty-eight days were needed for full curing but that tar could be applied after only three or four. "Yeah, I'm waiting four days."

"Good. Good. You can't tar that too soon or it won't stick. Are you using waterproof mortar in the tie holes?"

"Yes," I replied. "And Barry and I have also run the trench drain where the foundation is waterproofed and he's backfilling so you can walk right up to the foundation."

"Good. Good. It sounds like you're on top of things." Jack paused. "When's that damned tree going in? It will have to be planted before the framing starts or we'll need a crane to lift it over the roof. I don't wanna pay for that."

"They're delivering it next Friday and Barry says he can drop it into place with his backhoe."

"Good. Good. You make sure that thing doesn't die. It'll cost a fortune to put a new one in after that house goes up." He paused. "That is the damnedest thing I've ever heard of. Has anyone ever stopped to think what they're gonna do when that tree grows too big for the space it's in? Fuck no! Sometimes I wonder where the practicality is in the architect business." He paused again, seeming to come out of his brief rant and turned to me with more focus and gravity. "Okay, now we need to talk about next steps. I've chosen Ace Construction to do the framing. They've got a top-notch framer named Scott Donnelly. He'll be starting in three days so be sure to have good access for his men and tell Barry to level out a spot where an eighteen-wheeler can get near. Against my better judgment, I've let Ace talk me into panelizing this house."

"What does that mean, panelizing?"

"They're gonna build the walls as panels at a factory and deliver them prefabricated to the site. The floor and roof will be built as trusses by the same factory."

Then I asked, feeling insecure about my observer role, "What's Scott like?"

"He's okay. You'll get along fine. Think of him as your teacher. And don't worry. You're still my number one man. Scott will run his framing crew. You make sure he doesn't fuck up. And while he may not know it yet, he'll show you everything you need to know. Trust me." He smiled and winked.

THE NEXT DAY, Scott Donnelly arrived in a shiny black Saab. The sporty car looked strange on the jobsite, next to a row of dirty pickup trucks. Scott was a big man with a boyish face. He looked to be in his late forties but dressed as if he were in his twenties. He wore a white T-shirt, cutoff shorts and work boots. He moved fast as he got out of the car and walked around as if he was already in charge of the site. I felt strangely resentful of this.

I extended my hand. "Hi, I'm Andy."

Scott extended his hand back. "Hi, I'm Scott." He paused, gazing around the site as if I wasn't even there. "I'll be bringing my crew in here next week. I'm trying to case out where I'm gonna start and how I'm gonna set up my staging area." Then he talked, not really to me, more to the air. "I'm gonna build this house faster than anyone's gonna believe. It may look big, but I'm gonna knock this baby off in record time."

I bristled. Was Scott trying to prove something? To himself? To Jack? I sensed impatience on Scott's part, but I wanted to show him where Barry had leveled off the staging area and where the foundation was ready to accept workers. The visit took no more than an hour until Scott was gone and the day returned to its original routine.

That evening, I mentioned Scott's remark about finishing the house in record time and Jack said sternly. "Listen carefully. You watch him like a fuckin' hawk. If he starts to cut corners or if his quality looks like it's suffering because he's moving too fast, say something. If he doesn't listen, say something to me. I'll put a stop to that kind of shit. You got it?" He waited.

"Yeah, got it." I paused, still feeling insecure about my role. "Jack, do you think Scott might be trying to impress you for a job?"

"Andy, don't worry. Scott's got a big mouth. I need him for this job but nothing more. He'll frame this house and then he'll be gone. You'll learn what you need to learn from him and then you'll learn more from other people. You'll learn everything you want to learn here. I promise you that."

I focused on Jack's words. He was unwavering in his support for me. But doubts lurked in my mind. Why would he be so supportive of someone with no experience? Was it simply that he could trust me? Could it be that simple? Scott was a seasoned and experienced builder, someone who knew how to build houses. As much as I tried not to, I saw him as a rival. Despite Jack's assurances that he was not, he was for me. How could I feel secure when I knew so little; when my job consisted primarily of my simply learning? It was as if I were going to school, a rare school, and getting paid for it. As much as I wanted to believe Jack, my father's words fed the insecurity inside me: "Now remember Andy. This is a job, not a vacation. You're being hired to do some hard work. If you don't produce, Jack will fire you." I had to be aware of the possibility. It was a real threat. If Jack could fire his own son, he could surely fire me.

SCOTT ARRIVED THREE DAYS LATER with a construction trailer and parked it behind the house next to the temporary power pole. I dropped my work with the concrete crew to survey the jobsite's new addition. It was a dented and scuffed wreck. I peered inside to find Scott tidying up the trailer's one room. Blueprints were laid on the room's center table and a waste basket contained papers from previous projects. I could see that plastic tiles were peeling off the floor, and some file cabinets were bent and disfigured. "It may not look pretty, but it's dry," was all Scott said.

I made no reply. I'd never seen a contractor's trailer on a home construction site and so it seemed unusual to me. But what did I know? I preferred to remain silent than appear ignorant. I rejoined the concrete crew.

That afternoon, two new carpenters joined Scott and they began to take measurements of the foundation. I again dropped what I was doing and joined them. Scott introduced me to the two new faces. "Guys this is Andy. He's the G.C.'s rep on the job. Andy, this is Gary and Brian. They're my foremen. The rest of the crew will arrive in two days and we want to get the sill down before they arrive."

While the same age, Gary and Brian were different from the guys on the Rogers house; rougher, more worn than Eric, Neil and Larry. They shook my hand and offered a quick hello but showed little interest in any socializing beyond that. The three of us looked over the plans where Scott had already drawn diagonal lines noting distances between multiple corners in the foundation. Then they measured the actual distances on the finished foundation. Scott collected the numbers and compared them to those he calculated on his drawings. While he was studying his calculations, Brian and Gary set up a builder's level and began to measure the height of the concrete all the way around what was completed of the foundation.

This activity drew the attention of Red, who passed by to briefly watch. Despite his attempt at indifference, he seemed edgy as he watched. "This foundation is dead on. If they find any problem," he paused, and then added more forcefully, "They won't find any problem. This foundation is dead fuckin' on," before returning to his crew.

I nodded, not really knowing what to say. I had worked with Red and his crew and was developing an affection for his abrasive style. I knew that, although easy to anger, he was conscientious and took good care of his crew, and the crew worked hard. But now, I could see that Red's work was being evaluated. Most of the walls were now solid and they surely weren't going anywhere. The concrete itself was clean and smooth, no honeycombing. But I could see that the final test was in how well the concrete met the planned frame of the house. Was it *plumb, level and square*? These were the final measures of good construction.

Scott looked up from his papers and yelled over, "Brian, Gary, get me the dimension from that corner to that one again," as he pointed from one corner to another. "Then get me those two as well," as he pointed from one of the corners to two others. The common corner was the end of the outermost wall on the northern wing and it was clear he was detecting a problem.

It was clear to me and, most importantly, it was clear to Red, who walked briskly over to the corner to watch what they were doing. He didn't say anything and just stared at their progress. Scott joined us.

"I think that corner's out," he said, adding after a moment's pause, "a lot."

"The hell it is," Red shot back. "Let me see your numbers."

"Let's wait a minute and see what they come up with."

"If you made a fuckin' mistake, I'll thank you to get your shit straight before you go off criticizing my work. This is the best goddamned foundation I've ever poured."

Brian and Gary brought Scott some numbers and Scott compared them to his original measurements. "Yup, this corner's out, by roughly six inches. Not to worry, we'll cover it up with the framing."

Red's face flushed red. "No shit-ass carpenter has to fix my foundation. Let me check it myself you son of a bitch." I stepped back. Scott remained calm. Red was livid.

"Hey Jimmy," he yelled. The crew stopped, responding to the emotion in Red's voice. "Give me that fuckin' tape measure and help me measure this mother-fuckin' foundation." All activity on the site ceased. Attention was on Red and Jimmy. Even Barry noticed the commotion over the din of his bulldozer and came over to watch what was happening.

They pulled a tape from one corner to another, checked it, rechecked it, then pulled some measurements from other corners to the offending one. Red scratched his head as he wrote numbers on his own blueprints, worn from weeks of work already committed to the project. Finally, he screamed, "What the fuck happened here? Why is that wall out?"

I could sense Scott's satisfaction that his numbers had been validated. I felt a mix of relief that what looked like it may turn into a violent confrontation had been averted. But that sense of relief was soon replaced by another fear that someone was going to be blamed for this, and Red was going to tear into him.

"Jimmy, why is that wall out?" Red yelled. "We've been standing these forms dead fuckin' plumb. Who fucked up?"

Jimmy stiffened but didn't respond with equal fury. "Dad, that's the first wall we put up. There was a lot of activity as we set it. Excavating was working around us. But I'm sure that wall was straight when we stood it. Maybe Barry hit it with his backhoe before our pour."

"I didn't touch that wall Red," Barry quickly protested.

"You were digging right there," Jimmy countered. "Your bucket was swinging in an arc right across that wall. And you were working there late the night before we poured. When I left that night, that wall was plumb." Jimmy stabbed at the air towards the wall for emphasis as he said these final words.

"Don't pin your screw-up on me," Barry shot back, starting to get angry himself.

"If you fucked me up, Barry, I'll have your fuckin' head," Red was wild now. "No one's gonna blame me for this fuckin' mess. We've done a first class job here. Jack's paying us top dollar and he's getting the best money can buy."

"Red, don't worry," said Scott. "We'll cover this up and no one will know it happened. The extra won't be too much."

Red exploded, "If you think I'm paying for this mistake, you're out of your fuckin' mind. Get Sutton to pay for it. He's the mother-fucker that did it. I have no time for this bullshit." Then he stormed away. Everyone watched in silence as he walked across the jobsite, pushing things out of his way as he made a straight line for his truck and sped off down the driveway, dust stirring into the air as he left. Jimmy sheepishly looked at each of us and went back to his crew. Scott returned to his measurements and Barry returned to his bulldozer.

AFTER WORK, I PRE-EMPTED the evening phone call by stopping at Jack's house to debrief him on the day's events. Jack listened patiently and quietly as I explained the chronology. When I was done, Jack looked me in the eye and asked, "So, who's responsible?"

"Well, I wasn't here when they poured that wall. But I've been working with Red and I know he's doing good work. It seems to me that, even if Barry hit the wall, he should have checked it one last time before the pour began."

"So you think Red should pay for this?"

I got nervous. My answers now carried greater weight and I didn't like having to give a black and white answer to something that may be gray. "I think Barry and Red share the blame."

"No, that's not what I asked you," Jack fired back. "I have to charge someone for this and I need to make a decision. Who should I charge?"

I swallowed hard. "It seems to me that Red's the one ultimately responsible for the wall. So, even if Barry did something to his work, he has to assure its quality." I paused. I didn't like the finality of what I had said, taking Barry off the hook. "But, Barry should've told him he hit it. Barry could've helped Red catch the mistake. Is there any chance he could have hit the wall without knowing it?"

"What do you think?"

"I don't know, I've never driven a backhoe before."

"Take a guess," he said impatiently.

"Well, to move the foundation six inches, he must have whacked it pretty hard. He should have known."

"So what're you saying?

"I'm not sure. Red is responsible for the wall, but Barry should've told him he hit the foundation." I paused, adding, "if he really did hit it."

Jack sighed. "I'll take care of it. You look tired. Get home and rest up for tomorrow."

I felt I had let Jack down. Jack was paying me to be his eyes and ears on the job. I was not living up to my end of the bargain. As I pondered this on the drive home, I realized that I didn't even know how much this was worth. Maybe this was small change and not as big a deal as it appeared. But I also knew that this was a matter of pride and trust, not just money. Red was being graded on his work by this incident and his reputation and ego were being challenged. It was a big deal to him.

THE NEXT DAY, the concrete crew resumed their leapfrogging task of forming the final walls while I alternated between waterproofing and helping them. But there was a notable tension in the air. First, the out-of-plumb wall was now obvious. Where previously no one had noticed it, once identified, it called out, screaming to everyone that this foundation was now flawed. What was once thought to be perfect was no longer. And someone was going to be blamed for it.

Second, the site no longer belonged solely to Red and his crew. Scott and his foremen were busy laying the sill plate in preparation for the full crew. The two crews kept their distance and I breathed easier with that blessing. But after lunch, Scott approached Red. I saw an opportunity to act as intermediary and joined them.

Scott shouted above the din of the job. "Red, I need to talk to you about column footings." But Red ignored him, barking out orders to the crew.

Scott moved closer. "Hey, Red, can I talk to you for a minute?"

He turned to face him, saying nothing.

"Red, I need some column footings in the floor. Can we talk about placing 'em?"

Again, Red said nothing and just looked at Scott, offering no unsolicited advice much less any verbal comment. He was just going along, barely acknowledging that he was even being talked to. With the plans as a guide, Scott measured off the center of each column footing, placing a stake in the ground at each one.

For each, a hole would be dug and a box would be built to hold an extra foot of concrete just below what would eventually be the final floor. Each would support a load-bearing vertical steel post called a lolly column which would help carry steel I-beams that would run down the center of the house and carry the center of the floor trusses. In other words, these pockets were an important structural element of the house.

Scott placed the first marker, off of which the rest were measured. I pointed out that it didn't line up with two wall pockets that would hold the other ends of the I-beam. Scott was unflustered and quick to make the correction, but Red smiled, seeming to enjoy his being caught in a mistake.

After being marked, the boxes were built, ten in all, and Red added the footings to the planned pour that afternoon. I was surprised at Red's speed in responding to Scott's request when he barely spoke to the man. Either he was trying to undo any credibility damage he had suffered from the wall mistake or, I suspected, he was putting them in quickly hoping that Scott had still misplaced them.

For the next two days, Scott worked with his two foremen on the painstaking task of laying the sill plate; two-by-six pressure-treated wood that they bolted to the top of the foundation in the exact outline of the house that would sit above it. Precision was critical. Using long tape measures and a builder's level, the three carpenters took great care to make sure that the wood was perfectly level and square regardless of what the foundation did. At some places it needed to be shimmed up a quarter of an inch. At other places, they used their hammers to chip off a protruding piece of concrete. When done, the outside edge of the sill followed the outside edge of the foundation with only slight variation. It was a good foundation.

That is, except for the offending wall. Here, the sill began flush with the outer edge of the foundation but, over its length, diverged from the wall at a steadily increasing distance. By the end, it hung over six inches, a distance so great that Scott had to use a two-by-twelve to make sure he had enough wood to bolt to the concrete. The combination of the wider sill plate, the extended overhang and the long shadow it created served to exaggerate the mistake, a silent testament to the house's first major flaw. To anyone, expert or novice alike, it was obvious that something had gone terribly wrong along this edge of the house. No one talked about it.

AT NINE O'CLOCK the next day, a tractor-trailer arrived pulling a flatbed piled high with floor trusses, two-by-fours and plywood. Just ahead of the truck was Scott in his Saab. He quickly parked to direct the driver to where the load should be dumped. It was just the driver and Scott, and I wondered how they would get all that material off the truck without help. Scott walked up to the driver, still in the cab, gestured to a flat dirt area behind the house, exchanged a few words and stood back to watch.

The driver turned the truck around in a cumbersome five-point turn and then backed it into the position Scott had pointed out. He parked the truck, got out of the cab and released the straps holding the material in place. Then, he got back into the truck, revved the engine and accelerated hard. The truck lurched forward violently, forcing the loose material to slide back on the smooth flatbed. Not fully off on the first try, it hung precariously off the back of the bed. The driver slowly backed up and once again, accelerated hard, this time driving the truck out from under the material, which landed on the ground with a loud percussion. The scene was comical, and, I thought, must surely have damaged some of the trusses or plywood. Scott walked over to the driver, exchanged a few words and the truck drove off.

I joined Scott at the pile. "Okay," he said, eagerly rubbing his hands together. "Now we're ready to get this job started." His youthful enthusiasm was endearing. "Can you help me check the stack of material against the invoice?"

"Yeah sure." I was excited to inspect the new materials.

The two of us counted stacks of plywood and lumber and compared it to the list. Then we turned to the trusses, each marked with a letter to designate one of the seven sections of the house and a number to designate its place within that section. They varied in size, shape and length. I helped Scott count them off and then line them up in numerical order.

When we were done, I was amazed that none of the materials was damaged. We stood and admired the pieces that would soon be assembled into a house. The sense of anticipation was euphoric. The house was really going to begin.

WITH THE CONCRETE CREW finishing the final wing on the west end of the house and the sill plate laid on the rest, carpenters began in earnest. Ten new faces joined Scott and his two foremen. Some were carpenters, others laborers. Scott gave each instructions on where to begin and what to do. The task of moving the materials fell to the laborers. One of them became a source of entertainment for the rest of us. A linebacker for Penn State who was using the job as part of his summer workout routine, he would lift trusses alone that others, who were more interested in efficiency than maximization of effort, would pick up with assistance. When he moved two-by-fours, he would carry them four at a time, doing curls as he walked across the site.

The carpenters became a bee-hive of activity with Scott at the center, whipping the crew into a frenzy; giving instructions here, yelling corrections over there. At times, trusses were delivered to the wrong place, prompting loud complaints from the foremen and furious correction by the laborers. Ladders were stood in the basement, saw horses were set up around the perimeter. Trusses were laid in rapid succession and nailed to the sill plate. Plywood was then laid on top with glue and nails securing it in place.

I had caught up with the concrete crew in my waterproofing and began to spend some of my time with the carpenters. I had found concrete work impressive for its permanence. But, it was dirty, repetitive and moved at a glacial pace compared to carpentry. I was anxious for more rapid results. I felt I was returning to familiar territory learned in Nantucket. And these guys were my new teachers.

Over the course of the week, the acrid smell of concrete was gradually replaced with the sweet smell of wood and sawdust. The sounds of nail guns and hammers added new urgency to the din of activity. And I spent the day adding to that din with my new crew. I loved the immediate results and I loved the look of the expanding plywood floor. It was beautiful, a gleaming, bright blonde platform in the warm afternoon sun.

SCOTT BEGAN TO INTRIGUE ME. He loved to talk about construction. One day, he explained with great excitement how cement-coated nails worked. "You see, when a nail penetrates a piece of wood, it pushes the fibers aside," he was motioning with his hands, using his fingers to illustrate how the fibers bent when the nail passed by. "As they yield to the entering nail, there's friction. That friction heats up the glue on the outside of the nail and cements the nail in place. If there's no cement, the fibers expand and contract with temperature and water and push the nail back out."

When I asked him which tool he thought was most important for a good shop, Scott answered without hesitation, "The radial arm saw. It's the most versatile. I can use it for cross and miter cuts and then turn it sideways and use it as a table saw."

Scott also loved to be in the middle of the action, giving instruction. Carpenters would ask him even the most mundane of questions. It puzzled me that he always had an answer, always an opinion, no matter how trivial the issue: where to stack wood, what to do with wood scraps, which walls to stand first.

One day I finally asked, "Scott, why do you answer their every question? Don't you ever just want them to figure it out themselves? Aren't there times when it really just doesn't matter?"

"Andy," Scott began, in a fatherly tone. "Some people just like to have someone else do the thinking. They could figure it out, but they'd rather not. I'd rather they ask me than guess. If there's one thing to remember in this business: *never do anything for no reason.* Always think things through, especially when they seem trivial. Because that's when you'll do something that'll be a problem later. I want people to ask me what to do, because I want to know everything that's going on. Sometimes what seems a minor decision is really connected to other steps in the job and therefore important. I know the plans. I can see tomorrow's problems caused by thoughtless actions today. There's always a *more right* way to do things that will set up next tasks or leave you latitude to have flexibility in the future."

He pointed across the site, "Look at that stack of plywood. It's been sitting there for five days. If that were placed five feet to either side, Brian would have had real difficulty laying his trusses and it would have taken half an hour to move, and for no reason other than it was put in the wrong spot in the first place. Always think into the future. Always have a reason. Even if it's the most simple, always have a reason."

AS EACH WORKDAY ENDED, carpenters stored their tools in the trailer and laborers cleaned the jobsite. On his second Thursday on the job, Brian asked me if I would like to join the guys for drinks that evening. I accepted enthusiastically, pleased at the opportunity to hang out with them. In fact, I was eager to hang out with anyone. I had begun to feel lonely, having only Jack and my friends back in Boston to talk with. The guys on the concrete crew were the only locals I knew but I never saw them outside work. Brian wrote down the name of the bar—The Watering Hole—and told me to meet around 7:30. I put the paper in my pocket and turned to my cleanup.

After the crews left, I lingered to admire the work alone. I relished the solitude of being lost in the growing house. I enjoyed hearing the hollow sound of my footsteps on the new plywood deck. I admired the crisp angles of the floor as it jogged in and out. At several spots, holes remained open with temporary railings around them. Through two of them, spiral staircases would lead to the basement below. Three other holes awaited chimneys that would rise up through the entire height of the house. I climbed down and walked underneath, experiencing the newly enclosed space.

I was lost in my thoughts but awoke suddenly when I realized that I was not alone. Red and Jimmy were surveying the concrete wall that would forever be in the wrong place. Red calmly picked his teeth with a sliver of wood, while Jimmy just stared. I watched from a short distance.

"That fuckin' Sutton," Red muttered. "It's his fuckin' fault."

"If he had any balls, he would've admitted it. There's no way he could've hit those forms without knowing it. He must've really rung 'em," Jimmy added.

"Well, I'll be goddamned if I'm gonna pay a dime for some mud-pusher's mistake. He sits in that chair on his machine and thinks he's the fuckin' king of the world. I'm not paying for his mistake." Red was getting more heated as he spoke.

"What do you wanna do about it, Dad? This's a good job, one of the best we've ever done."

"Well, if push comes to shove, there's one way to really fix this mess. All it takes is a match; just one little match." Red let the words hang in silence as he surveyed the wall. Then, he turned, glanced with surprise at me and walked away. No good-bye, no more words at all. Jimmy turned to me and nodded solemnly as he walked away.

I stood frozen in place. Was Red serious? Was he really that ruthless? I packed up my tools and drove directly to Jack's house to report on the day, or more importantly, to report on Red's comment. As I drove, I realized I was shaking. Red's cold comment had unnerved me.

BY THE TIME I ARRIVED at Jack's house, I decided to forego the regular update and go straight to the threat. I pulled into the driveway, parked and walked toward Jack, who was mowing his lawn. He was dressed in jeans and an oxford shirt unbuttoned mid-way down his chest, the most unkempt I had ever seen him. He saw me coming and stopped pushing the mower.

I walked up to him and simply blurted out, "Jack, I think Red is threatening to burn down the house."

Jack didn't react. He didn't show alarm. He didn't show any concern at all. He simply leaned forward, resting his arms on the mower and said, "Tell me what happened."

"Well, we were standing around the job after everyone left. The sill plate and floor are down and the mistake in the concrete wall is pretty obvious. It was me, Red and Jimmy," I was trying to tell the story in coherent order, but I was excited. "We were standing there staring at the wall and Red said that he wasn't going to pay for this and that an easy solution would be to just get a match." I paused, "That's what he said, 'All it would take to fix this problem would be a match.'"

Through my whole description, Jack was still strangely placid. It confused me. When I finished, he calmly leaned over, turned off the mower and stood erect again. The immediate silence gave Jack's words greater emphasis.

"Andy, listen to what I'm gonna tell ya." Jack emphasized each word slowly. "Red isn't gonna do anything to that house because Red knows that if he does, he's gonna meet with a very unfortunate accident." His last words were calmly metered. It sounded less a threat as a fact. He paused to let the words sink in, never breaking his lock on my eyes. "Do you understand what I'm telling you?"

I was having trouble grasping Jack's full meaning and I was not sure that I wanted to. I didn't know whether to laugh or shiver. Was he serious? I simply nodded gravely and let Jack's calm become my own. I had delivered the message and Jack was telling me not to worry. So I wasn't going to worry. I wondered if I had been overreacting. One minute earlier I was in a frenzied panic and the next I was calmly secure that Red's threat was an empty one. Jack had taken it away by telling me that some deeper and darker force would keep him in line.

Jack waited a moment for me to adjust and then asked again, "Do you understand what I'm saying?"

"Yes Jack, I think so."

"Good," his demeanor brightened. "So, how's the rest of the job going?"

I explained the progress in framing, the material drop-off, the laying of the trusses and the installation of the floor.

"Make sure they use glue and nail that floor off good. Watch 'em closely. Make sure those nails are hitting the trusses. Also make sure that floor is dead nuts level. If Scott's pushing too fast, that's something he'll be careless about. And a mistake now will transmit through the entire house, all the way to the ridge."

"Yes, I'll keep an eye on it."

"Hey lighten up, Stuff. Things'll be okay. Do you believe me when I say that?" Jack was teasing me into smiling. "Keep up the good work. Have fun. Do you wanna have dinner tonight?"

"Thanks, but I'm meeting up with the carpenters tonight."

Jack gave me a curious glance that made me feel the need to explain. "Brian, the foreman, asked me to join the guys for a few beers. It's no big deal."

"Okay Stuff, have a good time. Don't leave your best in the bar. It's not the weekend yet. Still got one more day." Then he added, "I don't have to tell you that our business stays between us?"

I was disappointed at the question and rushed to reassure. "No Jack, I know when to keep my mouth shut."

Jack nodded approvingly, shook my hand and I left. As I drove home, I felt bewildered. I wondered if Jack thought that I was too naive for this kind of business. Maybe I was. I felt a great relief in being able to drop the difficult issues, such as Red's threat, on Jack and let him carry them. It was liberating. But, if Jack could make good on such a threat, to cause physical harm to Red if something happened, what kind of person was he? If this were so, what kind of world did he live in? Surely, not a world that was anything like my own. This realization created a strange distance between us in my mind. My admiration for him had been growing. It had always been growing. I liked his strength and the confidence it gave me. But should I be more cautious? Was this man truly dangerous? The question flowed through me and by the time I had fully considered it, I knew that in many ways it was moot. I was in love with the job and there was no way I could leave.

THE WATERING HOLE had a long thin bar with an extra room in the back for dancing. When I walked in I could see Brian and the crew at the far end of the bar. From the way they all stopped talking as I walked over to them, I sensed that their objective in inviting me for a few beers was to figure out how I fit into the whole scheme of things on the job. Brian bought the first round and soon we were all joking over nothing in particular. One guy was complaining about his girlfriend. They fought over him coming out tonight, so he decided to drink heavily. "I'll show her," he announced in defiance. Another guy was telling jokes. A third began to tell a story about a friend who had injured himself that afternoon.

"He fell off a horse and landed on his hammer claw. It dug right into his hip. He needed seven stitches!" Everyone grimaced, but the story set a theme upon which everyone could contribute. One after another, each tried to outdo the previous story. And the beer helped to create exaggerations in each successive story.

"I knew a guy who braced a two-by-six on his knee to cut it but misjudged the depth on his saw blade and cut right through the muscles and tendons above his kneecap!" Everyone squirmed.

"One guy I knew disconnected the safety on his concrete nail gun. You know, you're supposed to push in the barrel or it won't fire. So there he was, swinging the gun when it accidentally went off. A twenty-two caliber shot! He didn't realize what happened till he tried to walk and couldn't. His foot was nailed to the floor!" Everyone grimaced again, but they were also starting to get silly. I was skeptical that someone could shoot a nail through his foot and not know it instantly. "No it's true," he protested, "He was the foreman of a friend of mine." I gave him a look of disbelief, which another used as a chance to add his own story.

"No, these things happen. I know of guys disconnecting the safeties on their pneumatic nail guns and shooting twelve-penny spikes right through sheetrock walls. One guy, I heard, got a nail right in the head!"

This last story satiated everyone's appetite for construction horror stories. Another round of beer was ordered and the conversation turned to Scott and his running of the job. My ears perked up, curious how people who had worked for him saw him.

"I heard that Joey"—the owner of Ace Construction, another carpenter leaned over to explain to me—"told Scott to stay in the trailer to direct the work and not put on his tool-belt."

"Yeah right! Can you see Scott as a pencil pusher? There's no way he's not gonna swing a hammer."

Brian shook his head. "But Scott gets too involved in things that Gary and I can take care of. I think the job would run a whole lot better if he just coordinated the work and got out of our way. He's getting too damned old. Did you see him swinging that big twenty-five ounce hammer of his? That's too much hammer and his arm was hurtin' by lunch-time."

One of the carpenters put down his beer and began to mimic Scott, flexing his muscles like a body builder. "I'm Scott," he said in a false deep voice. "Watch me build this house all by myself." Then he turned his arms up as if he were lifting weights, puffed his chest out and added, "Tell me, which way to muscle beach?"

Everyone started laughing.

Brian continued, "He's moving too fast and makin' mistakes. Can you believe that floor truss we had to turn around today? He put the fuckin' thing down backwards. He personally put it there and then watched us glue and screw the deck on top. What a pain in the ass."

Gary said, "Well, at least we caught it. Can you imagine the shit storm if we found it later when the heating guys couldn't run their duct work through the chase? I'm not sure how we would've fixed it then."

Brian added, "The only reason we had that fuckup was because Scott was distracted. He's got enough to worry about with those panel makers. He should just worry about getting us the materials. We can put it together just fine thank you very much. Someone needs to rein him in."

This last comment directed everyone's attention to me. I wondered if I had just been set up. Was Brian trying to use me to control Scott? The beer was loosening everyone's lips and I felt pressure to say something, but I would not divulge anything that was better kept between me and Jack. And on matters related to the job, that meant almost everything. So I tried to divert the topic. " How long've you guys worked with Scott?"

"We all move around between crews. Joey likes to keep things jumbled up. I think he's afraid we'll form our own company out of his," said Brian.

Everyone laughed.

"Is that for real?" I asked.

Brian nodded, "It's been known to happen. Not often, but it can happen."

Another carpenter added, "Some of us are new. I've never worked with Scott before. He seems alright to me."

One of the older carpenters guffawed. "Give it time, greenhorn. You'll see what he's like."

Another round of beers appeared and as everyone grabbed a fresh mug, the topic turned to the out-of-plumb concrete wall and Red's culpability.

"Shit happens," one said as he shook his head.

"Red deserves a break. This is one hell of a foundation and he's doing a great job. This'll be easy to fix," added another.

"Yeah, but that was some blow up he had," said Brian. "He's got one hell of a temper. I heard that he once used a two-by-four to beat a contractor who didn't pay him." Another added, "And I heard that he once called in a load of concrete and filled the car of a contractor that tried to fuck him over."

"Yeah right," said Gary.

"No really. I heard that they just buried the car right there cuz the tow truck couldn't lift it."

Gary shoved him and everyone groaned in disbelief.

I shared their skepticism. People liked tall stories and these must have been the product of years of exaggeration, not to mention a night's worth of drinking. But there also must have been some truth to start it all. When Jack first introduced me, he had mentioned something about Red trying to repair a damaged reputation. And the threat about the match was still on my mind. Had I misjudged Red? I liked him and thought he worked hard. But did he have a more violent side? As with Jack, was I not seeing the true nature of the people that I worked with?

I decided to shift the topic to something completely different. "So is this the best bar in Danbury? Is this where you guys meet girls?"

"What girls?" one carpenter was quick to shoot back, to the approving laughter of the others. The beer was flowing very freely now and people were feeling very loose.

"If you want girls, you have to go down to Norwalk or Stamford," he said. "Around here, the girls leave when they turn eighteen and go to college. Then they don't come back until they're married. It's too quiet for single people."

"Great," I remarked, rolling my eyes. I was not sure how long my enthusiasm for the job would carry me without a girlfriend.

By the time the evening started to wind down, I had lost track of how many beers had been ordered. Brian settled the bill and told everyone he would collect at lunch the next day. Carpenters staggered out one by one until Brian and I were alone.

The bartender delivered two snifters of Grand Marnier. "One last one for the road?" Brian asked as he lifted his glass to toast. I did the same, working hard to get it down. I was never a fan of the stuff and I knew I had passed my drinking limit, but I also knew I couldn't refuse it. We finished our drinks, shook hands and said good night. I staggered back to my truck and drove home through the back streets.

THE ALARM CLOCK sounded at five-thirty and it took all my effort to lift my head off the pillow. I felt horrible. I couldn't tell whether I was hung-over or still drunk. I could taste the Grand-Marnier and it caused my stomach to lurch. There was no way I was going to be able to function on the job. I was in desperate fear of getting sick. I got up, brushed my teeth to rid myself of the sour taste, drank a large glass of water to clear out the cotton mouth and went back to bed. I fell quickly to sleep and was awakened at nine by the phone.

"Stuff, you sick today?" Jack's voice was abrupt.

"Oh Jack, sorry. I didn't go in today. I drank a little too much with the guys last night and couldn't get out of bed." I laughed.

"What kind of shit-ass excuse is that?" Jack shouted. "I hired you to do a job. I'm depending on you. You have a responsibility and part of fulfilling that responsibility means that you go to work." He paused and then added with a strong note of sarcasm, "Or am I missing something here? Is this your idea of professional behavior? Maybe you don't have the level of maturity and responsibility I thought you had? Maybe I can't trust you!"

I was caught completely off guard. On Nantucket, I had been able to miss a few hours of work for being hung over. I never had to report to Jack, only Neil, and Neil was usually the one I drank with. But I was stung by Jack's attack. "Sorry Jack. I am taking this job seriously," I said.

"Good," Jack said loudly. "Get your shit together and get your ass down to the job." He paused and then added with finality, "Don't let this happen again."

I was feeling even more like I was going to throw up. I struggled to say, "It won't," but he hung up.

I knew that I wouldn't be able to get into work. The hangover was too severe. I crawled to the bathroom, threw up and went back to bed. I wanted to sleep but couldn't. My body was reeling, and my mind was trying to sort out all that Jack had said. It made sense. I had left engineering because I didn't like the idea that I was easily replaced, that if I didn't do my work someone else would do it just the same. I wanted my work to be an expression of myself and I thought I had found it here. Jack had given it to me. But now I realized that there was another side to this coin. If I was doing work that was personally meaningful, then I couldn't just *not* show up. No one else could replace me. I couldn't have the challenge and satisfaction of being responsible while at the same time have the flexibility and freedom of being irresponsible. I had to make a choice, one that had never been demanded of me before. Or, I wondered, maybe I had never noticed it before. Maybe my carefree attitude in the past had been the reason that I had not found the job that would satisfy me. Maybe I needed to take things a little more seriously to find what I was looking for.

I never made it to work and Jack never mentioned it again. But missing work started me on a reflective weekend healing my over-indulgence. My emotions shifted from casual acceptance to embarrassment and shame. Jack had brought me down here and taken a chance on me. And now I had let him down. I resolved that I would not do that again.

WHEN RED AND HIS CONCRETE crew were alone on the job, they could move freely and at a pace that was set only by their contractual arrangement. But now, they would simply look across the site to see the carpenters bearing down on them. Concrete walls did not stand long before sill plates were attached and the flooring spread further towards completion. They had to keep pace, and they had to manage their tools and materials more carefully. Forms, dogs, braces, ties, all had to be neatly stored so as not to interfere with the carpenters. And movement of the two trades had to be coordinated.

This is where I found myself becoming more useful. Red and Scott maintained a quiet truce, no outward signs of anger or aggression, just mutual avoidance. This left me in the position of being the only one able to talk to both sides, and I liked it. Red and Scott called on me when they needed something from the other—progress reports, time schedules, access to certain parts of the job. I was the one with the answers. I had found an irreplaceable place for myself in the job team. I kept the peace, and therefore the progress on the job. I felt content. I was part of something, yet I was adding my own unique contribution. The plans were clear but the process for building them was not. I had no manuals, no specific education, no prescribed path to completing this work. No one was telling me how to do it. I was just doing my part as I figured it out, and of course, with the advice of Jack when I needed it.

I never mentioned the out-of-plumb wall to Red or to Scott. I avoided the topic completely as something that Jack would resolve. And neither Scott nor Red brought it up.

When the concrete foundation was finally completed and the entire house was ready to be framed, there was one last job for Red and that was to pour the basement floor. The space was accessible from the ground on the north side of the house, but the concrete trucks could not reach into the back portions of the basement. Red would need a concrete pump and would also need the carpenters to stay out of the way while he poured four sections in four days. He planned to move from east to west and he told me that he "expected the carpenters not to fuck me up." My job was to coordinate Scott and his crew out of his way.

When I first approached Scott about Red's plans, he was resistant. His answers were vague and dismissive. "Yeah, I'll see what I can do," or "I'm not gonna screw up my schedule for him." After persisting, I was able to work out a settlement. The carpenters would occupy the land on the south side of the house while Red's domain would lie to the north. A fuzzy line of demarcation extended off the east and west ends of the house. I would have to see that the boundaries were enforced and took it upon myself to coordinate with Scott's and Red's foremen. They were quick allies since they were as anxious to avoid a fight as I was. All concrete materials were moved to the north while all carpentry equipment followed the reverse course. All this was done while each side continued to do its work.

While playing mediator, I also joined either crew as I chose. While I had lost interest in the concrete forming work, I was fascinated by the idea of pouring a floor and asked Red if I could help. Red laughed, "So you wanna get dirty with us again, huh? Have you had it with those pretty boys upstairs?" Then he yelled to Jimmy so that his crew could hear, "Hey Jimmy, Andy wants to rejoin the big boys on the job when we pour the floor. Do you think he can hack it?" Everyone laughed. Turning back to me he said, "wear your worst clothes and be prepared for some kick-ass, back-breaking work. And then we'll make a man out of you."

PREPARATIONS WERE MADE to pour the basement floor—nearly ten thousand square feet in all. Lights were strung up in the back wings of the basement where the new floor had blocked out sunshine. Plastic was laid over the stone base of the first section—one quarter of the floor—and wire mesh was laid over that. Along the walls, a blue chalk line marked the final concrete floor height and at intermittent locations, stakes were driven into the ground, also marked with the final height of the floor. Finally, a metal strip was put in place, marking where one pour ended and the subsequent one would begin the next day. Everything was set.

Early Monday morning, Red and his crew waited with the usual air of nervous anticipation that preceded a pour. As we waited, Jimmy filled the time by sharing his pride in his craft. "You have to move this stuff quickly and get it in place before it starts to set up. It's not like carpentry where you can make a mistake and rip it out. Once it's here, it's here. That means that we have to do it right the first time. We have to be good. We have to work as a team. We have to react quickly to any unforeseen problems." He paused recalling a memory. "We once had a wall form start to blow out. Boy, you wanna see these guys move quickly. If it had given way, we would've had yards of concrete in a pile and a wall that wouldn't have been worth a damn. It would have killed the entire profit on the job just to get over the mistake. But we were able to brace it back while continuing with the pour." Pleased with himself, he added, "These guys are a great crew."

We were interrupted when one of the crew yelled, "Here comes the pump."

A large truck with a boom and a long coiled tube was rolling up the driveway. Red directed it into position in his territory of the jobsite. The crew began to unload the long, thick hose. The driver operated the boom, extending the reach into the basement, but he never got out of the truck. Just as with the cement mixers, the concrete crew did all the work with the cement company's equipment. "They're union," Jimmy explained. "They don't have to do a fuckin' thing." After a pause, he added, "And they won't."

Soon the first of two mixers for the day came rolling up the driveway. A member of the crew directed him into place. Red donned rubber boots, as did we all. I was given a shovel and was teamed up with two other guys, similarly equipped. Jimmy would direct the pour at the end of the hose. At the beginning was a large hopper into which the cement mixer started to dump its load. With a loud grinding noise, concrete was pumped out of the hopper and through the hose and was spitting out the other end. I and the others with shovels pushed the heavy material around the floor while Jimmy directed. "More over here; more over there."

One of the guys carried a stick with a nail on the end of it, which he used to pull the wire mesh up into the middle of the mix. As more and more concrete flowed, Jimmy kept directing it to the various points on the floor that needed it. With a trowel in his hand, Red smoothed the mixture along the line on the wall and around the stakes to mark exactly what height the concrete should rise to. Once enough floor was covered with the wet mud,

Red and Jimmy pushed a long straight metal bar along the top of the mix to get the right height. And once the rough height was set, Red used a screed—a flat, three-foot-wide blade on the end of a ten-foot pole—to smooth the top of the floor into the final height. Occasionally, he would holler to Jimmy that he needed more, and Jimmy would direct one of the shovelers to lob a lump of concrete into the low point for Red to smooth out.

On it went for over an hour. Concrete was dumped into the hopper, pumped through the hose, dumped onto the floor, moved with the shovels, directed by Jimmy and smoothed by Red. The floor was flush with the metal strip marking where tomorrow's pour would begin. Some of the crew began preparing the next section for tomorrow's pour. Jimmy, Red and two others stayed with the fresh cement.

"Now the finish work begins," Jimmy explained. "This is where you separate the men from the boys."

After waiting for the concrete to stiffen, Red put on knee pads, laid some boards on the floor and crawled on top. I couldn't tell what signal or sign Red used to know it was ready. He just knew and, with two large flat trowels, he began to smooth the surface of the concrete even further. Jimmy and the other two did the same. I watched, impressed with their concentration. Red made it clear that I could not help at this stage. "Sorry, Andy, this's where we earn our money. We can't afford a mistake." They were completely focused on the floor, working against the clock to get a smooth finish out of the material before it hardened. Never really speaking to each other, they worked their way around the floor, smoothing every inch. When they were done, they rested, and the remaining crew left.

Now it was just Red and Jimmy. They pulled a finisher out of their truck, a large motorized tool that looked like a lawn-mower with a fan blade on the bottom. After waiting for the concrete to cure even more, they turned on the machine, sending the fan blade to swirl on top of the finished concrete. Red walked the machine over every inch of floor, occasionally squirting water on top to soften it where it had become too hard to work.

The process took most of the day. When done, the floor had a shiny, smooth finish. Red and Jimmy wrapped yellow tape around the new floor to keep people away, packed up and went home. Rejoining the carpenters, I was energized from having watched something new. And I was exhausted as Red had promised.

THE NEXT THREE DAYS went like the first. I spent the morning with the concrete crew and the afternoon with the carpenters. I had seen the process in the first pour and, by the fourth day, would have rather skipped the job. It was hard work. My legs ached from pushing them through the heavy mix, and my arms, back, chest and shoulders ached from shoveling it. But I felt an obligation to Red and his crew. I had started with them. They had accepted me. Whether they needed me or not, I refused to leave them shorthanded.

Above the concrete crew's activity, on Scott's side of the territory, the house continued. While the plywood deck was being finished on the west end of the house, walls were being stood on the east. They were delivered in the same ridiculous fashion, sliding off the back of a tractor trailer, crashing to the ground in an enormous cloud of dust. Scott would take an inventory and direct the laborers to carry the wall sections to their allotted spots, where the foremen would stand them. The house was rising quickly.

BY FRIDAY, RED and his men were done. They collected their materials and loaded them onto the truck for final departure. I reflected on their work, summing it up as a wave-like rhythm between slow forming and fast pouring. This created a sense of satisfied relief following each pour and a sense of excited anticipation before the next one. Since there was always a last or next pour, there was also a balance between these competing emotions. Out of this balance, the team drew their energy. At any moment they could look back and appreciate what they had already done, something that was solid and permanent. At the same time, they could look forward to what they had yet to do, building more solid and immovable walls on which the house would be built. The concrete crew relished the notion that their work was literally and figuratively the foundation of the house. Other trades always followed them. But they were first, and theirs was the work upon which all else was built. Since they took great pride in their product, they felt that the best the other trades could do was to maintain their level of quality or diminish it. They "could not be improved upon," pronounced Red.

But now there was no work to look forward to here. The crew was wrapping up and leaving the job. They displayed none of the nostalgia at departing that I felt. I watched them joke with each other as they picked up stray dogs, forms and rebar. They tied the forms down neatly on the truck, more neatly than I had ever seen them. I was becoming aware of how temporary my participation in the team had been. Their eyes and minds were on the next job. I could see that they had already left this job mentally and emotionally. And so I felt that I was missing them already, although they had not yet left. As in Nantucket, I watched the job-end ritual playing out. They had done this many times before and would do it many times again.

I lingered around their trucks as they were finishing their cleanup, holding a few pieces of rebar and a bag of dogs as an excuse for being there. But really I was trying to time my presence so as to say good-bye. I felt embarrassed at my sentimentality, but lingered nonetheless. Once fully loaded up, Red turned to me and extended his hand. I reached for it eagerly.

Red held it, firmly, steadily. "Andy, it's been a pleasure working with ya. You're an honest guy and we appreciated the way you handled things. Hold onto that attitude and enthusiasm. It'll carry you far."

I felt embarrassed at the compliment and the surprising intensity with which Red delivered it. I was also embarrassed that the rest of the crew was now standing around me, watching in the same silence.

I waited long enough so as not to disrespect his intention and then replied, "Thanks. And thanks for teaching me concrete work." Turning to the rest of the guys, "Thank you all. I really appreciated the way you let me join you." The words sounded a little melodramatic.

Jimmy added, "Now don't let that asshole ruin our good work," and the spell of the moment was broken.

The crew laughed and Red was quick to add his sentiments "Yeah, fuckin' Scott. He's got his head so far up his ass he's oblivious to everything except what's got his immediate attention."

One of the guys was quick to finish Red's sentence, "Yeah and that's usually his dick." The crew burst into laughter again. Everyone shook my hand. I figured that I'd not likely be seeing these guys again, but didn't give up all hope. After all, I thought I had said goodbye to Jack on Nantucket. Perhaps we would work together on another job, if there was another job. One by one the crew returned to their trucks and started their engines. All were ready to go, leaving Red the only one left to get into his truck.

"Andy, think about what happened here. We've done good work, despite that bullshit with the wall. And you saw how some people behaved when their ass is on the line. Sutton screwed up that wall and didn't have the balls to admit it. Remember that. I'll take a hit for it and he won't even bat an eye. Think about what kind of person could do that. If it comes down to his ass or yours, he won't hesitate to make you take the fall. Watch your back my friend."

He stepped towards his truck, "Think about what I said." And then he yelled, loud enough for the carpenters to hear, "And don't let these animals fuck up the perfection we gave them. If they finish this house half as well as we started it, this'll be one first class fuckin' house." He got in his truck and drove away, honking his horn triumphantly down the driveway.

I walked back onto the deck. One of the carpenters yelled, "Hey, is that a concrete guy over there?" Answered another, "Yeah, I think Red left him behind." Brian added, "Let's call in a load of concrete and see if he can build us a house." Everyone laughed. Scott just watched from the other end of the house, continuing to direct the placement of wall panels that had been delivered that morning.

THE FLOOR DECK WAS COMPLETE and there was no need for the crew to work in the wave that had marked the process so far. In fact, working at multiple locations allowed the crew to break into teams that worked independently from one another. First, walls were stood. Once done, roof trusses would be added and then the plywood roof itself. This was the progression of materials to arrive on the job by the flat bed. But for now, it was the walls, and they were carried to the house by the laborers and assembled by the carpenters. It was moving fast but was too much for the size of the crew presently on the job.

As if on cue, a van arrived the next morning, "Ace Construction" printed neatly on the driver's side door. It stopped in the dust and six new men emerged from inside. I was struck by their appearance. They were older than the carpenters on the job. They appeared more experienced, tougher. I felt a sense of nervousness or even fear. My first reaction was that they looked like convicts.

Joey—the owner of Ace Construction—got out and signaled to Scott that he was leaving two guys with this job and taking the rest to another. Scott signaled okay and directed Brian to bring them over. The new guys didn't say a word; didn't show any emotion. They simply grabbed their tool belts and went where they were told. The tool belts showed their age as much as their faces. These were seasoned veterans.

The first man introduced himself as Chet. He was tall with long light curly hair, a weathered face, two days of beard and a worn belt that sported two red suspenders clipped to it. The other was Benjamin. He was shorter, five foot seven, with an even more weathered face, wrinkled from age, a bald head and a long dark beard, six or seven inches long. His belt was similarly worn and possessed many tools that I had not seen before. It jingled when he moved as the nailpullers, chisels and hammers tapped against each other. He seemed prepared for any possible carpentry contingency.

Since they came as a pair, Brian decided to keep them together until he got a sense of what they could do. He gave them one laborer and told them to start nailing the top plate to the walls that had already been built. This was a job that required no understanding of the blueprints. It was a task that any carpenter would know how to do and was required on every wall as a way to tie them together. I watched them as I continued to work with Brian's crew, standing walls just ahead of them.

Benjamin took charge. He instructed the laborer to collect two-by-sixes and stack them on two horses that he told Chet to set up. Benjamin set up two ladders and the power for his saws—he brought two. I could hear his deep southern accent, "Chet, let's set up right there. I'll call out numbers, you cut." Chet silently nodded and prepared for his part of the task. They were very methodical, and to my eye, they were slow. But they did work that would not likely have to be replaced. They checked the walls for *plumb, level and square* before adding the top plate, which surprised and impressed me. Many would have just started adding the plate.

During the break, I introduced myself and struck up a conversation. "Ben, is it?"

"Benjamin," he said dryly.

"Sorry?" I asked.

"Benjamin," he repeated. "Just wanna set things right from the start."

"Okay, Benjamin," I said. "Where are you guys from?"

Benjamin explained that he was from Louisiana. Chet was from Texas. They had both been traveling the country looking for work and met a month earlier on a jobsite in New York. They decided to break out on their own but found work hard to come by, so they answered an ad in the paper for Ace Construction.

I was surprised. The idea that Joey was simply putting new hires on this job bothered me. I had assumed that all these guys were part of an organized crew. With this revelation I thought a little less of the value that Ace Construction offered to the job.

"Why do you have two saws?" I asked Benjamin.

"One's a worm drive and the other's, well, the other's just a regular circular saw. I prefer the worm drive for cuttin' below my shoulders and the other for cuttin' above."

This kind of simple practicality seemed a common thread in all his views. The more I got to know him over the days that followed, the more interesting I found him. He lived by a code of his own, and laid out his logic carefully in his slow southern drawl. For example, he didn't believe in banks, preferring to bury his money in mason jars. He reasoned, "Why should I pay a bank for the right to sell my money to someone else?" He didn't believe in insurance companies. "All they want to do is place a bet with me. They bet I am *not* going to die or get in a car accident. I bet that I am. And if I win, they pay someone else. That seems a fool's bet to me." He said all this in a matter-of-fact fashion. One day a carpenter asked him if he had any kids. He replied, "Yes, the Lord has blessed me with four children. One in Texas, another in Louisiana and two in Tennessee." He then calmly added, "I fulfill all my fatherly responsibilities and provide child care for each one."

Later, when Chet told me that Benjamin had plucked someone's eye out, I asked him to tell me the story. He explained, "Well, the gentleman was bouncing my head off a pool table. I could think of no other way to make him stop. So I reached up and grabbed what I could. It happened to be his eyeball." Then with a smile and an air of satisfaction, he added, "he stopped."

WITH THE ADDITION of Chet and Benjamin, the crew was now in full swing and the house was growing rapidly. Proportion and scale were starting to materialize as the architect's vision was becoming a reality. And the architect, William Simon, came to the job now with more frequency.

I found him a distinctly different presence on the job. In stark contrast to the tradesmen, William would arrive neatly dressed in pressed slacks, shiny shoes and smooth shirts. He was tall and thin; his hair was neatly combed and his manner of speech showed that he had an educated background. I listened intently to William and tried to learn from him, but I first had to master his new language.

He spoke in a very enthusiastic and descriptive way, using a vocabulary different from the one I had been learning so far. He talked of "the multiple elements of the structure" and "the elegance of the west elevation's vertical lines" where the carpenters talked of "wall trusses on the north wing" and "jack studs supporting the headers on wall number A-45." William saw dimensions and characteristics of the overall form. The carpenters saw the individual pieces that were beginning to comprise the whole. William saw form, function and aesthetics. The carpenters saw structure.

Scott found him amusing. When William spoke in terms that at times drifted into the poetic, Scott would say something to bring him down to earth.

William would gush eloquently, "Look at the receding elements of these multiple forms, drawing the viewer deeper and deeper into the interior spaces. The viewer is transformed into a participant, experiencing the house as it unfolds its inner secrets bit by bit." Scott would respond drolly, "Do ya have any idea how hard it's gonna be to make the sheetrock corners on those posts line up, William?"

The difference between the two perspectives struck me and I mused about it over break with the carpenters. Brian expressed the now familiar opinion that every architect should spend some time working the trades. "That way they won't design these stupid details that cost a fortune to build for no reason. Think how cheaply this house could be built if an architect knew something about framing, plumbing or electrical work."

Benjamin waited for Brian to finish and then added, in his now familiar accent and formal manner, "Well it's important for the process that those who design be different than those who build. That allows them to be creative and unrestricted by the restraints of the material world." His speech had a tone suggesting it was the product of great thought and possessing great wisdom. It made me smile.

Brian retorted, "Yeah, they're unrestricted by the material world all right. That's my fuckin' point."

"But Brian, I think you're missing the point," replied Benjamin. "Think how boring this house would be if everything were in eight foot dimensions to match the size of a piece of sheetrock or plywood. That twelve-inch jog on either side of the front door may seem a pain in the ass to you, but it adds to the feel of the entry. If a carpenter were in charge of designing it, he might design the wall straight through because it's easier to frame. But then, taken to the extreme, designs would be guided more by ease of construction than by artistic effect." He sat and pondered either his last or his next comment, I couldn't tell. Everyone who was listening gave Benjamin his undivided attention. Finally he added, "Actually though, I feel sorry for architects."

When no one responded, I finally volunteered, "Okay I'll bite. Why do you feel sorry for architects?"

"Well," Benjamin pondered aloud. "Architects design something that they can't make into reality. They need builders to do it. William's an artist, just like a painter or a sculptor. But while he develops the idea and design for his art, he can't work with the medium. An architect is like a painter or sculptor who needs someone else to do the brush strokes or chisel work."

"Damn straight," said Brian. "Without us they'd be nothin'. And what thanks do we get? None. When this house is done, it'll be William Simon that'll get all the credit, not us."

"But wait a minute Brian," Benjamin answered back. "William deserves the credit. A house is much more complicated than a painting or a sculpture. A division of labor is necessary to get it done, but it's his vision that's guiding us. We're building an idea; William's idea. It's not ours. It's his. And that makes all the difference in the world."

I thought about Benjamin's words. But, as I watched William on the jobsite, he showed no signs of frustration. Scott's comments, which seemed designed to accentuate his disconnect from the physical construction of the house, rolled right off his back and he never wavered from revealing his excitement at seeing his ideas become reality at our hands. He enjoyed his place in the process and I admired him for that.

AFTER LUNCH, THE CREW was fully set up and hard at work. Compressors were humming, horses erected, saws and drills plugged in throughout the site. At the same time, the clouds that had been threatening all morning finally opened up. It was a real downpour. There was not enough roof for cover yet and it took at least twenty minutes to get everything protected. Most importantly, the first shipment of windows had arrived that morning and were stacked on the open deck. So a majority of the cover-up effort was devoted to protecting them from getting soaked. Once everything was covered with plastic, some of the crew ran for their cars while Scott, Gary, Brian and I collected in the trailer.

Drying himself off, Gary turned to me and said, "I hope Jack'll appreciate what we just did for him with a bonus." He was smiling as he said it, and I thought it was a wisecrack.

"What's the bonus for?" I asked.

Gary exploded, "Because we just saved his fuckin' windows. I think that's worth some fuckin' money, don't you?"

My face flushed. Out of the corner of my eye, I saw Scott smirking.

I shot back, "I don't think you need to get paid extra for doing your job and I'm sure Jack feels the same way."

The two of us stared at each other while the others waited in silence for the standoff to end.

Finally, Gary backed down. "Well, we're all pretty wet here and we did it for the sake of the job. That's all I'm saying."

"And I'm sure Jack'll appreciate it as he sees fit."

"Well we just need to get dried in as fast as we can," Scott said. A day of rain added one more day to the achievement of that goal. Everyone was sent home and I had nothing to do but linger for a while in the trailer and then try to kill the day. No one got paid. I hated rainy days.

That evening, Jack and I talked during our regular phone call. We began with the usual, "How's things going out there, Stuff?"

"Moving along fine."

"Yeah, I stopped by last night. It looks like it's coming together. I'm not sure I like a few of the things William's got going, but it's impressive. And, it looks clean. Keep on top of that. I don't wanna see any cigarette butts, coffee cups, soda cans! Nothing! Got it?"

"Yeah Jack, I've got it," I said, used to that priority by now. I was surprised that he had checked on the job without me. His time on site had been noticeably limited, at least to me. But, I was too anxious to talk about the outburst from Gary. I explained the story, concluding, "I was angriest at the way he demanded the bonus. If he asked politely, maybe we could've talked about it. But, it's your money and he's got no right to demand it. Especially if he's just doing what he's supposed to do. It kind of defeats the purpose of a bonus, doesn't it?"

"Andy, let me explain something to you. I think Gary knows he was out of line and that's why he yelled. He was just testing you to see how far he could get. You were good not to give in. You passed the test."

"Thanks," I said, but I became mad as I thought about it. "So he was just tryin' to get away with it? That pisses me off! I thought I could trust him. Now I can't!"

"Andy, put it behind you. There's no need to give Gary another thought. He's not worth it. See him for what he is and now deal with him that way."

I was still mulling over the deliberate ambush in my head when Jack added, "Andy, think of it this way. If you're walkin' down the street and you see a piece of dog shit on the sidewalk, what do ya do?" He paused; I waited. "Well I'll tell ya. You step around it. And do you get mad at the dog shit? No! You just step around it and walk on." He concluded, "Just step around Gary and move on. That's who he is. Learn that and deal with him that way from now on. Believe me when I tell ya."

I laughed at the comparison between Gary and dog-shit, but then grew serious again. My worries over a rivalry with Scott had been resurrected. "But there's more. Scott smiled when it happened. I still think he sees me as a threat or he likes fucking with me too."

"Listen to me, Stuff. No one, and I mean no one, is gonna stand between you and me. Fuck Scott! Fuck him!" Jack was adamant. "Scott's just someone I need right now. Don't worry about him. Just learn. Do you hear what I'm telling you? Don't worry about him at all."

I wanted to believe him, but I was still suspicious. I had to admit that I couldn't do what Scott was doing. I now knew that it would have been crazy for me to start my own company. I was learning so much and was still not sure that I could learn all that was needed. But Jack's support and praise carried me along. His confidence in me became my confidence in myself. And with that connection, with him behind me, I could do anything. And in return for this profound gift, I wanted to please him. I wanted him to be proud of me.

I MARVELED AT EACH STEP that brought the house closer to what it would eventually be. The floor created a sense of the boundaries of the house. It was smooth, flat and perfectly square at all its corners. The walls created a sense of space, the shape of the house coming into greater clarity. They defined the inside of the living space both in relation to what was now outside and to what would become other rooms. The master bedroom was divided from the study was divided from the living room and so on. Each wall created greater dimension and complexity to the house as a space where people would live, sleep, dine and entertain.

The roof trusses then finished the definition of what was inside and what was outside. Designed to specific engineering specifications, they formed the final shape of both the ceiling and the roof above. Then with the plywood and the waterproof plastic or tarpaper laid on top, the house became watertight and we now finally had a sense that we were *inside*. While fully "dried-in" required roof shingles, windows and doors, we could now work unimpeded by the weather.

I knew by the drawings what the house was supposed to look like as each piece found its rightful place. To me, it was more than just knowing the drawings; I understood them. They made sense. There was a pattern and symmetry to things that I could put together as some over-arching logic, William's logic. I was learning how he thought. Because he designed a particular detail on one end of the house, it only made sense that another detail on the other end of the house be done in a similar way, even if he hadn't drawn it.

William's design was very angular and balanced. Once the exterior walls were in place, I could see how every element, all the way to the ridge, became defined. The ridge-line would always run down the center of two opposing walls no matter how they were arranged. Because of the many jogs in the house, the ridge line stepped back and forth as well as up and down with each change in the location and distance between the opposing walls. Then the valleys—places where two pitches met to create a trough where water drained—would form whatever angle the meeting roof-lines required. The roof was pure geometry and the walls defined it. To me, it was beautiful in its aesthetics and in its logic. I could see its shape before any trusses were stood. And therefore I could see if a truss was placed incorrectly.

One afternoon, I watched as the crane placed a group of trusses on the walls and the carpenters began to separate them and nail them into place. Most of the trusses were straightforward, as the carpenters merely measured the four foot overhang from either end and nailed them to the opposing walls with metal brackets.

But on one corner where two roof-lines met at a jog, the trusses didn't cross the entire house. These trusses were unlike any others that had yet been installed and Brian searched for the truss drawings to figure out how to place them. I stared at the individual pieces and began to assemble them in my mind until they completed the final shape. Before Brian could return, I directed Brian's crew to lay them out, waiting to nail them off in case I had made a mistake. When Brian returned, drawings in hand, he saw what had happened. He looked up, looked down at the drawings, looked up again and smiled. He stuffed the drawings into his tool belt and climbed back up on the roof laughing, "Andy, screw the drawings. You're staying with me."

OVER THE WEEKS, I began to notice that carpenters occasionally disappeared from the crew. Nothing was said. The carpenter simply stopped coming and another replaced him. When I asked Scott, his replies were usually brief. "Oh, he didn't work out," or "He's been assigned to another job." I accepted the answers but grew suspicious about the underlying reasons and the brevity of his answers. Over lunch, I asked Brian.

"Well let's see, remember Roger? He wanted more money and Joey told him to hit the bricks. He hates being told he's not paying enough. And with the market as it is, he can just go out and get a replacement. And remember Marc? Scott was riding him because his work was sloppy. Marc didn't like it so he called Scott an asshole back at the office. Joey didn't like him anyway, so he canned him too."

I wondered about the dynamics of running a business this way, letting people go with so little thought. I liked working with Brian and Gary and thought it would make sense to keep the crews intact so as to create camaraderie. But this led me to also wonder about how I fit in the world of carpentry. Were my notions of loyalty misplaced?

Brian added, "Not to worry Andy, they'll find work. I'll bet they've got jobs already. And Joey'll get some new guys and bring 'em as soon as we need them."

Brian's prediction came true the next day when the "Ace Construction" van pulled up again and three men stepped out. Again I was struck at their age and weathered appearance. I guessed that they were in their fifties but wasn't sure if they were really that old or just showed the wear and tear of much experience. They were definitely the toughest guys I had seen so far. Scott and I greeted them.

Riley spoke first, introducing himself. He had light sandy hair, pale blue bloodshot eyes, and two days growth on his face. He was tall and spoke politely with a western accent. His work pants and flannel shirt were worn and his hands were rough and strong. He looked like someone who had worked in construction for a long time. He explained that he had spent many years as a carpenter but had spent most of his career running concrete crews for a large commercial construction firm in Denver.

"Times been tough back home," he explained, "so the three of us just drove east until we found work. Around Pennsylvania, we heard that y'all were building homes up in this part of the country so we headed on up. We just got in yesterday, saw your ad and rented a room over in Brewster."

Scott nodded as he listened to the story. Perhaps he had heard such stories before, but I had never met someone who lived like this. I felt both amazement at Riley's story and nervousness at the kind of person who lived such a life.

"This is Arthur and this is Dennis," continued Riley. "They drove out with me."

Dennis extended his hand. He was clean-shaven except for a mustache, his hair was neatly combed and he was dressed in jeans and a clean, white T-shirt. He also had a strong accent and he was less reserved than Riley when he spoke. He looked around. "Goddamn, this is what I call a house! I think we found what we've been lookin' for." He smiled, oblivious to Scott who did not smile back and was instead eyeing them all with suspicion.

Arthur was the biggest and quietest of them. He had dark skin, dark curly hair and a large frame. He was chewing tobacco and leaned over occasionally to spit by his side. He appeared nervous and kept shuffling his feet and looking down. He spoke slowly, explaining that he had left his wife and two kids back at an Indian reservation in Albuquerque, New Mexico. "There's not much good payin' work back home," he explained. "I'm here to make as much money as I can and just get back to my family."

"Well, we'll see if we can help you do that," said Scott, turning to the jobsite in a signal that introductions were over. He called over to Brian and Gary, "Here's three new guys for ya. Split 'em up. Brian, put Arthur with Benjamin and Chet. Gary, put Riley and," he paused looking at the third man, "What was your name again?"

"Dennis."

"Yeah right, put Riley and Dennis on the guest bedroom wing. Let's see what they can do."

It seemed a cautionary statement, a warning that he wasn't sure what to think of them yet. Once the carpenters left for their assigned places, Scott looked at me and said, "I don't know what rock Joey got those guys out from under. But if that's the best he can do, things must be getting pretty tight out there." I had no reply. I didn't know how to evaluate them as I was only now learning the range of personalities that worked on a jobsite.

THE CREW WAS DIFFERENT with the recent additions of Benjamin, Chet, Riley, Dennis and Arthur. The old and young guys mingled, but the distinctions were clear. I could see it in the language and the way they worked. The older guys formed themselves into clear roles, one would do the measuring and the nailing, another would do the cutting. They knew how to organize themselves and get things done. They had different expertise and they knew when to defer to another for that expertise. Arthur emerged as the most skilled carpenter when it came to detailed work. Riley was better at organizing the larger bulk work. Dennis liked following orders, as did Chet. Benjamin was extremely detail-oriented and possessed extraordinary patience in his work.

And they spoke to each other in expressions that could charitably be called "colorful." If Arthur, for example, received a piece of wood that was cut just a little bit too long, he'd ask for his cutter to remove "a taste." This was usually followed by a spit of his ever-present chewing tobacco. He was considerate enough to always spit it out the nearest available window or doorway.

Riley and Dennis asked the cutter to take off "a cunt hair." Taken even further, one day Dennis asked that a "red cunt hair" be taken off. This, it appeared, was new to the other carpenters, as evidenced by Arthur's askance look.

"Come on," Dennis protested with a smile, "everyone knows that red cunt hairs are thinner than blonde or brunette."

Arthur replied, "And you've come to this conclusion after careful inspections?"

Dennis grinned widely, "You bet. All in the name of better building."

This got laughter from all within earshot. That was what I noticed most about the older guys. They worked in a casual and steady rhythm that mixed work with banter. Jokes would be stuck into everyday activities with natural ease. One day, Dennis broke down in mock sobs as a country-western song—the older guy's favorite kind of music, which was not easy to find on Connecticut radio stations—listed off the sadness of the singer's life. Soon, the others were sobbing along with him.

With the older guys, Scott became more tentative in his practice of barking out orders. Previously he would not hesitate to instruct a young carpenter on the smallest of details. "Put those horses over here." "Stack that wood over there." "Don't forget to check for *plumb, level and square* before you start." "Use two nails every twelve inches when nailing off that jack stud." At times, he would even put on his nail belt and show a carpenter how to do what he wanted. But with the older guys, Scott was less dictatorial. He would give more general instructions and then step back and let them work it out. "The plans call for a doorway at six inches from the end wall. Be sure to leave enough room for the light-switches and the casing." "The wall panels for this section of the house just arrived, here's the plans, I'll have the laborers bring them over, where would you like 'em?"

Where the older guys worked steadily and slowly, the younger guys ebbed and flowed and still needed Scott's guidance. They moved more erratically. Most days they worked feverishly. They liked to listen to rock and roll, and they liked to play it loudly. It fueled their energy to work hard. Sometimes these days were successful. But sometimes, they resulted in mistakes that had to be ripped out and fixed. These annoyed Scott, as they cost materials and time. But in the end, it was hard for me to tell who really worked faster overall.

SUBCONTRACTORS STARTED TO CHANGE the character of the jobsite as well. Jack would give me a day or two's notice and they would just show up. My job was to coordinate them and make sure they kept moving.

First, the masons arrived to build the house's three chimneys and five fireplaces. They set up shop in the basement, mortaring together towers of blocks that rose through holes in the first floor deck and reached towards other holes waiting in the still forming roof. They were Italian by birth and spoke in broken English. Jack had sung their praises as being top-notch craftsmen who brought their skills from Europe. They were friendly if I approached them, but otherwise stayed to themselves.

Then there were the plumbers. Freddie Carlucci was the head of "Carlucci Plumbing and Heating," a company made up of himself and his two sons. They were honest, hard workers. More importantly, they were friends of Jack's. They had helped Jack build his house, not only installing the plumbing but also helping with the actual construction when tasks required more hands than Jack's two. They began to run their waste lines for the toilets, sinks, tubs, washers and showers. These lines were connected to a sleeve in the foundation that led to what would eventually be the septic field Barry was digging one hundred feet downhill from the house.

The heating and air conditioning system was installed by Fairfield Heating, Ventilation and Air Conditioning Company (or HVAC). Nigel Parsons introduced himself as the president of the company and he had multiple crews to prove that he was, in fact, in charge of something more akin to a company than the family operation of Carlucci. Underneath the first floor deck, his crew was installing ductwork to the eight zones in the house.

One subcontractor with whom I developed a particularly close bond was the salesman from the local lumberyard, Ridgefield Supply Co. Philip Morgan was a cleanly dressed, mild-mannered guy. He wore button-down oxfords and khakis. He spoke in a way that revealed that he was educated, talking about current events and business issues. Most importantly, he understood the concerns that I was facing and taught me the complexities of ordering materials from the forest to the mill to the wholesaler to the lumberyard and finally to me. I bought basic materials from him—framing lumber, plywood, nails—but also turned to him for the more difficult items to find—special moldings, stainless steel screws, copper screening. Jack had stressed that I should solicit others bids at times but said that he had struck a deal with the president of Ridgefield Supply which insured that we would always get a good deal from Philip. And more than pricing, Philip just gave me good thoughtful service. He would stop by the job "just to check out how things were going." When he did, he would call beforehand to ask if there were any materials that I needed. There usually was, a box of nails, some Tyvek sheeting, a sheet of plywood.

While most of the subs didn't know each other before the job, they knew the routine and where their tasks would overlap. At times this overlap created tension, such as when a plumber drilled a four inch wide hole through the framing that a carpenter had built, or when the HVAC crew ran some ductwork through a space that the plumber had hoped to use for a waste line. These disputes were usually settled with a jobsite pecking order.

Masons were first. Their chimney had to go straight up, period. Ductwork had the next right of way. Bends in ductwork slowed the efficiency of the system greatly. Waste plumbing could rival ductwork when it required a steady downward grade allowing gravity to feed towards the sleeve in the foundation. Next was water plumbing. Although straight lines were preferred, water pressure could overcome bends. Electrical work, which would come later, was always last. And carpenters were left with the task of having to fix any framing that was inevitably cut, drilled or removed in the process.

While this pecking order had a clear logic, I still found myself negotiating disputes among the subcontractors. And where possible, I tried to identify places where future conflicts would occur so as to head them off. Sometimes I was successful, other times not. Either way, there was always a show of complaining. It seemed a way to gain points for winning future disputes, because coming in second in one of these disputes always meant more time, more work and therefore less profit.

I also assigned myself the task of short projects. Some were my sole responsibility, such as watering the tree in the middle of the house. But as more subs came on site, small projects were often necessary to fill in the gaps between them. If some small pieces had to be made to keep the carpenters going on the roof vent, I would devise an assembly line and make them in bulk. If there was a project that required special materials, they were on the job before the carpenters needed them. If the plumber was installing pipe in a place that required some adjustment in the framing, I would either do it myself or make sure that the work was completed before the plumber got there. This required that I walk the job a lot. I carried a mobile phone so that I could take a call anywhere, from the roof to the basement to the back lot. I felt I knew everything that was going on at the job and I was making sure it went smoothly. No one was telling me to do this, to take on this new role. I was just growing into it. I saw needs and I was filling them.

ONE DAY, JACK MADE a surprise visit to the jobsite. This was rare and was usually associated with some other business. But this time, he had no obvious purpose or agenda for showing up. And even more of a surprise, he didn't come in his Blazer but rather in a brand new, black BMW sedan. It was a dry day, no mud, and he pulled up to the trailer and stepped out. His entry drew the attention of everyone on the jobsite. Barry got off his bulldozer to admire the car. Scott came out of the trailer to greet him and I put my tools down to join the three of them.

"Nice car, Jack," admired Barry. "It looks like a shark."

"Yah think so?" Jack smiled back. "This is one fine piece of machinery. The power in this German motor is incredible."

"A far cry from when you were building race cars I'll bet," replied Barry, his admiration in full display.

"What brings you out to our neck of the woods, Jack?" asked Scott.

"Just thought I'd come and see how things're going," said Jack. Laughing, he added, "So, how's things going?"

"Come check it out," I responded, eager for the chance to show him around. "It's coming along nicely."

Barry returned to his work and Scott, Jack and I walked the job. We toured the perimeter first, admiring the overall shape of the house as the roof was being completed. Then we walked inside, surveying the carpentry work. Jack offered a suggestion. "I don't know why you're doin' your stud wall corners that way. I like California corners myself." He then proceeded to show us a configuration of two-by-sixes that would create the corner he was describing. Scott and I observed attentively, but something seemed odd to me. I already knew how to do this from Nantucket. And I wondered how an experienced framer like Scott could not know about them. But Scott was appreciative in his response.

At other spots in the house Jack made more suggestions and we, his audience, were dutifully appreciative. There was a relaxed tone to the walk as the three of us spent about thirty minutes reviewing the jobsite.

Then Jack shifted tone abruptly. "Okay, what's the story with that laborer over there?" He sternly pointed to the linebacker for Penn State holding a broom. "I've been here for half an hour and I haven't seen him move once. He's just been leaning on that goddamned broom."

"Jack, I'm sure he's been sweeping," Scott explained. "He's our best laborer. Things are a little slow right now. He's most useful when wall panels need to be moved around the site."

"That's true," I added. "He's amazing at lifting stuff. When we move wall panels, he carries one side while three guys carry the other."

Jack shot back. "I'm not paying your guys to stand around doing nothin'. Fire him."

"But Jack, he's a good laborer," Scott protested.

"I don't give a shit. I'm not running a charity here. I don't want him on my job. Get him the fuck off."

"Okay Jack, if that's what you want," Scott replied. I was as surprised as Scott at this display. I knew Jack could shift moods quickly, but this was the most dramatic shift I had seen. He was furious. It was startling and unnerving.

With the mood broken, Jack added "I'll just walk the site on my own. Don't let me keep you two from your work." The message was clear. We were dismissed. Scott went back to the trailer and I rejoined the crew, bewildered.

Jack walked around the site, stopping to stare at something, talking with some of the carpenters and then moving on. His visit lasted about an hour and all the while, the entire crew seemed distracted by his presence. When he was done, he waved to me and drove off. There was a collective sigh of relief when he left.

THE DAY PROCEEDED AS USUAL, but Scott and I were both put off by Jack's sudden fury. At the end of the day, Scott called me into the trailer, "Andy, can you arrange for Jack to come to the job again?"

"What's up? You can call him just as easy as I can." I was surprised that he would want to see him so quickly but not surprised that he might want to avoid making the call.

"I can if you like," he said sheepishly, "but I just thought it would be easier if you asked him if he could give us some help. I negotiated a price with Allied Trusses when we started. It's part of our price to Jack. But now they say there are extras that'll require an additional billing. I can't get them to budge and it might help if Jack was here when we talked."

I could understand Scott's assessment that Jack would be helpful in a negotiation. He always got what he wanted. "Sure I can ask him."

"They're sending a representative out here next Tuesday at ten o'clock. Can you see if Jack can come by earlier so I can explain the details?"

"Sure I'll call him right now." I picked up the telephone and explained to Jack what Scott wanted. Through the entire conversation, I was watching Scott, taking cues on what to say. I hung up with Jack agreeing to come.

"Thanks Andy, I'm sure this'll be a minor issue that we can clear up easily."

By Tuesday, I was happy to have Jack coming out, as the crews were making good progress. Scott stayed in the trailer the entire morning and the day before poring over the drawings and the bills. Scott's boss, Joey, was also there, having arrived just fifteen minutes earlier. When Jack arrived, I handed the piece of lumber I had cut to someone on the crew and walked over to join him.

"Hey Stuff, how's it going?" he said, in a jovial mood.

"Look around. I think it's coming along well. We've got the framing close to complete, the roof should be sheathed by next week and the masons, plumbers and HVAC are going at it downstairs."

"Good, good," Jack smiled, "I guess you've got things under control." He laughed jokingly, repeating, "don't yah? don't yah? Let's take a quick look see!"

Although it was nine o'clock and Scott was waiting for him, Jack let me lead him around the jobsite, introducing him to the various tradesmen. He admired everyone's work and was open with his praise. The tour ended at the trailer when he turned to me, "Okay Stuff, let's get this over with. I want you to watch this closely. You may learn something."

Jack hardened in his demeanor as he passed through the threshold of the trailer. Scott looked up from his paperwork. "Hey Jack, thanks for comin' out. This shouldn't be too difficult to resolve, just a minor misunderstanding. But Joey and I appreciate your lending a hand."

"Hello Joey, Hello Scott," Jack said as he extended his hand to each of them. "Why don't you explain to me what's goin' on."

"Well Jack, the short of it is this; we gave the architectural drawings to

Allied and they developed the truss and wall panel schematics. But some of the dimensions of the final drawings were wrong. We were able to correct some of them here on the job, others were caught before they left the factory and they repaired them there. We say it's Allied's mistake, they say it's ours. I think we have a legitimate case. We had to spend time and money to fix the mistakes and they should reduce their price. They say we owe them money because they had to change the panels from what was originally spec'd."

"So who approved the drawings? This seems straight forward to me," Jack said.

"Well, it's not that simple, Jack," Scott continued, Joey quietly observing from the corner of the trailer. "We got a price from them and approved it, but we didn't have all the final drawings yet. And we didn't really have a formal approval process. There was no official sign-off on the drawings."

"I see, so you think that because you didn't sign anything, you're not responsible?" Jack's question had an accusatory edge to it that caused Scott to hesitate and Joey to stand up straighter.

"No, it's not as simple as that Jack. Let me explain."

But Jack continued, "Explain it to me in a minute, but first, I'd like to know something." Narrowing his eyes, he turned towards Joey, and asked, "Are you guys falling behind on your cost estimates? Is that why I'm here? Am I here to help dig you out of a hole?" The air in the room chilled. "Or, are you preparing me for extra costs?"

I paid close attention. Was Jack being paranoid or was he uncovering an underlying agenda? By Scott's stunned look, I sensed the latter. Joey saw his hesitation and stepped in. "Jack, if there's a mistake in our pricing, that's our problem and we'll eat it." As he said "we" he looked directly and deliberately at Scott. "But we're working together here to build the best house possible for the Winslows. That means that we want the best quality at the best price. I'm sure you'd agree. So, with that in mind, we'd appreciate any help you can give us. We genuinely believe the mistakes were honest ones, but that Allied went ahead with flawed plans. We think that the ultimate measure of how the panels should be built is in the original blue prints. Whether we approved the engineering drawings or not, we paid for panels that matched the blueprints. And they don't. It's as simple as that."

Joey appeared annoyed at having to step into the middle of this discussion so strongly and the whole time he was speaking, I watched Scott regain his composure and prepare himself to step back into the discussion.

Jack simply crossed his arms and listened with the same firm but controlled demeanor he had adopted since he first stepped into the trailer. His composure had not changed one bit, and Scott was scrambling, having been caught off guard by his intensity. I was impressed at how Jack could so easily knock someone off balance by his tone, his demeanor. I had seen this before. He controlled the mood of the discussion. I admired that ability and privately wished I could do the same.

"So it's your problem and I'm here to help?" Jack replied calmly.

"We'd appreciate it, Jack," Joey replied. Scott nodded.

"What would you like me to do?"

Scott now stepped back in. "Here's the original price estimate." He was showing Jack some paperwork, pointing to figures. "Here's the amount they say they spent to correct the panels at the shop. And here's the amount we had to spend to fix the ones here on the job." Then he softened in his tone, "What do ya think is a fair settlement?"

"Well," Jack guffawed. "What's fair here? I'll be goddamned if I know."

Scott quickly said, "Well then, we think you should stand firm on recouping the costs we spent here and not pay them for corrections back at the plant. As a last resort, I'd suggest splitting the difference of the overall costs we both incurred."

I shot a quick glance at Scott. *Jack* was to stand firm? That caught me by surprise. But to my equal surprise, Jack did not react. He simply paused, then nodded, then looked back down and stared at the estimates. He looked up after a few moments and asked, "What time does this guy... what's his name?"

"Al Freedman," Scott said.

"And what time does Al Freedman arrive?"

"Ten o'clock."

"And he knows these numbers?"

"Yeah, we've been discussing them over the phone."

"Okay then, we've got fifteen minutes. Tell me about the rest of the job while we're waiting." Jack leaned back against the wall, arms still crossed.

Scott told about the progress of the job as it compared to his schedule. He gave estimates that had the job coming in on time, a time schedule that he was also quick to point out was fast for a house this size. Jack said nothing and just listened. Scott filled the fifteen minutes with as much information as he could. Finally, a car pulled up behind the trailer and Scott stepped outside to greet Al. Jack looked to me and winked. Again, my admiration for him grew. I watched attentively.

Al entered in a suit and tie, not a common image on the jobsite. He carried a briefcase and set it on the floor extending his hand as Scott introduced him around the room.

"This is really coming out nicely," Al said. "Your order has taken quite a bit of our capacity over the past month and it's a pleasure to see it coming together. This is an image we rarely get to see from the plant."

"It's one hell of a house," replied Jack. Contrary to his sternness with Scott and Joey, Jack was now calm and collegial. "We appreciate your help in bringing it together. We couldn't have done it so fast without your panels."

"Thanks Jack," replied Al. "It's been a pleasure working with you on such a signature home. I hope we can do more like it. And I hope we can straighten out this misunderstanding to our mutual satisfaction."

"I'm sure we can, Al," said Jack. "These things happen and it's best to work together so we can develop long-lasting relationships. That way, we all make money." Jack's words put everyone at ease. Again, he dominated and established the mood. He added, "And if we can work well here, I've got plenty more work to talk to you about."

More of Jack's bravado, I thought. As far as I knew, there was no other project. But Jack kept his business private and it was quite possible that there was.

Al opened his briefcase and pulled out some papers. "I'll cut right to the chase. No need to be hard-nosed about this. I'd like to propose that we split the difference. As I understand it, you estimate these to be your costs. And these are what I estimate ours to be. We spent a little more than you as represented by that figure," he pointed to a number on his sheet, "and it seems more than fair that we share the load in correcting this mistake."

Jack calmly leaned back and I waited for his counter offer. I thought this all part of the negotiating game. One side makes an offer and the other comes back and they teeter back and forth until they settle.

"Well, I'm sure you think that's fair, but we really think the mistake is yours and not ours. I've come here with the expectation that you'll absorb the costs for your work at the plant and then we can talk about reimbursement for our work here. That's where I'm starting from."

Al stood still, staring down. He didn't seem to know what to say. I watched, impressed at Jack's boxing him into a corner. I knew that Jack was taking a strong position and it appeared that Al had been caught off-guard, expecting a more middle of the road tack.

After a moment's pause, Al looked up perplexed. "But, and correct me if I'm wrong here." He looked at Scott, then at Jack. "Scott suggested yesterday that the labor costs here were negligible and that we just needed to resolve my plant costs. I was trying to be generous in response to that offer by making a similar good faith offer in reply."

Jack's face stayed calm, but I saw him twitch. Al stepped back from his papers and spoke very slowly, "In all due respect to everyone in this room," he met each person's eyes as his gaze revolved around the room. "I'm not used to doing business this way." He looked at Jack, "Jack, I sincerely want to maintain a professional relationship. But have I been the subject of a bait and switch? Yesterday I discuss one thing with Scott. Today you enter the negotiation and we're discussing something else. Tell me what's going on here?"

Jack just leaned back, almost smirking as he crossed his arms. "Well Al, it looks as though we have a little misunderstanding here." He looked at Scott and Joey, then slowly extended his hand and Al took it, looking confused. Jack said, "Al, I can see your point clearly now. Your first offer was very fair and we'll work it out from here. I'd like to thank you for your time and apologize for any inconvenience." Handing him his card, he added, "If there's anything else I can do, please don't hesitate to call."

I was confused. What was I missing?

Al now looked around in a way that showed he sensed what was happening, or perhaps what was about to happen. Apparently desirous of escaping before anything changed, he replied in kind. "Thank you Jack. I have other stops to make. It's been a pleasure." He gathered his papers into his brief case, shook everyone's hand and walked out to his car. We waited in silent anticipation as Al's car started, backed out of its spot and departed.

Once gone, Scott started to move towards the door but Jack loudly said, "You're not goin' anywhere! You're gonna stay right here and explain to me what the fuck just happened!" His voice was controlled but fierce. Scott froze. It scared me and I decided that I didn't need to hear this. I made up an excuse that I needed to get something at the lumberyard but Jack stopped me too. "You're gonna stay right there and listen to this." I backed up against a corner of the wall, wishing I could fade into it. Joey watched quietly from his corner.

"So what the fuck was that?" Jack reiterated loudly.

Scott was contrite, "I'm sorry Jack, I messed up."

"You didn't mess up! I'd say you fucked up! And more importantly you fucked me up. My reputation is very important to me and you just made me into a sleazy contractor. How the fuck did this happen?"

Each time that Jack cursed, he spit the words out.

"I'm sorry Jack, I talked to Al yesterday and we talked about these numbers but I didn't think we'd come to any kind of firm conclusion," Scott meekly replied.

"You didn't know you reached a fuckin' conclusion? What the hell does that mean? Was he right or was he wrong? He seemed like a straightforward businessman to me, not prone to making things up." Then very slowly and deliberately, Jack asked, "Did you, or did you not, have an understanding with him yesterday?"

Scott's voice was getting softer with each increasing decibel of Jack's fury. "I didn't think we had an understanding. But I can see how he might've thought we did."

"I'm not buying any of this bullshit!" Jack looked at Scott and then at Joey. "You know, when I run my business, my word is my bond. Screw this bullshit about being absolved of responsibility if you didn't sign off on the goddamned drawings. And screw this shit about having understandings but not being sure. If you can't be sure about what you said to him, how do I have confidence in what you're sayin' to me? What kind of businessmen are you?" He looked at Scott. "Huh?" And then with more force at Joey. "HUH?"

Before they could reply, he continued, "It looks to me like you two are about to lose some money on this contract and you want me to eat it. Well there's no fuckin' way that's gonna happen. Do you think I'm that fuckin' stupid?"

Joey started to speak, but Jack stopped him. "Save it Joey! Just fuckin' save it! I know where you're coming from. You need to make a profit." Then he turned to Scott, almost scrutinizing him, "But you! I don't know what your fuckin' problem is. You're supposed to build me my fuckin' house. It's that simple. Where am I missing something here?" He paused, "And then, you bring me into this whole fuckin' charade. Are you tryin' to steal from me?"

I felt awful. Scott was being degraded in front of me. While I admired and wanted to emulate Jack's ability to control situations, this had gone too far. I needed to get out. "Jack, I have to meet with William about the door detail. He's expecting me." This was only partially true. William had told me to drop by anytime. And this seemed like a good time.

"Fine, get outta here. Joey, if you need to go, that's fine too. Scott and I are gonna continue this little talk."

I made my escape, not waiting to hear Joey's response. Outside, I could see that the crew had heard the shouting and knew something was amiss. Brian signaled a curious look and I just shook my head and mouthed the word "later." I got into my truck and drove to William's office, calming down as I drove through the twisting roads into town.

I conducted the meeting with William, not mentioning a word to him about what had happened. But to my disappointment, my business was completed in only twenty minutes. William had taken the initiative to draw up a new door schedule, answering all of my questions. Reluctantly, I drove back to the jobsite. My heart sank when I pulled up to the trailer to find Jack's car still there and the door to the trailer still closed. It was still going on! How could it still be going on?

As I got out of my truck, the trailer door opened and Scott stepped out. I felt a range of emotions—sorrow and embarrassment for Scott mixed with a certain amount of surprise that he had stupidly put Jack in an embarrassing spot and brought this on himself. I cautiously asked, "Scott?"

Scott turned to me and shook his head, which was hanging low on his shoulders. "I can't talk to you right now, Andy." He walked over to his car and drove off.

Jack stepped out of the trailer and growled at me. "Did you get what you needed from William?"

If Jack knew I had run away from the demolition he had wreaked on Scott, I didn't care. Jack was taking Scott apart bit by bit, and while I didn't want Scott to go through that, I certainly didn't want him to go through that with an audience. And even more certainly, I didn't want to be that audience. It seemed cruel.

Jack walked to his car, turned to me sternly and added, "Keep up the good work. The house's lookin' good." And he drove off.

AT LUNCH, THE CARPENTERS wanted to know what happened in the trailer. Brian told me that Joey left immediately after I did, his face showing signs of distress that were clear to everyone. "So what was all the yellin' about?" he asked.

Riley knowingly explained, "Boys, you just witnessed Scott getting taken to the wood shed. That's obvious enough. And since Jack was the one who took him there, we can only assume it had to do with money."

Dennis whistled, "Man, there was some serious shit going down in there. I could hear the yelling from the guestroom. I wouldn't wanna be on the receiving end of what I heard." He looked to me to add to the comment, but I remained quiet.

"Well, Scott was gonna get it sooner or later," added one of the carpenters. "He was movin' too fast and makin' mistakes."

They were hitting the target but not the bulls-eye. They knew that mistakes were being made but had evidence of only a few small issues that were evident on the job. They had no idea of the extent of the problems that were being resolved back at the plant. I didn't even know until this morning, and even then, it wasn't fully clear to me. But I was relieved that they were figuring it out on their own. I didn't want to tell anything that would betray Jack's confidence and I didn't want to admit anything that would embarrass Scott. I needed time to digest what had happened, and without any clear sense of what I should or should not say, I decided it was best to say nothing.

All I would offer was that, "Scott and Jack had a misunderstanding on some pricing issues with Allied." That seemed innocent enough. When pressed further, I was honestly blunt, "I think I better keep the details to myself right now."

After lunch, work resumed without Scott on the job. The foremen knew their tasks and the materials were on site waiting to be assembled. Interior walls were being completed. Final plywood roof sheathing was being nailed down, tarpaper was covering it over and a line of red cedar shingles were added as a drip edge—William preferred this to a stock metal edge. The last remnants of summer were being enjoyed with this outdoor work.

THE NEXT DAY, Scott came to the job briefly in the morning to get everyone organized on their day's tasks but then left by eight o'clock. His absence was noticeable. The work continued as before, but we all took on new responsibilities to fill Scott's void. Brian, Gary, Riley and Benjamin gave more direction to their crews. I took more charge of the plans when questions emerged.

That afternoon, Jack asked me to stop by the house before heading home. I was looking forward to more explanation of what happened with Scott and figured that the face to face meeting meant that Jack had something important to discuss. When I arrived, I was greeted by Jack's wife, Jane, who directed me downstairs to Jack's office. Jack was seated at his desk.

"Stuff, how's it going?" Jack warmly greeted me.

"We're carryin' on since yesterday's commotion."

"Well, that was quite a scene wasn't it? Can you believe those two? Scott gets caught tryin' to fuck me and Joey just hangs back and lets 'em take the fall."

"I don't understand what happened."

Jack laughed, "Well, as near as I can tell, they were about to lose some serious money on the truss contract because of Scott's screw ups. So they wanted Al to negotiate the extra costs from me. That way, I might take responsibility for paying at least some of them. They were so fuckin' clumsy."

I shook my head trying to put it all together. Jack resumed, announcing, "Starting tomorrow, Ace Construction's off the job." He let the words hang and my mind raced to consider all the implications of such a change.

"Are we gonna stop the job?"

"No, we're gonna carry on with some of the guys, others'll go and we'll hire some more."

I shook my head again, this time to wake myself to my senses. "Wait a minute, you've got people who'll stay? Who?"

"The Colorado guys, Benjamin and Chet. They're all quitting Ace and coming to work for us." The word "us" rang out in my ears. "They asked me to hire them about a week ago and I'd been mulling the idea over for a few weeks before that. I was payin' Ace Construction for nothin' more than putting ads in the paper. Can you believe they were just pulling people off the street and throwing 'em on the job? I could've done that. And when Scott fucked up the panel order, I was at a loss to understand why I was paying them at all."

He stopped and looked at me. "But the question for me is, do I have your commitment to run this job?"

I was stunned but sure. I could not let him down. I stared straight back at Jack and said "Yes Jack, I'm with you." I was thrilled that I was being brought deeper into his confidence.

"Good. Good. That's what I wanted to hear. Good things are comin', Andy. Just you wait and see. Things are gonna happen."

He discussed details about the job, but my mind was elsewhere. I was spinning with the recognition that I was now going to be running the job. Jack kept talking, but my mind continued to ponder this thought. Finally, I interrupted, "Jack, how am I gonna run those guys? They're all twice my age. And they won't listen to someone as inexperienced as me."

"Andy, there are many ways to run a crew. You just have to find the right way for you. Think about it. You can run people by fear. You can run by respect. You can run 'em by being liked. Everyone has to find his own way and I think you're finding yours. Neil used to try to run by fear and he couldn't do it. He just pissed people off. But you run by respect. You know those plans and how to organize the crew and they know that. Believe me, they'll help you. Just let 'em. And they like you. And so do the Winslows, and so does William. Believe you me, that'll go a long way in getting things done."

"But you said I was too green when I got here. I haven't learned that much."

He leaned back in his chair. "Well, look at what you've done. You made friends with Red. That was no small feat and it really impressed me. And the other subs like you. You're getting the job done. I'm not sure how, but you are." Then he smiled at me and chuckled, "Well, I've seen one way you do it. I've seen it a couple of times. When you don't like what someone does, you turn on your Boston snootiness."

Embarrassed, I guffawed, "What's that? Gimme a break."

Jack laughed back, "Yeah, your Boston snootiness. You have this weird way that you shut people down. You don't say a fuckin' word. You just do it with your manner. I wish I could bottle that. It's somethin' you can't fake." He laughed again, "That's what I call it, Boston snootiness. What do ya think of that?" He was grinning widely, teasing me into greater embarrassment.

"I think it's...," I paused, unable to find the right word. "I'm not that way." I was embarrassed, laughing in protest. We were both laughing. After we settled down, I asked, "What's gonna happen tomorrow?"

"Well, for one thing, Scott won't come to the fuckin' jobsite." He laughed loudly. "He and Joey will sit in their office and figure out what the fuck just happened."

"You told 'em already? That must've been awkward."

"They saw the writing on the wall. Did you see how quiet Joey was at that meeting? He knew they were blowin' it. I really don't think he was surprised."

All the while he was talking, I was slowly realizing that I had entered the deep end, and I clung to Jack's words for support. Jack had been scheming this whole thing, watching the signs, and I had no idea it was happening. I couldn't even be sure that he hadn't provoked the whole confrontation with Scott. I had not read a thing. It made me uncomfortable that I was so oblivious. Again, the thought returned to my mind, was I a babe in the woods here? And if I was, all I could do was ride this out and see where it went. Jack was in the driver's seat. I would concentrate on the house and let Jack work out the other messy details.

"So tomorrow, get started as you normally would. We'll need to buy tools. So I'll come by around nine. How's that sound?'

"We'll lose the trailer. We'll have no place to store them."

"We'll use the box truck. It's been sitting at Sutton's place since Nantucket."

"And what if Scott shows up?"

"He won't. But if he does, throw his sorry ass off the job." Jack laughed.

I felt ill at the prospect.

MY NEW CREW OF FIVE arrived for work as usual. The rest of the crew did not. It felt lonely, empty, and I couldn't tell if that was because of fewer people or because of my new responsibilities. I reassessed the priorities, set the men up into two teams and sent them to work outside the house.

"We need to get this dried in as soon as possible," I announced. "Dennis and Arthur, can you finish up the drip edge over the guestroom? Benjamin and Chet, can you start figuring out the trim detail? And Riley, can you help me figure out what tools we'll need to buy?" I raised each set of instructions as a question. I didn't feel comfortable ordering people around, or at least these people, these seasoned veterans, each one nearly twice my age.

Dennis and Arthur climbed up onto the roof where drip-edge shingles had been stacked the previous day by the previous crew. Benjamin and Chet set up in the middle of the house with the radial arm saw and began to cut cedar for the trim. Riley and I began developing a list: a table saw, two chop saws, a sawbuck, two drills (one a hammer drill), two sawzalls, a drill press, two compressors and four nail guns. Finally, I stopped. "Riley, Jack's not gonna spring for all this. Let's prioritize and we'll see what we can get."

Riley smiled, "Then I guess the half-ton pickup is out too?"

I smiled. Out of the corner of my eye, I saw Scott's car pulling into the driveway. My stomach tensed as I braced for a scene.

Scott got out of his car in a rush. He walked into the trailer, grabbed some papers, stepped outside and locked the door. All eyes were on him as he passed through the house to the radial arm saw, which Benjamin was using. Pulling the plug, he announced "This is Ace Construction property. You've got no right to use it."

"No problem Scott you can take it away any time you want," I replied politely.

"I'll have it outta here this afternoon, as well as the rest of our tools." He paused as if to say something more. But he just stared at me for a moment. He seemed bewildered or panicked. I couldn't tell if he was going to yell at me, or swing at me. I felt stronger having Riley, Benjamin and Chet by my side. "Fuck you all," he blurted out and walked briskly to his car, leaving a hasty cloud of dust as he left.

"Well, nice to see you too, Scott," Benjamin chuckled as he reached over and plugged the radial arm saw back in. "Stop by any time."

The crew laughed and went back to work.

AT NINE O'CLOCK, Jack arrived and the entire crew gathered around him. Riley was first to speak, "Jack, you won't regret this. You've got a top-notch crew here and we're gonna make you some good money." All the others seconded the statement, giving their own versions of "You bet Jack," or "You can count on us."

Jack was magnanimous in reply. "Good. I'm glad to hear it. I know we're gonna put together the best goddamned house-building team in Fairfield county. And then you'll see the work come pouring in. If you guys wanna make money, this is the way to do it." He turned to me and asked, "Any word from Ace?"

"Scott was here earlier," I said. "His basic messages were: stay out of the trailer, don't use their tools, he'll get them out of here this afternoon, and, ah," I hesitated for effect, "and, oh yeah, fuck you!" Everyone laughed. For me, it helped to laugh. It made me feel more secure with this change. It was what I thought I wanted from the very beginning—to run the job—but now I was scared to have it.

"Fuck us, huh?" said Jack. "No fuck him! He had a good thing going and he blew it. Fuck him! And he better get that piece of shit trailer outta here too. I can't believe I let him put that eyesore on this jobsite in the first place. We'll get the box truck and some of our own tools here this afternoon."

"We'll need to get the power and the phone out of it. I can take care of that this morning," said Riley.

"But he locked it." I replied.

Riley rolled his eyes, "Yeah right."

"Good," Jack said. "Andy, where do you wanna set up your office?"

"In the common room." It was in the eastern wing, what would eventually become the children's playroom, and from there I could see much of the jobsite.

"Great, we'll set up your phone, get you some power and build you a desk," Riley said.

AS JACK AND I were driving to the contractor's supply, he asked, "How're ya feeling?"

"A bit scared, but all-right."

"Good. You've got a good grasp on what's going on and good rapport with the crew. Keep it up. And don't let Scott get to you. He's a lot of noise, just noise. You've got the start of a good crew. Put an ad in the paper and hire three more carpenters and two laborers. These guys'll work well, but be careful. Don't get too chummy with 'em. You'll need to keep a little bit of distance if you want 'em to respect you. Do you hear what I'm tellin' you?"

"Yeah Jack. I hear ya."

"Good. Enough about that. Now you can go spend some of my money. How does that sound?"

After an hour-long shopping spree, tools were loaded into the back of my truck. It was a carpenter's Christmas dream. We bought a table saw, sawbuck, two chop saws, three drills, two sawzalls and a builder's level. Jack said he had two compressors and several nail guns at his house and we could rent any specialized tools as needed. But, he warned, "take good care of these tools. They're now your responsibility. Label them with 'S&S' somehow and make sure they're packed away every night."

When we arrived at the house with the new collection of tools, we found Arthur, Benjamin and Chet putting the finishing touches on my desk; an impressive piece of design and construction. It had a sloping top, three shelves underneath, two electrical outlets along the side and the phone jack attached on top. It was quite sophisticated and modern in its look.

"Now that's what I call a desk," Jack exclaimed. "Who designed this piece of artwork?"

Arthur quietly announced, "I did," as he spit his chewing tobacco out the window.

"Well, that's one helluva piece of work. Andy can run World War III from this command post." His praise felt genuine and his enthusiasm heartened everyone.

But later, he warned me, "That desk's a bit over the top. I'd rather not think about the time and materials that went into it. Keep an eye on that kinda shit. We've gotta get our feet on the ground here. We can allow a little slack right now. But keep a careful control on the work."

I could see his point over costs, but in the desk, I saw a genuine attempt by the crew to start anew. The trailer would soon be gone as a command post and they had built a new one. To me, it signified more than just a place to work, but a new beginning for the house, for S&S Custom Builders and for me.

That afternoon, the remnants of Ace Construction were carted away, the tools first and then the trailer. In its place, Jack parked the box truck.

Several months later, I found the trailer abandoned on the side of a back road outside town. Looking inside, all signs of its previous owner had been removed. I was annoyed to see it disposed of this way. I wondered if Scott was similarly abandoned. I would never find out.

I WAS NOW IN CHARGE, but in my mind, I didn't quite think of it as *my* jobsite yet. It was still Jack's. In a way, this gave me comfort. It lessened the burden of things to worry about. I would defer to Jack on matters of most concern. In particular, it was Jack's role to hire subcontractors and handle financial matters. I saw my role as facilitating the process. I was, in a way, there to guide and coordinate the crews and then grease the skids so that it all came together. I adopted my role with serious diligence.

I began by carrying a notebook with a continually evolving list of things "to do." When something was completed, I crossed it off with a pencil that now seemed permanently placed behind my ear, while usually in the same motion adding at least two more items. The list was a constant presence, a physical reminder of how much the job crept into my whole life. I would take it home and add things as I was having breakfast or watching TV. I kept it by my bed, and would jot down thoughts that came to me in the middle of the night. I had to do this. The job was just too complex to rely on my memory. It would require all that I could bring to the task.

I placed an advertisement in the local newspaper for help. I wasn't exactly sure how to pick new crew members but I met with each person who replied. I was amused that I was now on the opposite end of the interview process that I'd been in just a year before. And I was asking the same questions. "Tell me about your previous history; do you own a car; do you have your own tools?"

But, more than standard questions, I remembered something Neil told me on Nantucket, that "no one knew everything and anyone who said they did was a liar and not to be trusted." While I thought it a bit strongly stated, I found a kernel of truth in the sentiment and walked the prospective candidate through the job to see his reaction. If the carpenter was unimpressed by the scale and detail of the project, I was unimpressed with him (and they were all "hims"). I wanted to find people who were not cocky prima donnas, but rather people who would genuinely like to work on *this* house because it was different, special. That was how I saw it, and that was how I wanted others to see it.

After I met with each applicant, I called Jack to discuss his qualifications and salary. Jack would tell me how much to offer as an hourly wage. And he was always adamant that each was to keep their wage private and that each was to be told that he was an independent subcontractor; there were no benefits and no taxes. Everyone accepted the deal as standard routine in this business.

I hired three carpenters and two laborers. Max was a middle-aged family man; an ex-hospital administrator who didn't like working for a big company. His corporate background showed later when he pulled out the *Wall Street Journal* to read at lunch-time. He had taken a stab at starting his own general contracting firm and found it hard to locate enough work to support his wife and two children. But, Max pointed out, his wife was an executive at IBM and money problems were not an issue. Simon was in his mid-twenties. While a little mentally slow, he was easy-going and quite peaceful and I thought he'd get along well with the others. Carl was an older gentleman; had been a carpenter for over two decades and seemed content at that level, not wishing for the headaches of anything more. He seemed honest, straightforward, and trustworthy. He always wore overalls and carried himself in a very unassuming manner. This led to jokes from the crew that stereotyped him as a bit of a bumpkin. He took it in stride. The two laborers were local kids who had just graduated from high school and not yet moved on.

LATER THAT WEEK, a Cadillac with Colorado plates arrived on the jobsite. Out stepped a tall blonde man with a strong build and intense manner. His name was Olaf and he was a friend of Riley and Dennis. "They told me there was work out here and I've driven out to see if there's room for one more," he explained. "I just arrived this morning and here I am!"

Again, I was amazed. Who would simply drive across the country to inquire about work after receiving a phone call from his buddies? Riley and Dennis were quick to vouch for his credibility. And, after talking with him, I liked his positive attitude and energy. I asked Olaf to come back after lunch while I called Jack for advice. I liked that these older guys were more experienced, which to me meant more professional.

Jack deferred, "Well, what's your assessment?"

"Well, he seems like I can get along with him. He has a car full of tools that look experienced. The other guys vouched for him."

He responded quickly. "Don't put too much stock in that. This guy's their friend and they're all here for the money. While that can be a good

motivator, it can also cause people to do things you should be careful about."
With that warning, he turned the decision over to me. "Well, do what you
think best. I'm not at the job. I can't make that decision. Can you look me
in the eye and tell me he's worth hiring?"

The way the question was phrased, I felt as though I was staking my
reputation on Olaf, a man I barely knew. But Jack was turning over
responsibility of building the crew to me. I felt pressure to make a decision
and I wanted to follow my gut in making it.

"Yeah, Jack, I think we should hire him."

After lunch, I gave Olaf my answer.

"Great. When can I start?" he asked.

"Whenever you get settled."

"Now's as good a time as any. Just tell me where." Olaf grabbed his tool
belt from his trunk.

I laughed. "You don't want some time to settle in; find a place to live?"

"Naw, I'll move in with the boys. They've rented rooms in a flophouse
over in Brewster. It sounds a little rough, but the price is right. Maybe with
so many of us here, we'll be able to get an apartment. But I wanna keep my
expenses down. And that includes down time. So, if it's all the same to you,
I'm ready to get to work."

I admired his enthusiasm and his experienced tool belt. In particular, I
admired the tool that hung where his hammer should have been. "What's
the deal with that?" I asked.

"Oh, that's my hatchet. You'd be surprised how solidly the flat end can
drive a nail when it's in the right hands."

This, I had to see. And so did everyone else. At lunch, Olaf demonstrated
how he could indeed deliver a crushing blow with this tool. With one tap to
set a twelve-penny nail, he followed with a single powerful strike and sunk
it. He let others try to do the same. I found the hatchet much too heavy
to deliver any kind of accuracy in my swing. Others found similar trouble.
But Olaf was only too happy to demonstrate again. He even pulled out a
sixteen-penny nail and attempted the same feat for his admiring audience.
It took several tries, but he was finally able to do it, once.

In the process, he also revealed some of the drawbacks of his tool. First,
if he missed his target, delivering only a glancing blow, the nail shot to the
side like a bullet. Second, if anyone was unfortunate enough to walk too

closely behind his wind-up, he would find himself greeted by the business end of the hatchet. Olaf would be given a wide berth when his hatchet was in use.

WITH THE EXPANDED CREW in place, I found myself the center of questions and activity and I loved it. I knew the plans and could answer specific questions about what to do. I could also look beyond the plans and appreciate the order in which things needed to be built, and the interconnections among them. I remembered Scott's advice to never do anything without a reason and tried to think as far ahead as I could with each answer. I began to visualize not only the house as it was designed in the blueprints, but also the process by which to get it there.

I felt a responsibility for the job and identified more and more with my new role as a builder. I was feeling a growing confidence in my nightly conversations with Jack, my direction of the crew and my interactions with the subcontractors. I talked easily with them all, sensing that I could get them to do as I wished. I felt a growing balance in my role.

AS I GOT BETTER AT MY JOB, I slowly began to realize that I had neglected other parts of my life. I had been in Connecticut for almost seven months and had devoted myself almost entirely to the job. But I suddenly woke to the fact that I was lonely. So I determined to fix it, much as I would fix a problem on the job. To make friends, I signed up for a volunteer group in Norwalk; the place where the guys had told me to find girls. At the first meeting, I was greeted by Sharon, the most beautiful and intriguing woman I had seen since moving to Fairfield County. Where in the past I would have been intimidated by someone so desirable, I resolved to meet her and get a date. I signed up for the first project that the group was organizing and upon arriving, quickly found her.

I surprised myself at my bold determination and careful maneuvering. When it wasn't too obvious, I found ways to work next to her and talk to her. If there was a chance to catch her glance, I capitalized on it. I learned that she worked as a travel agent but really loved to cook. She grew up in one of the more wealthy towns nearby, but carried none of the airs one might expect from such affluence. Her casual manner put me at ease and I sensed she was feeling comfortable opening up to me. By the end of the afternoon, I had talked her into a motorcycle ride. By the end of the evening, we had dinner, exchanged phone numbers and planned to see each other again. Soon, we were dating regularly.

Later, Sharon would laugh that I didn't ask her to go on a date, but rather told her that we were going on a date. This was not my usual way of behaving. I was usually more shy, more reserved. Her descriptions sounded like someone else. But after months of developing my confidence, I was determined not to let someone that I found so attractive pass me by. And I didn't. I knew who I was and what I wanted. The job was changing me. With Sharon in my life and the job going so well, I felt balanced. I was happy and content. And things seemed to be falling my way. I didn't question how this came to be or why. I just basked in the rhythm that was carrying me along.

Jack shared the same balance too. He began to occasionally skip his evening phone calls, something he had never done before. And those that we did have, had become more casual. In one of the more informal calls, he started, "How's the job going Stuff?" I answered, "fine." Jack seemed satisfied with the abbreviated response, joking, "Good, you've fooled 'em for another day!" And that was it. He said goodbye and we hung up.

ON RAINY DAYS, the crew worked inside. There were small details to be framed throughout the house. Bathrooms and the kitchen needed soffits— boxed out sections above the cabinets. Some rooms required closets. And the large entertaining rooms called for their various shaped ceilings. The dining room called for a tiered ceiling where a rectangle in the center (built to the same dimension as the owner's custom made dining table) rose ten inches above the outer perimeter. Within this space would be a custom-built lighting fixture that would cast light around the entire area. The study called for three recessed sections, creating the effect of beams crossing the room. The entry had a pyramid shaped ceiling, rising to a point at the center of the room.

And the living room and master bedrooms each had a tray ceiling, beginning as a pyramid-shaped ceiling but stopping at a flattened top, the sides sloping inward at forty-five degree angles from the flat ceiling which started two feet off each of the four outside walls. In the living room, it rose from a height of eight feet to a height of twelve feet. Two sides of the tray were formed by the trusses that spanned the room. But Benjamin had to build in the other two sides of the tray. As he began, he discovered a flaw in the original trusses. The slope on one side of the ceiling was too close to the wall.

"Andy, how much wood do I need to put on the slope to get three quarters of an inch on the horizontal?" he asked.

I pulled out my calculator and began to work the trigonometric functions, calculating the sine, cosine and tangent of the ceiling dimensions, and answered his question: "0.563 inches."

Benjamin just stared, deadpan. "That's all well and good with your fancy little calculator there. But, let me ask my question again, how much do I pad the ceiling to get three-quarters of an inch? And this time, I'd like a number I can use."

Carpentry worked in dimensions of sixteenths, eighths and quarters. "Okay, I see your point," I smiled. I calculated a few more numbers and answered, "Pad it down five-eighths of an inch, light." Light was shorthand for subtracting a thirty-second of an inch.

THE HOT AFTERNOONS of the summer began to give way to milder days of September and October. And these were glorious days to be working outside. The leaves were turning, and in the process, they were filling the air with the rich organic smells of fall. The best days were the warm ones of Indian summer. I found it pure heaven to stand on the roof or scaffolding and feel the warm sun through my clothes. The thickness of the air softened the sharpness of the sounds of nail guns, compressors and saws. And the valley below, painted in the rich colors of a New England October was a joy to behold.

In one meeting about some interior details, William stopped mid-sentence at a sight in the field just beyond the house. A fox was prancing through the tall grass. Its gait was alert, alive, its red fur ablaze in the waning sunlight of the season. Everyone's attention shifted outside through the openings in the wall that would eventually be filled with glass. I could imagine this scene being reenacted after the house was completed. It gave me a glimpse of how the design would work for bringing people together and allowing them to interact with the outdoors.

But, while we enjoyed this open-air view, I had an overriding awareness that winter would soon arrive and every step to make the inside world distinct from that outside was critically important. All work was concentrated on getting really dried-in. This meant completing the roof and overhang and installing the windows and doors. Until then, although protected from the rain, we would be subject to the constantly blowing wind and decreasing temperatures. This would be my first winter outside.

THE DRIP EDGE had been completed, allowing the roofer to get started with the asphalt shingles. But finishing the overhang was no small affair and took painstakingly long to complete. The house had seven hundred and fifty feet of roof edge defining its outer perimeter. And the overhang between this perimeter and the walls was four feet around the entire house. In all, we had to cover up nearly three thousand square feet of overhang with one-by-six-inch, tongue-in-groove poplar. And to add to the difficulty of the task, William had designed a custom vent detail around the entire outer edge. Where most houses used a stock vent that could be nailed up with ease, this house had an intricate lattice detail that, while attractive, required a great deal of time and effort. With the winter looming, this detail became a source of great frustration as it significantly delayed our moving inside.

While not necessary for getting dried in, the deck that ran along the entire north side of the house had to be completed in order to install the doors. The overall theme of the house was Oriental and this deck was one of the centerpieces of that effect. It was to be built with large dimension, rough cut lumber, which I had delivered to the north side of the house in several loads so as to minimize carrying it while onsite. First, the support posts were eight-by-eight inches square. They were to be seated on large rocks that were pulled from the old stone walls on the property.

Each rock was mortared onto a concrete pier that sank below the frost line. Through the rock, a hole was drilled to allow a piece of steel rebar to extend from the concrete through the rock and into the wooden post so as to tie it all together. Drilling the hole through the hard Connecticut granite was a difficult challenge and I rented a large hammer drill that required two of us to hold it.

While watching this maneuver, Freddie Carlucci remarked that he had broken his cheekbone doing a similar task. He was drilling over his head with his "hole hawg" when it bit and snapped into his face. He showed no scars or other physical signs of the accident. If he had, I am sure he would have worn them with pride.

Once the pier-rock assemblies were completed, each post had to be contoured to fit the shape of the rock, so that it looked as though it were "growing out of the rock" as William described it. I gave the job to Benjamin, given his penchant for detail. Using his circular saw as a carving tool, he free-handed his cutting of the bottom of the post to follow a line he had traced to mirror the rock's shape. Holding the saw tightly and pulling back the safety guard, he dragged the spinning blade sideways across the wood, shaving it out as he moved. It required a lot of trial and error so he left the post long and cut it to length after he had created the right fit to the rock.

He carved out a section of wood, tried it on the rock, retraced the line and tried again. In the middle of the process, Arthur looked on and warned, "That's not very smart. It'll bend your motor axle."

Benjamin replied, "Yeah, and using any tool will wear it out!"

Arthur shrugged, "Suit yourself," and walked off.

Benjamin turned to me, his helper on this project, "The manufacturer doesn't decide how to use my tools. I do! A tool can be used any way I want. It suits *my* ends, not someone else's."

Turning back to his carving, he continued, "Ever seen someone cut a circle or a cove on a table saw? I'll show ya sometime. I decide how to do what I wanna do. Tools are merely devices to help me do it. Remember that. They're not for anyone else to decide but the user."

Completing his patient carving, Benjamin admired his work, having created the effect that William desired. I could find no gaps between the posts and the rock. One grew out of the other. And with the posts in place, assembling the structure and decking proceeded quickly. Four-by-ten lumber formed the lintels and four-by-eight lumber formed the joists. Topping it all off, two-by-four redwood was used for the decking. It created a beautiful effect and I made sure that the nailing pattern looked as much like rivets as the decks in Nantucket.

But the process got bogged down with the railing. William had created a complex design. An eight-by-eight inch top rail would split at each post, revealing a one-inch sloped channel between successive pieces. The corner was a confusing complex of interconnecting joints. Benjamin and I stared at the drawings and could not figure out how this was supposed to work.

I made a phone call to William, who began to explain the "conceptual elements" of the design and the effect he was trying to create. With each of his points, I was becoming more confused. He was speaking his own language and I could not understand what he was trying to say. Each attempt at asking him to clarify pushed us further from an understanding. Finally, after fifteen minutes of ineffective explanations, I stopped him and asked, "Can I try a different tack here?"

William sounded as eager as I was to find a common language, "Sure, fire away."

"Okay, can you position yourself squarely in front of your drawings?"

"I am," William replied tentatively.

"In detail E-1, we're going to focus on the third post from the top, at the inside corner, as our point of reference."

"Okay, I can do that." William still sounded hesitant.

"Now, the railing coming in from the top, let's call that 'A.' And the railing coming in from the left, let's call that 'B.' Got that?"

"Yes, I'm with you so far." William was sounding a little more cooperative.

"Now, there are eight segments to your joint design in the detail. Let's label them. First, let's differentiate those four on the upper tier from those on the bottom tier, as you've drawn in detail E-2. You still with me?"

"Yes, keep going."

"The upper tier we'll call one through four and the bottom tier we will label five through eight."

"Gotcha, keep going."

"Now, going back to E-1, let's call the upper tier segments one through four starting from the upper right quadrant and moving clockwise so that four is in the upper left. And then let's call the lower tier the same way, with five being in the upper right and eight being in the upper left."

"Okay, okay, I've marked my drawings. Now what?"

I was getting excited that we were finally getting through to each other.

And I sensed that William was getting excited as well. We were talking in a common language, my language. "Okay now, tell me which number segments go with rail A, which go with rail B and which stay with the post."

"Excellent!" William exclaimed. "Excellent! Let's see." He paused and then began, "segment six stays with the post. Segments one, five and eight go with rail A. And segments two, three, four and seven go with rail B." William started to laugh, "Bravo, Master Hoffman. Well done. I think I actually enjoyed that."

I laughed too, feeling euphoric at having bridged the language barrier with William and solving the problem without him having to drive out. That saved time and money. I explained the results to Benjamin in the exact way that I had discussed them with William.

"Damn!" Benjamin remarked in his southern drawl. "You got all that out of him over the phone?" He paused, staring at the drawings. "Damn!"

WITH AS MUCH EFFORT as possible being devoted to the deck and overhang, another crew set about the task of installing the windows and doors. Open space on the job was becoming scarce and the windows had been taking too much of it for weeks. Forty-five windows in all, they were soon to be joined by a delivery of forty exterior doors. Most of them were glass French doors—actually two doors side by side.

The house was first wrapped in Tyvek, a wind and vapor barrier, and the crew installed the windows working clockwise around the house. With relatively minimal effort and time, the house was completely transformed. Sound and wind that used to travel so freely between one side of the wall and the other was now restricted. Inside, the air became still, construction noise became dulled, and the house took one more step in its progression towards providing security and protection to those within.

As each window was installed, I admired the form of the final rooms. If the sense of the atmosphere inside the house had been unclear to anyone until this point, it was no longer. The extremely tangible sign of progress filled me with excitement. It also demonstrated how the construction process could ebb and flow. With the same amount of work, some steps showed great progress while others did not. The overhang was moving at a laboriously slow pace. But with a corresponding amount of effort installing windows, the change was breathtaking.

Next came the exterior doors, which arrived just as the last windows were being nailed into their openings. The crew continued with their clockwise rotation to install them. The first thing I did after the first doors went in was install a set of lock hardware. I stood back and admired the shiny brass handle and latch. The house could now be locked and it was showing clear signs of its final finish.

That afternoon, Jack made a brief stop at the jobsite to admire the progress.

Taking just one step inside, he bellowed, "Who the hell installed this lockset?"

"I did Jack," I replied sheepishly.

"Andy," his tone softened, "Put that stuff away. We'll put it on when the house is done. This is finish hardware and we still have lot of rough work to do yet. For now, just toe nail a piece of wood to the floor." He pulled my hammer from my tool belt and held out his hand for some nails. Kneeling down, he drove them diagonally into a two-by-four on the floor. "There, those toe nails will keep the wind and honest people out."

LATE NOVEMBER BROUGHT colder weather than usual. And this brought a vivid taste of what was to come. Each successive morning that my alarm sounded, the sunlight outside grew dimmer. Eventually, I had to string the jobsite with temporary lighting so that the carpenters could see their work in the early and late hours of the day.

We began to arrive in increasingly thick clothing. I bought a full body insulated jump suit made by Carhartt. Like the pants, it had pockets for carrying utility knives, pencils and nail sets and canvas loops for carrying hammers. And like the pants, it took a few stiff weeks to break in.

To warm the job, I rented potbelly stoves. Each came with a large propane tank that had to be replaced each week. It was an expensive item for the jobsite as the heat quickly dissipated through the still unfinished overhang of the house, the one and only priority of the crew.

I hated that they had to work outside during the gradually colder weeks, but until the overhang was complete, there would be no warm refuge. The carpenters understood this too. Areas of the house where the overhang was finished felt different from those that were not. The restraint of sound and wind gave the space a stillness that, whether true or not, gave the room a sense of being warmer.

As cold as it felt spending the entire day outside, gradually it got colder. That slowed the job down and I didn't like it. People moved at a slower pace, constrained by the increasing layers of clothing that restricted their movements. Extra time was devoted to arranging lights for work during the early morning and late afternoon hours as the days got shorter. Deliveries of material would sometimes be hindered by fresh snow.

When temperatures dropped below freezing, a warm room had to be built to keep glues, paints and caulking from freezing. Plastic was stretched around a two-by-four frame with a potbelly stove inside. An electric heater was added for warming overnight.

As the temperatures got even lower, the compressors were put inside the warm room to keep them from seizing and the crew huddled closer to the stoves. One day, after warming myself against a stove, Benjamin calmly informed me, "Andy, I think you've got a bit of a situation on your right side." I looked down to see flames consuming the zipper flap that ran up my entire side. Quickly extinguished, the fire left little damage to the suit itself, merely burning the flap; what I would look upon as a battle scar.

I quickly understood what Eric and Larry meant when they teased me about outdoor work reducing my enthusiasm. I longed for the warmth and brightness of the summer and fall. In those days, there was nothing better than working outside. At those times, I would think of my past life spent at a desk and feel fortunate for the chance to be in construction. But in the winter, I felt the opposite. I could endure, but it was harsh. There were mornings that were especially foreboding. One morning, I awoke to a dark bedroom, sunrise not beginning for another thirty minutes. Outside, wind howled and the weatherman on my clock radio announced, "It's going to be a cooooold one today." I shivered as I forced myself to get out of bed and longed for the warm offices of EEC.

Despite Sharon's protestations, I grew a beard, perhaps to reflect my tempered mood, or perhaps just out of the drudgery of the winter days. As I looked in the mirror each morning, I saw someone else looking back. My hair was unkempt. I saw no need to shower before the start of the day. My burned Carhartt jumpsuit showed no style at all. No one would possibly mistake me for a college educated engineer.

BY EARLY DECEMBER, the house's exterior was complete—windows, doors, overhang, trim and roof. One last step was the siding and we were in a decidedly bad period of the year for this step. But despite the cold weather, the exterior finish—stucco—had to be completed for the job to proceed. Given that above-freezing temperatures were needed to apply the wet mortar mix, the subcontractor draped tarps over the house and kept the space warm with propane heaters. This task also brought the out-of-plumb foundation wall to its final completion. Using pressure-treated wood, we reconnected the six-inch overhang of the house to the foundation well below it. The stucco completely covered the repair and the house was made right again. No one could tell that the mistake had occurred. We had now reached the all-important milestone: we were dried-in.

ONCE DRIED-IN, attention was completely devoted to finishing the interior. The carpenters framed interior walls; electricians ran their wires and installed switch boxes, outlet boxes, and circuit breaker panels; plumbers finished their pipes and the HVAC contractor installed the air handlers, condensers and duct work. These were the finishing touches, the aspects of the house that would make it a home to be lived in. With this shift in progress, Maura Winslow started to show up and inspect the work. But unlike the Rogers' house, I, and not Jack, was Maura's escort and guide. Jack and I never discussed my taking on this responsibility. It just happened. In yet another sense, the job was mine.

I could see the importance of these visits. The details of the house had not been clear to Maura from the blueprints. She could not see the three dimensional rooms from a two dimensional piece of paper. But now the rooms were taking enough physical form for her to see what was developing and to decide whether she liked it. She also brought friends and interior designers with her as she walked the house. Alternatives were discussed and I found my role on the site evolving to include that of an intermediary between their change ideas and the technical feasibility of making them real. I was consulted to explain the trade-offs and consequences to particular design proposals. When the designers for example, suggested rearranging the master bathroom, I described what they had just done in physical terms, first the positive, then the negative.

"We can take out this wall and move that one," I explained. "They're not load-bearing so it's not a major issue. We'll also have to move the plumbing which you can see has already been installed. It will give you a nice open view through the bathroom, allowing light from these windows to penetrate more clearly. But if you leave the front door to the master bedroom open, you'll be looking straight at the toilet." I then placed everybody near the entry to demonstrate what I meant.

"Oh dear, we can't do that," one of the designers replied, and the discussions resumed.

In counseling on changes, I kept two concerns at the forefront of my mind. First, I wanted to remain true to William's design. Second, I didn't want to outright reject an idea from the owner. It's not that I would not do either. I just tried to avoid doing them. Usually, I was successful. My status as the builder always trumped Maura's designers who, in fact, knew very little about construction.

But as they became more involved, William became less so. Drawings for details in the bathrooms and kitchen came from an evolving cast of new designers. These drawings were usually incomplete and changed often. Soffits were added, moved, taken out, rebuilt. Drawings came in piecemeal and were often more conceptual than architectural. This left me to figure out dimensions and conflicts with other design elements that were taking place. It was frustrating, but I kept sending carpenters to all ends of the house to add details and prepare for the house to be plastered.

One afternoon, the designers made the decision to slide one of the windows in the guest bedroom two feet down the wall and to add an extra window near what would be a reconfigured bathroom. I hated the idea, but was cautious as usual, trying to point out the consequences of the change. I warned that moving the exterior window would cost a little more as this was a bearing wall and that the window and stucco were already installed. I also cautioned that the new window would have to be special-ordered and would take a few weeks to acquire. And finally, I warned that the exterior elevation would be altered. It would lose the symmetry that it shared with the adjacent elevations. I was trying to protect William's design.

But the interior designers dug in. Maura listened to all sides impassively. When everyone had stated their mind, she pressed me on whether this was doable. I answered, "Yes, we can do anything you want, but I really don't think it's a good idea."

Maura answered, "I appreciate your concerns. I'll pay the extra costs. I don't think the effect on the outside aesthetics will be that bad. And frankly, I'd rather have the house look better from the inside than the outside. Do it."

I felt no personal challenge to the decision. I had made my recommendation clear and she had chosen not to follow it. "I'll take care of it," was all I said.

When Maura and the designers left, I felt compelled by loyalty to break the news to William. I called and asked if he was planning to come out to the job anytime soon. William said that his afternoon had an opening and that he would come right out.

When he arrived, I walked him through the house to show the progress, ending at the guest bedroom.

"Okay William, Maura has made a change here that I want to explain." I described the new design and the process by which it was made.

"Ugh," William muttered as he shook his head. "This will destroy the interior flow of this room and the exterior form of this wing."

He walked around the room, looking at it from different perspectives, growing more agitated with each step. He took out a notepad and began to draw possible alternative designs.

"I'm going to call her and discuss this. Don't make any changes until I get her to consider some alternatives."

"Okay William. But I'll need to order that window soon. Otherwise it'll hold up the plaster." Then I added, "I really don't think she's gonna budge on this. I explained the disadvantages and she stood firm."

"But she doesn't understand the overall impact of what she's doing. I think I can get her to see." William was stiffening in his resolve.

"If this is what she wants, why not just give it to her?" I winced as the words came out of my mouth. I knew they were not going to be taken well.

"Young man," William stated firmly, "this is more than just moving a window and some walls. It lacks integrity. It violates all of the rules of architecture that have guided my design up until this point. She may not see the implications now, but she will later." He paused and then ended with finality, "My job is not to *give* the owner what she wants. My job is to *tell* the owner what she wants."

I had no retort. This was a battle I wanted no part of. I would build whatever I was told to build.

That evening in my conversation with Jack, we considered William's point of view.

"He's a professional," Jack said. "He was hired to design a house and see it through construction. That's what he's doing. You gotta admire his sticking to his guns."

"Yeah I guess," I said. "But he's so aggressive and opinionated. He should be more flexible. He can't tell the owner what she wants. That's condescending."

"It may be. But that's what makes William who he is. I'd love to have listened to his conversation with Maura."

"It just seems to me that I listen to the owner's idea, I tell them the implications and then I let them make their decision. If they still want it, I might tell them I don't think it's a good idea. But, if they still want it, I'll do it. If they want to paint the house bright purple, I'll tell them it's a bad idea, but if that's what they want, that's what they'll get."

"Andy, keep in mind your position and how that allows you that luxury. Your job's to build the house they tell you to build and to do it at the lowest cost. We're invested in the structure and the process, but not in the final design. Don't get me wrong, I don't wanna build something ugly. But, I'll give on the design where I won't give on the structure. I won't put my name on something unless it's first class quality, rock solid." He paused, "Think about it. If Maura wanted you to put only half the studs in the wall, would you do it?"

I laughed at the ridiculousness of the question. "No."

"Well, to William, this is the same. He's standing up for the integrity of his part of the process."

"Yeah, I guess you're right."

"You think so?" Jack said chipperly. Then laughing, he added, "Yup, you gotta admire his integrity…all the way up till he gets his ass thrown off the job."

And that is exactly what happened. Within days, Maura informed Jack that William's services would no longer be needed. She would finish the house with her designers, and with me.

WHERE THE DESIGNER'S or William's plans were responsible for most design elements, some issues required more personal input from Maura. These included things like where she might listen to music, where she would like to operate the security system and where she might like to have telephone jacks. Questions became awkward. "Which side of the bed do you want the phone jack and light-switches on?" This often led to a discussion involving who slept on which side of the bed and what their personal sleeping habits were. Or, at another point, I had to discuss whether to put a phone jack near the Jacuzzi tub, and this led to discussions of how the tub might be used.

Outlets were spaced according to the building code but additional outlets were added based on Maura's expected floor plans. Some were in the walls, others in the floor. But she soon tired of the tedium of these decisions and waved me off with, "Oh, Andy, just deal with it."

So I walked the job for hour upon maddening hour with the electrician deciding where to place light-switches when entering a room and when to tie them with switches on the other side for leaving. I knew that mistakes in this would annoy the owners for years. There were hundreds of switches, outlets and recessed lights to be placed in very precise locations. Many of the rooms had several lighting possibilities including sequences of recessed lights in the ceiling, wall washers for art, switched outlets for floor lamps, cabinet lighting and exterior lighting (both against the house and ornamental lighting on the grounds). Such complexity necessitated sometimes as many as six light-switches in a single location. I worked hard to develop a logical system that would be consistent throughout the house so that any future user could figure out which switches did what after using just a few rooms. I understood the gravity of my answers given that they would directly affect how the house operated forever.

I found it odd that all discussions about the final form of the house were with Maura. Her husband Randy was never involved. Maura joked, "All Randy cares about is his nice big shower." And that is what he got—eight feet by four feet of tile floor surrounded by marble walls and ceiling and four shower-heads hitting his body from the top and sides. But the lack of direct involvement of the man in the house led me to muse whether this was by design. I would imagine the men sitting around the locker room at the country club snickering among each other saying "Hey, guys, I know a way to occupy your wife for a year—build a house," to which they might all burst into laughter.

ONE MORNING, I ARRIVED at the jobsite first, unlocked the gate and drove up the long winding driveway. As I sipped my hot coffee, I turned on the temporary lighting and lit the propane heaters. The phone rang early, before the rest of the crew arrived, and startled me out of my quiet and solitary routine. No one ever called this early.

"Winslow site," I answered in my practiced way, still trying to wake up.

"Stuff, I'm glad I caught you. I tried to get you at home before you left. You get up early. That's good." Jack's voice was quick and agitated. I knew something was urgent, at least to Jack.

"Yeah, I leave around six-fifteen to open up and get settled before everyone else arrives." The coffee I had picked up on the way to work was still full. I was using it to warm my hands while I cradled the phone on my shoulder.

"Well, we've got a little situation," Jack began. "If Olaf and Max show up today, I want you to throw 'em off the fuckin' job."

I was startled but said nothing, the silence speaking for my bewilderment.

"They've quit to go out on their own. And I don't trust them." He accentuated these last words. "If they show up to pick up their tools, tell them to get the fuck off the job. Don't let them talk to anyone." Then he added an ominous warning, "We may lose more people."

I was trying to put it all together. I could understand not trusting people, but these two were part of the crew. "Wait a minute. What's going on here? They always seemed trustworthy to me. And anyway, if they're leaving, that's their decision. And if they wanna meet with the guys, they can always do it after work."

"Fine, let 'em meet after work. I'm not gonna make it easy for 'em. And don't be so sure about trusting those fuckers."

I bristled.

"That Olaf in particular. He's as two-faced as they come. He came to me last week and told me he wanted your job. How do you like that? He said you couldn't handle the guys. He said you may know the plans and how to deal with the subs, but these guys were capable of producing much more if the right foreman was pushing them. Whadaya think of that?"

I wasn't sure whether I was being warned that I couldn't trust Olaf or he couldn't trust me to run the crew. Or, was he making this up to get me to distrust Olaf? "I'm not sure what to say to that."

"Don't know what to say, huh? Maybe you better keep a closer eye on what's going on around that job." Jack's voice was sharp and his mounting anger was now shifting to me. It shocked me awake.

"Jack, I've done my best here. I'm not trying to sound insolent, but if you're uncomfortable with the way I'm doing my job, tell me." The words came out without direct thought. I was angry at being challenged when I had been feeling so good about the way things were going. I knew the pace we were maintaining on site, but I had no reference point by which to judge if we should be going faster.

"Andy, I'm pleased with what you've been doing. You've come a long way. You're now getting a hard lesson. Trust no one in this business. I mean NO ONE! I've gotten where I am today by protecting myself against getting screwed. These guys won't hurt us if we don't let 'em. But, it's a good lesson for you to see that this isn't like the professional world you left behind. You've gotta always watch your back!"

I was processing it all. Maybe I had grown too comfortable with the crew. I liked them and felt I managed best by having people like me too. Maybe I was opening myself up to being duped. Did I need to change my style? Or did I just have to be more on guard? I knew that I couldn't manage by fear as Neil tried. Could I still be myself and get done what I needed done? In one single moment, my confidence was damaged. Or, more accurately, in one call from Jack, my confidence was damaged. He said he trusted no one. But then how did I fit into that? He said he trusted me. Which should I believe?

"Are you okay?" Jack asked.

"Yeah, Jack, I'm fine," I said glumly.

"Good. Have a good day, Stuff. Hang in there. It can't get any worse, right?"

"I guess not. Talk to ya later."

I hung up the phone. Cars were streaming up the driveway, finding their usual spots in the courtyard. The guys were climbing out in the dark morning, everyone sipping their coffee, holding it in both hands for warmth. Max and Olaf were not among them. The crew walked to the areas of the house they had vacated the evening before and began to set up for the day's work. Power cords were unrolled, tools plugged in, lights arranged.

Riley approached me. "I presume you've heard about Olaf and Max?"

"Yeah, Jack just told me," I said somberly. "That's too bad."

"We tried to tell 'em it's a bad idea. They may not like working for someone else, but Jack can bring in the jobs and we can't. I think we all decided to take the certainty of steady, good money over the uncertainty of more but likely sporadic money."

"So you guys considered going with 'em?" I knew I shouldn't take this personally, but it was a shock to me.

"Not really. They asked, of course. But they had nothin' to offer. Two guys going out on their own would be tough enough. How can five or six guys make a go of it? In the short term, there just won't be enough work to make it worthwhile. We wished them luck. I think they're gonna need it."

"Yeah, I'm disappointed to see them go, but hope they do well."

Riley tipped his cap and walked off to his work area. I turned toward my desk. Max's truck pulled into the driveway, Olaf in the passenger seat. I walked to the edge of the house and waited for them to get out and walk up. "Jack's pretty upset with you guys. He told me, in no uncertain terms, not to let you on the jobsite."

"Aw, come on," Max replied. "I hope it's not that bad. This is just business."

"Not to Jack. He's taking it personally. He takes business very personally."

Olaf laughed. "Is he afraid we're gonna steal his crew the way he stole it from Ace? Tell him we tried, but these guys're too afraid to go out on their own. I told 'em there's too much money out there to be sharing it with someone like Jack, but that's their business."

"Well, that's water under the dam now, isn't it? I have to ask you guys to leave."

"No problem, Andy," Olaf said. "We've got no beef with you or Jack. We just need to get our tools. They're in the box truck."

"Grab what you need." I felt no animosity towards them and chatted as we walked across the site. They grabbed what was theirs, loaded the pickup truck and left.

While we talked, I felt a pang of resentment, not knowing whether Olaf was being sincere in his good wishes or not. In fact, the revelation that Olaf could be smiling to my face while talking me down to Jack made me suspect all the older guys.

In more ways than one, they were out of place here. They often complained of the tree-lined streets. I thought this one of the more beautiful aspects of life in New England. The trees created a canopy, making the winding streets into tunnels. I loved driving through them, emerging on the other side into some other reality, some other town, a river bed or a hilltop vista. But the Colorado guys hated it. They complained that they couldn't see the "big sky." "I have no sense of where I am," complained Riley. "Wherever I am in Colorado, I know where I am. I can see the mountain ranges, the mesas, the valleys. And I can see where I am in relation to them at all times. Without that vantage point, I feel lost."

The worst of it was that they lived in a flophouse in Brewster. I heard the stories they told of the other characters who lived there; prostitutes and drug dealers plying their trade. Benjamin told me how one resident stored his needles behind the communal toilet and became hysterical, "almost homicidal" Benjamin said, when they disappeared. I couldn't imagine what it must be like, and I couldn't imagine why anyone would endure it unless they were sacrificing to gain something. And they were sacrificing to make money.

MORALE WAS DROPPING. I felt it in everything. There was less energy in the conversations among the crew, less vigor in the way people attacked their projects. Coffee breaks dispersed more slowly and start-up dragged out. The weather, the departure of Olaf and Max, the distance the guys felt from home, anything could have been the cause. The solution, I decided, was a Christmas party and I proposed the idea to Jack.

"You want to do what?" Jack asked incredulously.

"The guys are far from home. The job's been going on for seven months. The working conditions are cold and dark." I didn't even consider mentioning the loss of Olaf and Max. "We need a reason to celebrate and make them feel like they're part of something. Christmas is a good reason to celebrate a good year and," I added "I want to build a reliable and committed work force out of them."

Jack looked at me and laughed. "So you want *me* to pay for dinner and drinks for these guys?"

"It wouldn't be a lot and I'm not suggesting an open bar." I laughed, "Not with these guys. They'll drink you dry. But a chance to meet outside work, and celebrate what we've done might improve morale." I was smiling and arguing my case with great passion; enthusiastic, but patient.

"Okay, Andy, set it up." He said grudgingly. "But I'm not gonna spend a fortune here. Call around for a room at a hall or restaurant." He laughingly added, "I don't want these guys mixing with the general public."

Pleased with myself, I got up to leave when Jack stopped me. "Andy, don't get too excited. Be careful about these guys. They're not like you and me. They're not looking to make friends or build a company. They're here to make money and then they'll go home. They're nothing more than migrant workers. Don't forget that. I'll give this idea a try. But remember, if they start to get messy, if things start to get out of hand, this party's gonna end and fast. Got that?"

"Yeah Jack. No problem." I knew the danger that Jack was warning me about. These guys drank a lot and I had no illusions about their capacity to get rowdy. I had heard their stories. But I also felt that they were people who missed their families, who felt at least some connection to me and the job and would appreciate a chance to have some relaxed time with Jack.

I called several local restaurants, gathered prices, ran them by Jack and settled on a date, December twenty-first. It would fall two days before everyone's plans to fly home for the holidays. I announced it to the crew.

"Jack's taking us to dinner?" Dennis squealed.

Arthur joked, "Is he giving us our pink slips as a Christmas present?" They all laughed.

"Merry Christmas, guys," I said. "It's just a way to celebrate the holidays and a good year. Whether you like it or not, we've become a company and we've done some good work. Why not stop and appreciate it?"

"Does this mean I have to go out and buy a tie?" Dennis joked.

"Yeah and I'll go dig out my Christmas suit," added Riley, "the one with the red cap and reindeer." They all laughed more as they broke from their coffee break and returned to work.

I ARRIVED AT THE RESTAURANT early, checking the final details. A small room had been reserved, a buffet lined the back wall, the bar was in the main restaurant and a waitress would bring us drinks. All was in order as the crew started to arrive. In contrast to their usual work appearance, they looked positively formal with button-down shirts, cotton slacks, and combed hair. Each seemed a little uncomfortable in the setting.

The waitress soon appeared and before long everyone had a drink in his hand. Most preferred beer while a few opted for something stiffer—usually whiskey. People talked about life out west, winters in New England, sports, families, personal histories. I ordered a beer and mingled until Jack arrived. He entered with a wide grin and greeted everyone loudly. He was wearing a button-down oxford, cleanly pressed, a pair of tan khaki pants and a blazer. Attention drew to him quickly and the crew gathered around. He was in good spirits, enjoying the attention and asking about everyone's satisfaction with the work. He also answered questions about himself. The crew was very curious about his past, as was I. We were enthralled as he told about the garage he once owned and the race cars and drag bikes he built—Harley-Davidson drag bikes, to be precise.

Conversation drifted to the job and Simon asked if Jack had let out the contract for the insulation yet.

"Not yet," Jack said. "But you don't need to worry about that. I've got it under control."

Simon persisted. "My brother and I have done some insulation work and we'd like to know if we can submit a bid."

Jack seemed put off. "This'll be top-notch work. The insulation would have to be tight and thick. We'll want R-30 in the ceiling, R-19 in the exterior walls and R-11 in all the interior walls. You'll have to pack the window frames. This won't be a small job."

"R-11 in the interior walls?" Simon asked.

"Sound-proofing. Remember, top-notch work."

"Okay, whatever you want." Simon assured him that they could do it and Jack agreed to think about it. But there was reluctance in his voice.

Riley made another pitch. "Jack, it's clear to us," he looked around the table for reassurance as he spoke. "That we're coming to a point where there could be no work while the insulation and plasterers have control of the house." His words slowed and he spoke deliberately, as one who sensed he was treading on thin ice and had prepared his speech. "Please understand, I'm not complaining and I'm in no way trying to threaten, but we've been talking and we're concerned about the prospect of having down time. We came here for full time work and we need it to justify our time here. If there's down time, we'll have no choice but to look for other work. I hope you understand our position. We've got no desire to leave you hangin', but we've gotta think about ourselves and our families."

Jack was calm. "Listen, I understand your position and I'm here to tell you not to worry. I'm working on a restaurant renovation in Milford that'll easily get us through any slow time, if there is any. It's a nice project—indoor work while the weather is coldest." Jack let the news out like a perfectly timed tidbit.

"What kind of renovation work?" Riley asked.

"An Italian restaurant. You like Italian food?" Jack laughed and the crew relaxed a bit, pleased that Jack had come through with a contract when it was needed most.

Arthur had been very quiet during the conversation. But with several empty whiskey glasses in front of him, he interjected, "Jack, how about you givin' us the project as a contract instead of payin' us by the hour?" It was a sudden statement, out of place and out of the flow of the conversation.

Jack paused and trained his eyes on Arthur. "Well, what's in it for me if I just give it to you?"

"Well, you'll get the work done fast," Arthur replied quickly.

Jack was again slow and deliberate in his response. "Well, maybe that's true, but how will I be sure I'll get quality? My name's on the project and I need to be sure the work will reflect my standards."

"Andy can still act as your overseer on the job," Arthur replied. "If there's anything that doesn't meet your standards, he'll be right there."

Jack reflected, letting silence hang in the conversation. But with each passing moment of silence, I felt tension building in the room.

Finally, Arthur broke it. "Jack, let's call a spade a spade. You've got a helluva good team here and you're payin' by the hour. Pay us by the contract and see what we can really do."

"So, are you telling me you're not giving me your all right now?" Jack's eyes narrowed as he shifted his large frame to face Arthur squarely across the table. It was a simple yet intimidating adjustment. No one moved as Arthur stared right back.

"Jack, we're not cheating you," Riley interjected, glancing disapproval at Arthur who was simultaneously defiant and glad for the diversion from Jack's attention. "This is business. We give you an honest day's work for an honest day's pay. If you work with us on a contract basis, we can give the project more of our time because, hey let's face it, we have nothin' else to do here. We've been working for you for seven months now and I think you've been satisfied with our quality, haven't you?"

There was no reply from Jack, only a cool gaze as he waited for Riley to finish what was on his mind.

"Andy's got a lot to focus on with the Winslow house. And he's doin' a first class job. But we can run ourselves too. We've been doing this for a long time. If you'll allow us to work some projects on a contract basis, you'll get more work done and we all benefit. And isn't that what we're all here for?"

I squirmed. Since Olaf's defection and Jack's question of whether I was getting too close to the crew, Riley's praise could be construed as an endorsement of my being too easy on them.

Jack replied. "And if I don't agree to contract work, are you gonna leave?"

"No Jack, that's not what we're saying. We wanna work with you. We think Olaf's a fool. We know you're able to bring in contracts that we'd never be able to find. And we wanna keep this relationship going. We're merely making a business proposal here. And you're free to accept or decline it, much in the same way that you'll consider Simon's offer to do the insulation."

Jack turned to Arthur. "You feel the same way he does?"

Arthur's gaze and his nod didn't mesh; the former revealing that the latter was grudgingly given.

Jack just stared back, waiting. Then he turned to everyone, "And the rest of you?"

Everyone nodded and said yes.

"I'll give it some thought." Then Jack raised his glass. "I propose a toast. To the success of S&S Custom Builders and everyone who makes it what it is. To lots of work and money to send home to your families."

Everyone raised their glasses and toasted, "Hear, hear."

A confrontation that could have ruined the night had been averted and I breathed a sigh of relief. Conversation rolled into other topics and people continued to drink. Soon the party was winding down and I bade good night.

THE NEXT MORNING was filled with stories of a night that went on long after I went home. The guys couldn't stop talking about it and I listened intently to their stories, each told with admiration and respect. From what I could gather from the many versions told, each clouded by great quantities of alcohol, Jack and a group of the guys went to a strip joint.

Benjamin explained in his usual formal way, "Chet was drunk and had somehow offended one of the patrons. I'm not sure what he said or did, but clearly this individual took some offense to it and decided to share his displeasure by trying to punch him. He would surely have succeeded if Jack had not yanked Chet out of the way and stood in front of him."

I looked at Chet who shrugged sheepishly, "I don't remember any of this."

Dennis added quickly, "Yeah, I'll say. You were gone. But without Jack, your ass would've been grass!"

Benjamin continued, "I wouldn't have taken on Jack, I'll tell you that. And the gentleman who took the swing at Chet apparently felt the same way. He wanted no part of him and backed off the moment he stepped in."

Even Arthur added some favorable reviews, "Yeah, that old Jack still has a lot of piss and vinegar in him. That was somethin' to see."

On the telephone later that morning, I asked Jack about the evening and got only the bare facts I had already heard from the crew. He relayed the story without much fanfare. "Chet was too drunk and had accidentally bumped into this guy. It was nothing. It just needed some clarification." Then he paused, laughing, "So I clarified!"

I was surprised. Jack was the one who had warned that we would leave if things got out of hand. He was still, in many ways, a mystery to me. I had heard bits and pieces about his rougher side but had never seen it for real. For example, over pool games, Jack talked of earlier days making money in pool halls. I never fully believed it until one day when I watched him perfectly execute a masse shot. Striking the cue ball directly from above, he was able to make it roll out into the table with enough back spin so that it circled back around a blocking ball and struck his object ball. Most pool halls will stop you if they see you even trying to set up this shot since it's so hard, and can result in a broken cue, torn felt or both. That he could do it spoke volumes about where he might have learned it. Here was a chance to see him in the raw and I had missed it. I was hungry for details. I was amazed that the night could end with such admiration from the crew after the confrontation with Arthur had looked so ominous. It looked as though the crew had forgotten all about it. But Jack had not.

"All in all it was a good night, Stuff. But did you learn something from the evening? You need to keep an eye on those guys. Think about the ultimatum in the restaurant. They may act like they're your friends, but they're out for themselves and if you or I stand in their way, they'll step on us without even thinking about it."

I didn't like believing that I was working with people who were so untrustworthy. In fact, I refused to believe it, at least to the extreme that Jack did. And I was pleased with the party. It brought the guys together in another setting and, despite Jack's suspicions, I hoped that it might have helped to foster the trust that Jack found so elusive.

"Riley might be okay. I'll talk to him about his proposal," Jack said. "But honestly, I have no interest in letting this restaurant job out as a contract. We can't trust 'em yet. They could just up and leave at any moment. They have no ties, no reputation to maintain." He paused, "And that Arthur, you keep a particularly careful eye on him. He doesn't say much, but he's thinking. He's a snake in the grass, that one is."

Against Jack's firm conviction, all I could do was consent, "Yeah Jack, I'll keep an eye out."

"Andy, don't worry about it. These guys are old and experienced." Pausing, he added, "and jaded. Your heart's in the right place. Just be careful. People in this business'll eat you for lunch without thinking about it." Jack sounded supportive and fatherly. It helped soothe the hurt I was beginning to feel—that maybe I could be taken advantage of.

"Oh and Andy, tell Simon that I like his proposal. Can you believe he and his brother put together a proposal and dropped it off at my house this morning? He's anxious for the work. Frankly, I think he underbid it. But, let's keep that to ourselves for now. If he gets into trouble, I think we can slide a few thousand his way."

I smiled but kept my mouth shut. Maybe Jack was showing a heart after all.

"Oh, and free up this afternoon so we can go look at the restaurant. It's called Via Via. They'll be ready for renovations very soon."

BEFORE THE WALLS were covered in sheetrock, there was something I had wanted to do since I began the Winslow house. I knew that it was not uncommon for renovators of old houses to tear open a wall and find something left behind by the original builders; a chisel, a watch, a coin, a hand written letter. The discovery is always met with glee, a message from the past, a gift handed directly from a builder in one era to a builder in another, both connected by the same structure, one adding to the work of another. I wanted to start such a chain. I wanted to leave a personal mark beyond my name on a course of shingles or on a sheet of plywood.

When the rough framing was done, and the framing, plumbing and electrical inspections were completed, I built a time capsule out of birch. It was mitered on all corners so there was no exposed wood edge to delineate the top, bottom or sides. It was a perfectly smooth, faceless, and mysterious box, certain to arouse the glee of future builders who might one day tear apart the walls we were now building. Each carpenter made a deposit, something to mark his time on the job. With the mementos packed inside, I tacked a group picture of the crew to the inside lid, added a brief letter telling who we were and sealed the box, hopeful that it would not be reopened for decades or even after I am dead.

I put the box aside for the right moment to hide it within a wall and we packed up our tools to leave. And with this final act, the house was ready for the step that marked the shift from rough framing to finish carpentry. The crew would leave the house in one form and return to it in another. The Via Via renovation would keep us busy while the house was turned over to other subcontractors who would prepare it for the finish carpentry we would return to do.

To celebrate, Sharon and I went to New York City for a formal dinner and a show. The house had become very much a part of our growing relationship. On weekends, we would often stop by the job site to check on subcontractors. She liked coming to the site. She knew the progress and more importantly, knew how it affected my moods. When I had a tough day, she heard about it. When I had a good day, she helped me celebrate. This time, she helped me celebrate. I felt that one chapter was closing and a new one was opening.

FOR THE NEXT TWO WEEKS, I began each day at the restaurant overseeing the renovations and ended the day with a visit to the jobsite to check on progress. Via Via was by all appearances an ordinary Italian restaurant. One could easily drive by it without noticing it. But, inside the food was considered the best in the region, prepared by the owner, Gino, a nervous man who brought his craft and his family from Italy. Gino wanted to expand the space both to handle his growing clientele and attract more. He also wanted the renovations done quickly since every day that he was closed cost him money. He went to great lengths to keep work moving. He fed the crew to minimize breaks—Italian food for dinner, lunch, even breakfast. We had garlic oozing out of our pores. He even let some of the guys sleep in an extra storage room so they could start earlier and work later. I didn't object. I wanted the job done quickly as well.

I breathed easier each day when I left Via Via and returned to the Winslow house. But that was only in the metaphorically sense. Insulation is unpleasant business. Installers cover every inch of their skin and face to protect against the fiberglass dust that finds its irritating way into every cubic inch of available air. Despite such precautions, they often end the day with itchy skin and a hacking cough.

Simon and his brother supervised the delivery of an entire tractor-trailer load of insulation and moved it into the garage. Roll upon roll of pink filled all four bays.

As they worked their task, I was reminded of how this step changed the Rogers House. But this time, with my longer tenure on the site, the transformation was more vivid. Where there were no rooms before, only transparent stud walls, rooms appeared, defined by walls now filled with pink fiberglass. Sound was deadened, newly hidden corners offered welcome places of solitude. Despite the snow outside, the propane heaters warmed the space into a hospitable environment that enabled Simon to work in a T-shirt. The Winslow House was becoming a home.

But for all the excitement that this transition created, a problem was beginning to emerge. Simon was falling behind and it was becoming clear to everyone but Simon. I reminded him of the two week deadline, and he replied, "No problem. We've got it under control."

"Look Simon, you're one quarter done but you've used up a third of your time."

But Simon was impenetrable. He kept smiling and working at the same calm and relaxed pace.

One morning Jack warned me. "Get that guy moving! He's gonna cost us money if he doesn't pick it up!"

I conveyed the message and still, Simon proceeded at an unchanged pace and demeanor. It was as though his joy at working this contract could not be shattered by his pending failure to meet the contract's deadline.

When the promised completion date was two days away, Jack flared, "Andy get that asshole moving! The plastering crew's ready to go. Offer him anything you have to, but get his ass moving!"

I warned Simon about his contractual agreement; that the plasterer was coming in two days and he needed to be out of the way. And I added, "Look, I'll give you a thousand dollar bonus if you make the deadline." The money perked him up and he promised to try.

But the deadline passed and Simon was still not done. I negotiated a compromise with the plaster contractor, Michael Lapre, to start his crew on one end of the house and follow the insulation moving from east to west. Michael didn't like this and protested loudly, more it seemed over the principle of having been promised an empty house and less about any real inconvenience. For four days, Michael complaining unrelentingly to Jack. Jack in turn leaned on me and I leaned on Simon.

WHEN SIMON FINALLY FINISHED, Jack was livid. "Is that guy retarded? He showed no regard for the schedule or his promise to stick to it. By moving at his own pace, he might as well have been reaching into my wallet and taking out dollar bills one by one. Who knows what extras I'm gonna hear about from Michael."

"I don't know what to tell ya Jack. He was in his own world. I couldn't get him to budge."

"Well, I know what'll make him budge. Fire his sorry ass!"

I was caught off guard and momentarily speechless. I had never fired someone before and really didn't want to. Scott had handled all past personnel issues. Worse still, I liked Simon. "Jack, I really don't think that's necessary. No harm was done."

"Yeah, maybe. But he could have cost us plenty. And he still might. He's a liability. Fire him." Whether this was a sudden reaction or he had given it careful thought, I couldn't tell. But he was adamant.

Michael's annoying complaints now made me angry. While Simon's delivery of the contract was late, I didn't see any real damage to the process. "Look, Michael is just a pain in the ass. But he has no grounds for an over-charge."

"Andy," Jack said sternly, "Fire him! Fire him now!"

"Okay, Okay, Jack, I'll take care of it."

"Today. Tell him today. I want him off my job." Jack was getting angry.

"Well, he's gone for the day. I'll have to tell him tomorrow."

"First thing! Tell him first thing in the morning. Come by the house before you go to the job and I'll have a check for him. It'll be his final payment and he's gone. Got that?"

"Okay Jack." I felt horrible. Again, I questioned whether Jack's toughness was extreme. And again, I questioned whether I was tough enough.

All night, I played out the act of firing Simon over and over in my head, each time envisioning a different scenario. What if he asks for a full explanation? Could I give it? I thought that firing was a severe punishment, but I had to carry out Jack's instructions. What if he gets angry? I was not prepared to get into a fight. The mere thought of it got me out of bed to pace the room. What if he starts to cry? I was only half-sure that wouldn't happen. This was going to be horrible. I was telling someone that he had screwed up badly enough to be fired, that he no longer had a job, that he wasn't good enough to work for S&S, for me. The scenarios went from the plausible to the implausible. What if he doesn't leave? What if the rest of the crew backs him and refuses to let me fire him? What if, what if, what if? The possibilities never stopped playing out in my mind. I finally drifted off to sleep and awoke with the alarm, my mind right where it had left off.

SIMON'S FINAL PAYMENT was sealed in an envelope and taped to Jack's front door. I picked it up and left, relieved at not seeing Jack and having to discuss this more. On the way to the jobsite, I practiced my lines, how I would break the news to Simon. Although I was frustrated with the way Simon handled the time schedule, I knew I couldn't convincingly defend the decision. So, I decided to deflect all reasoning to Jack.

I waited at the jobsite, sipping coffee and chatting with Michael while watching his crew get to work. Some of the rooms had already been covered in the off-white layer of sheetrock. As with the Rogers house, I was sorry to see all the hard work being covered up. The framing, the wiring, the plumbing, so much work would never be seen again. But it was fun to watch the crew work. One set of guys carried the sheetrock in and hung it on the ceiling and walls, using a router to cut out the outlet boxes and light fixtures. Another set of guys walked around on metal stilts which allowed them to run continuous tape (with their taping "banjos") across the ceilings and down the walls. Getting a smooth seam was very much an art form and the speed with which they did it belayed the reality of just how hard it was to do. They finished by applying a skim coat over the whole surface and once painted, you could never tell where one piece of sheetrock began and another ended.

Soon Simon arrived and he joined Michael and me with a smile and some small talk. He was feeling proud of having tackled such a large job and shared his pride with everyone. Michael, on the other hand, showed his displeasure at having to work around him by not talking to him directly, pretending he was not there. It was childish and petty, traits I now saw as part of Michael's character and I had grown to dislike him. Simon complimented Michael on his crew's work before excusing himself to the garage to clean out his tools and the last of the insulation.

This was when I had to do it. I willed my feet to follow and I entered the garage to find Simon surveying his materials.

"Simon, I have something for you." I handed him his final payment.

"Oh, thanks. This'll sure come in handy. The margin was tight, but we appreciate the chance to do such a big job. Who knows what opportunities this'll open up?"

"Simon," I pulled the word out of my throat, "I've got to tell you something that I'm not happy about."

Simon sobered at my discomfort.

"Jack's really upset about your being late." My voice was now softer, less forceful and direct. "He wants me to let you go."

Simon instantly began pleading. "Oh Andy, please don't do this! Please don't! I need this job. I was a little behind but it didn't cause that much of a problem."

I felt great compassion for Simon and felt horrible at having to do this. I knew that if I wavered, I would lose the will to do what I needed to do. I couldn't go back to Jack and say I couldn't fire Simon. That was not an option. "Simon, it's Jack's decision, and he's made it final. I'm sorry but there's nothing I can do. I have to let you go."

But Simon did not relent. His pleading took many forms, each one I had to reject. Finally, he asked, "Can I talk to Jack? Can I reason with him? This is so unfair."

"Sure, you can try." While I knew that I was partly abdicating my responsibility, I felt that I couldn't speak entirely for Jack. If Simon wanted to confront his judge and jury, why shouldn't he? I was only the executioner and I was not relishing the role.

Simon shook my hand and awkwardly wished me well before turning to leave. The energy and enthusiasm he previously possessed were gone, and I felt horrible for having killed them.

All I could muster in reply was, "Good luck." I knew I wouldn't see him again.

I trudged slowly back to inspect Michael's work. When he and his crew were busy in the eastern wing, I quietly hid our time capsule in an insulated wall in the western wing yet to be walled in. There would be at least one bright point of the day.

ALTHOUGH SIMON SHOULD HAVE rejoined the crew, no one asked about his absence. They asked about progress of the house, they knew that Simon was done, that he had fallen behind, but they didn't ask about him. It puzzled me. I wondered if they knew what had happened without asking. Or maybe they just didn't care.

Finally, I sat with Riley during lunch and announced the firing as matter-of-factly as I could, hoping not to give away any naiveté. "I had to fire Simon the other day."

Riley chewed on his Italian sandwich, took a sip of his soda and nodded, "Yeah, we figured he was cut loose."

I continued with my matter-of-fact tone. "I liked him, it was too bad."

Riley said. "Yeah, he was a nice guy. But business is business."

That was it. Nothing more was said. I supposed that I was to learn something from this, a sort of Darwinian inevitability to the construction business. But I couldn't give up on just how hard it was to fire Simon and how much it hurt to hear him plead with me.

Later Jack told me. "Your friend Simon called today, asking for a second chance."

"Yeah, I thought he might. What'd you say?"

"I said NO!" he answered abruptly. "Andy, listen to what I'm about to tell ya. Never give someone a second chance in this line of work. If he screwed up once and you give him a chance to do it again, you have no business running a job."

As always, his logic seemed harsh. But, it appeared that no one else saw it that way. The crew accepted his dismissal as normal. If this was the way it worked, then I had to learn.

THE CREW PACKED in long hours on Via Via, working from six till eleven. I was glad, counting each hour on this job as one more towards getting us back to the Winslow house. As Michael's crew finished the walls, the flooring subcontractor began laying oak floor in the rooms they had finished, moving from east to west right behind them.

When both subcontractors were finished, the house was ready for our return—three days before Via Via was finished and those three days were agony. I wanted out. I wanted to get back to what was now waiting for us. When the day finally came, I left and never looked back. I felt no sense of accomplishment with Via Via except that it was in fact done. And that meant that this minor deviation from my primary task was over.

We returned to the Winslow house the next day. I had already arranged for window trim, door trim and baseboard to be delivered. The newness of the space, transformed by the smooth walls and oak flooring thrilled us all. There was still a lot to do, but the house was showing its final form. I organized the crews to begin trim-work while I worked out a schedule to take us to completion. New, finer-tooth saw-blades were fitted into the saws; thin writing pencils replaced thick carpenter's pencils and everyone prepared for the more precise work that would take us through completion. This was the first time I had even talked in terms of actually finishing the house.

JACK CALLED TO ASK ME to leave Thursday morning open to visit a possible new project in nearby Redding. I was pleased that he was including me in a high-level business meeting. But I hadn't even considered the possibility of working on another project. All my attention was now fixed on finishing the Winslow house. How could I think of another?

He had arranged for us to meet the home's architect, Robert Devereaux, and owners, Bill and Lucy Shaw. We were being asked to assume responsibility for the house from another contractor named George Saunders, with whom the owner had become dissatisfied—not an enviable predicament for the owner. I could only presume that Jack's services would come at a premium at this stage in the project. But Jack also said that he was a friend of the owners. He had built their house in Nantucket before the Rogers' house and wanted to help them out of this jam. I remained defiantly disinterested. All my attention and pride was attached to the Winslow house. Nothing could change that.

But Jack tried. He brought several pages of blueprints for the new house to the jobsite on the morning of the visit. "Come on over boys, I wanna show you one fuckin' monster house."

The carpenters gathered around the drawings and raved openly.

"Those're impressive proportions Jack," Riley said.

"Yeah, I'll say. That house's bigger than anything I've ever worked on," added Benjamin.

I only glanced at the drawings, paying them little attention.

"This alone will carry us through the next two years, and then some," Jack said triumphantly. "You guys wanted work. I give you work. Can I count on you if I accept it?"

"Shit yeah," said Dennis. The others concurred.

"Good. Then I'll plan on your support and we'll build the biggest fuckin' house in Connecticut."

More of Jack's bravado, I thought to myself. I resented his suggesting that any house could be more impressive than this one.

Jack rolled up the blueprints and handed them to me. "Take good care of these, will ya?" I cradled them under my arm and followed Jack to his truck. Despite my reluctance to go, I felt important as I stepped in. This was a business meeting and Jack was including me. We drove through the Connecticut countryside until we reached the locked gate of the Shaw site.

SENIOR

THE SHAW HOUSE

"I learned this, at least, by my experiment; that if one advances confidently in the direction of his dreams, and endeavors to live the life which he has imagined, he will meet with a success unexpected in common hours."

HENRY DAVID THOREAU, *Walden*

ACK AND I WAITED ALONG the roadside in the rolling hills of Redding,
Connecticut. A locked gate blocked our entrance to a snow-covered
driveway, leading through what had once been farm fields. The road
disappeared over the crest of the hill, hiding the construction project that,
unbeknownst to its present contractor, might be reassigned to us. It was an
unusually mild March day, one of those temporary respites from the frigid
New England winter. The sky was cloudless and bright blue, the warm sun
reflected off the snowy white fields and a gentle breeze helped to begin a
light thaw. The half-foot of snow on the ground had gotten heavy, a soft wet
topping covering the fluffy blanket below. The conditions were perfect for
snowballs, which I threw to pass the time. I used the surrounding trees and
barns for target practice, leaving white pockmarks on all within range.

"Hey, Nolan Ryan. Let's get serious. Here they come." Jack pointed to
an approaching car, the only car we had seen in the ten minutes we had
been waiting. Coming to a stop before the gate, a well-dressed man got out
and introduced himself as Robert Devereaux, the lead architect in the firm
designing the house. "I just got into LaGuardia this morning on the red-
eye," he said. "Sorry for being late."

"How are things in L.A.?" Jack asked.

"A lot warmer than this I can tell you," Robert laughed.

But I was annoyed. Los Angeles! Why would anyone hire a California-
based architect to design a Connecticut-based home? I was constantly
consulting William for clarifications in his drawings. It was inevitable.
With such a large and complex project, there were always mistakes, missing
information or conflicting designs. In fact, I had learned that the best way to
hurt an architect would be to build exactly what he drew. It was impossible

for any architect to think of everything before work had begun. And even if such a superhuman task were possible, the owner or the site conditions always prompted changes.

Robert unlocked the gate and invited us to follow. We drove up separately, Jack and I in Jack's Blazer, Robert in his rental car. On the way up the driveway, Jack handed me a portable tape recorder. "Take verbal notes to keep track of what he says so we can document this conversation." It seemed an unnecessary task but I said yes. I was impatient, wanting to get back to the Winslow job to supervise the trim work and continue with the materials I had to order.

As we cleared the crest of the hill, however, all those concerns were pushed aside. What lay beyond was larger than any home project I had ever seen. It was enormous, rising high and wide out of the snow covered field. The imposing house sat alone, no other houses were within view. The windows had not yet been installed nor were the holes into which they would fit been cut out of the walls. It was a large brown colossus of plywood with a blank and foreboding look. A feeling of dread began to grow inside me.

Two aspects of the house struck me before all others. First, the ridgeline on this house—should I call it a house?—rose at least fifty feet above the first floor deck. That's five stories in a normal office building! The entire roof was covered with blue plastic tarps to keep water out until the permanent roofing could be installed. And, where most houses might be covered with one or two tarps, and the Winslow house by eight to ten, this house was covered by at least twenty. Second, the shape of the house looked gothic with two cylindrical turrets on either side of the front door. They were at least twenty feet in diameter and rose the full height of the building. Turrets, I thought. I've never seen turrets on a house before!

I had no time to process the images unfolding before me, so I made a conscious effort to look relaxed. Robert got out of his car, a smile engulfing his face. He was unabashedly proud of his creation as it was now taking shape. "What do you think?" he beamed.

I was amused by the obvious show of pleasure. William had never hidden his child-like excitement either. They both seemed in direct contrast to the hard-nosed demeanor of everyone else in the construction business.

Jack, true to his part, was cool and confident. "It looks like an interesting project. Your chimneys are a strong statement." Looking at the scrap and material piles strewn around the yard, he added, "Their site management leaves a little to be desired." I knew Jack's bravado by now and he was putting it on full display.

The shape of the cone that topped one of the turrets and the height at which it was perched fascinated me. I quickly calculated that if I fell from that ridge, I could die. I wondered what other dangers this house would present.

To my right, the house stretched for one hundred feet and to my left another one hundred and twenty. But, I also knew from my quick scan of the drawings that this was only half of the final house. Another wing had yet to be built. Dread inside me was turning to fear.

"Why don't we go inside and I'll show you around," Robert said as he walked to where the front door would eventually be. He unlocked a padlock, slid a sheet of plywood to the side and led us into the entry hall. I followed, the energy in my step flagging.

Once inside, my eyes adjusted to the darkness as I tried to consume all that was around me. One of the house's seven fireplaces greeted us to the right. The scale of the space made it clear that this house was different from anything I had ever built, or seen built, before. The ceiling rose twelve feet over our heads. I could look through interior walls for the extent of the house, but there was clutter everywhere. I had trouble identifying the floor plan.

Beginning the tour, Robert explained, "We decided to have the house balloon framed so that we could accommodate multiple heights on the separate floors."

I had heard of this technique before but thought it was mostly abandoned in favor of the more common technique of stick framing, where you build one floor at a time, each floor standing on the one below it. That was the only kind of framing I had done. In balloon framing, the entire exterior walls were built-in one continuous piece and the floors were added after. I could see how this would build a stronger house, but at what cost?

Robert continued, "The structural engineers decided that the house needed a steel infrastructure to carry several of the important load-bearing elements as well as the ridge beam."

My head spun. Structural engineers! Steel infrastructure! I had never needed structural engineers and had used steel in only small ways, mostly lolly columns and flitch plates, steel sheets sandwiched between framing lumber to make stronger beams. It dawned on me that this was not a large house as much as it was a small commercial project. My fear began to turn my thoughts away from the house and towards Jack. What was he getting us into? What was he getting *me* into?

As the window openings were still boarded over, the only light that illuminated the space came through the blue tarps on the roof. This cast an eerie hue through the house. Water from the melting snow dripped into the house at random spots. The dripping echoed throughout the interior as the water cascaded from floor to floor, finally puddling in the basement below. Each stop on its way was audible.

Some of the second-level floor had been built. Where incomplete, there was an unobstructed view to the ridge. I gazed up at the height of the ridge beam and followed the rafters down to the walls. I guessed the rafters to be twenty-four and thirty-feet long. I had never seen such lengths before. They had to have been special-ordered framing lumber. Even the basic materials for this job were a challenge!

I looked inside one of the turrets, up fifty feet to the peak and down twenty feet to the basement floor. That made the total drop nearly seven stories! From top to bottom was a disorganized collection of temporary landings and internal bracing to hold the cylindrical shape together until the space was filled with a wrap around staircase. Drops of water ran along the bracing, dripping down successive levels. Above, I could see that the carpenters had built a platform from which to build the cone-shaped roof.

My fear continued to mount. I was trying to put it all together, but the information was coming too quickly. This house needed temporary structures in order to build the final structures! And it had curves! How was I going to supervise the building of curves? We'd built an ornamental curved wall at the Winslow house. But this house had cones and cylinders that were structural parts of the house. And further, I could see that in this cone at least, the roof was made of clear pine rafters in four-inch-thick dimensions; very expensive wood. If anyone made a mistake on that, it would cost plenty. There was no room for error. The rough framing was also the interior finish. These were usually two separate trades, now merged into one!

Robert startled me out of my growing bewilderment by calling attention to the other side of the entry. Beaming with even more pride—if that was even possible—he said, "Come see the Great Room and the work they're doing inside." He pulled open another locked sheet of plywood.

My eyes again took a moment to adjust. The room was darker than the entry and the air carried a reddish haze that clouded what could be seen. The only light that penetrated the darkness came in thin beams from holes in the exterior plywood walls. In the light beams, I could see that the haze was actually fine sawdust. Across the room was a potbelly stove with stacks of wood scraps waiting to be burned. From all signs, this room was being used for a lot of woodworking.

The far wall stood forty feet away and the two side walls were twenty-five feet apart. The ceiling was nearly twenty-four feet over the floor. Two large steel I-beams crossed the ceiling, resting on steel columns that ran through the stud-framed walls on either side. Large wooden joists crossed from each I-beam, forming the floor above. The words "Great Room" echoed in my mind; an appropriate title. It was large enough to engulf the entire house I grew up in.

Robert turned on the temporary lighting that was strung along the ceiling. It illuminated the projects that were creating all this dust. And with what I saw, the fear inside me turned to terror.

On the left side of the room lay the sixteen foot wide cone roof for the second turret, still being constructed. Lying on its side, it looked more like the cowling of an airplane than the framing of a house. The redwood rafters spiraled out from a center block and the shape was being finely tuned into a curve with belt sanders. It was exquisitely complex. But what impressed me even more was the question of how I was going to know how to do that. I had to figure out how to build the curve, I had to build it on the ground first, I had to build temporary structures to put it in place and then I had to install it at death defying heights!

On the right side of the room, the carpenters were building an eyebrow skylight, an elegantly arched window that again showed a level of skill one would put into fine finish work, furniture or perhaps even a boat or plane. They had built a mockup of the roof and the window was taking shape on top of it. Measuring twelve feet across, the window gently rose from the roof, curved over and then rejoined the roof. A carrying beam had been built-in the shape of the curve of the window, out of which were strung curved rafters that radiated back to the roof in a graceful slope.

Next to the skylight, they were constructing a similarly shaped but smaller arch that would house a bathroom vent, two feet wide. And on the floor were stacked seven more, each made of redwood with copper screening in the face. This much work for the bathroom vents! Normally, such vents were handled simply by punching the PVC pipe through the roof. In more elaborate cases, you might wrap them in lead-coated copper. But in this house, each bathroom vent would get a treatment that would take at least two days of labor. I shuddered. How much detail does this house have? This will take years to build. And even if I had the nerve to do it, where was I going to get the skilled labor to pull it off? The thought returned: What was Jack getting me into?

Behind the skylight, the framed wall was sheathed on the inside with plywood. On the plywood was an intricate, full-scale structural drawing of one of the trusses that would cover the indoor pool. The trusses were to be triangular, measuring twenty-six feet wide and fourteen feet high, with cross braces filling its inside. The drawing showed details down to the placement of bolts, carrying braces, interconnecting purlins and steel connecting plates. The drawing alone was the product of a significant amount of work. I could only imagine what the actual trusses would involve. How was I going to learn all this and then supervise others in building it?

And with these images, the terror within me was now complete and total. I continued with the tour but no longer spoke, not because I had nothing to say but because I was no longer capable of speech. I was in a trance. My body floated along, taking in the surroundings but no longer actively participating in the discussions.

Jack was unfazed. He viewed the scene dispassionately, shaking his head in disapproval. "There's no need for all this work to be taking place in here. These guys are just trying to milk out the winter by holing up in here. Look at that truss drawing. What a ridiculous waste of time and money."

I tried to adopt Jack's confidence. But to me, it seemed reasonable. If I were to supervise this kind of work, this room seemed perfect for fine carpentry through the winter. I tried to dispel the terror that the room had created for me and replace it with Jack's assessment of its wastefulness. But I could not. I just continued to stare at the intricacy of the projects around me. Milking out the winter or not, this was some of the finest woodworking craftsmanship I had ever seen. How in the world was I going to replace these guys? This was nuts!

Robert endorsed Jack's sentiment. "Yes, we've been worried that they've been wasting too much time and money in here." I could see that Jack's discrediting the previous contractor might validate Robert's and the owners' decision to take the drastic step of switching construction companies midway through the project. And given that architectural commissions are based on a percentage of the construction cost, if this house was running over budget, his relationship with the Shaws must be strained. Any strain in the relationship would limit the latitude for designs yet to be introduced. At least being able to blame Saunders for the cost overruns would help his cause.

ROBERT TURNED HIS HEAD, responding to the sound of another car approaching the house. I froze in a panic; the other contractor! It would be bad enough to have to meet him under such unpleasant circumstances. But I couldn't stand up straight and face him as his replacement in my presently disheveled state. I hoped that no one could notice any outward change in my appearance, but inside I was overcome. I wanted to be someplace else. I needed time for my mind to accept all that I had seen and my body to return to my own control.

With Robert's announcement, "It's Bill and Lucy," I sighed in relief.

We walked to the front entrance and watched the car approach. I was now intrigued with the coming introduction. What kind of people would build a house like this? Were they going to be modern-day Roosevelts or Vanderbilts? Interest in the Shaws helped me to begin to regain my senses. Emerging from my trance, the first thing I noticed was the tape recorder running in my hand; a tape recorder that contained no dictation or record of the meeting because I had not spoken one word into it.

Looking out at the snowy driveway, I was struck by how unassuming the car was. Or at least it did not measure up to what I had quickly anticipated of the financiers of this house. A couple in their early fifties got out and walked quietly to the house. Bill was a genial-looking man with kind features. He wore a brown winter coat and a baseball cap, brown hair emerging from under it. His face projected a youthful, athletic energy and he wore wire-rimmed glasses that gave him a studious look. Lines marking his face suggested that he smiled a lot. He appeared neither stuffy nor powerful as I would stereotypically expect. He seemed like any guy you might meet as a neighbor. Lucy was thin and had a head of white hair that seemed premature for her age. She wore an equally non-descript tan coat and projected the same youthful energy as her husband.

But for the moment, their faces were stern and somber. Bill extended his hand and Jack took it. It felt like some kind of clandestine meeting, planning the overthrow of the contractor of this job.

Bill spoke first. "It's so good to see you again, Jack. I can't believe the mess we've gotten ourselves into. George Saunders is just taking us for a ride." He spoke in quick, agitated sentences. "He came highly recommended but he's lost it. I don't know, maybe he's going to retire, maybe he's just getting old, but this project's out of control. His quality isn't there and his costs are through the roof. He's going to take me to the poor house."

Lucy followed. "Oh, Jack, I wish we could've gotten you from the start. You did such a wonderful job on our house in Nantucket. I understand you were tied up with Maura Winslow's house, but if I knew then what I know now, I would've gladly waited till you were free." Her eyes began to tear.

Jack spoke calmly, reassuringly. "Things'll be all right from here. We're wrapping up the Winslow house and we'll be able to put a team on this job whenever you say go." Turning to me, "This is Andy Hoffman. He's the best supervisor I've ever seen. If anyone can take over this job, it's Andy. I place my complete trust in him."

For the first time, I resented his bravado. I was terrified and he was not giving me the strength I needed. But it worked with the Shaws. I could see their eyes soften as they shook my hand. "Hello, I'm Bill Shaw. Please excuse my outburst. This has been very stressful. I'm glad you'll be taking charge of this." Pointing to Jack, he added in a lighter tone, "This guy's the best builder I've ever seen. He's just incredible."

I suddenly felt conspicuously young, too young to be taking on this job. But, I could see that Bill didn't share that view. He had complete faith in Jack's assessment of all things related to construction.

I turned toward Lucy and extended my hand, unsure by her look whether she shared Jack's assessment and her husband's faith. Shaking my hand, she said, "I'm looking forward to working with you on this. Saunders has kept me completely out of the loop and there are a lot of changes I want to make as soon as you get started."

As always, the confidence Jack exuded infected those around him; that is, with the notable exception of me. Lucy's words, "as soon as you get started," rang in my ears. This was apparently not an exploratory meeting. It was really going to happen. My fear began to swell again. I was always impressed at how Jack could promise people incredible things with the utmost confidence. He always delivered and I attributed it to his skill at convincing people to do what he wanted of them. But this time I was worried because delivering on this promise was up to me. I knew that we weren't ready for this house. The Winslow job still had months to go. While I lacked the belief that I could supervise this house, I didn't see how I could run both jobs at the same time. Furthermore, I was unsure that we would have the manpower to staff both jobs. I was reaching an inescapable conclusion. This job was just too far over my head. I couldn't do it.

But Jack kept promising as we walked through the house. "We can whip this project into shape. I can see where they've been driving the costs up. The quality is pretty good, but I've seen that little spa they've built for themselves in the Great Room. There's no need for you to pay for that."

After finishing a walk-through of the first floor, we approached a ladder to go to the second floor.

Bill stopped, his face blanched. "I'll wait here."

Jack was clearly annoyed. "Do you mean to tell me that they haven't given you access to the second floor yet?"

Bill sheepishly turned to me, "I'm deathly afraid of heights. If I see the ground in any way, I freeze. I can't go any further. There's no way I could climb this ladder even if I wanted to."

Jack assured him, "One of the first things we'll do is make an enclosed stairway so you can take a look at what you're paying for." And with added urgency, he turned to me. "Make a note of that. That should be your first priority."

It was this kind of take-charge attitude that had endeared Jack to Maura Winslow and Alfred Rogers. It was also what now annoyed me. I had become frustrated on the Winslow house lately as Jack's jobsite involvement had dwindled to a minimum while he worked in his home office. And with the potential addition of this job, the thought crossed my mind that maybe I was being taken advantage of.

Bill waited below as the rest of us walked through what was available of the second floor. From this vantage point, I could see the rafters more closely and the four-by-ten redwood outriggers that were being added at the tails to protrude beyond the outside walls and form the finished overhang of the house. More complexity! More special-order materials! It was endless!

After a brief tour, we returned to Bill on the first floor and considered how to terminate the contract with Saunders and bring S&S in. Jack felt strongly that the termination not happen for at least a month, "Andy will need to come to the jobsite and learn as much as he can from the supervisor."

Bill was very animated in his opposition. "I want that asshole off this job! I want him out of my wallet! I want him out of my life! Now! We don't need another month!"

"Bill, be patient," Jack said. "There's a lot going on here and the more we learn before the switch, the better you'll be in the long run."

"You're right." Bill acquiesced. "I'm not thinking clearly. I can't tell you what a relief it is to have you here!"

We ended the meeting with more reassurances from Jack and a plan for he and Bill to talk later that evening.

AS JACK AND I DROVE BACK to the Winslow house, I tried to understand the terror that had gripped me and what it meant. Was it a sign that this was too much for me and that prudence should dictate that I pull out? Or was it a test of my courage, the natural response to a challenge that was a stretch but within my reach if I dared? I was both excited at the fantastic proportions of the project and petrified that I couldn't do it.

Jack broke my silent worry, "Hey Stuff, what do you think?"

"I don't know, Jack, it's a pretty complex job. The Winslow house is all straight lines and right angles at heights I can manage. This job is huge." I was trying to sound professional but my weak and deflated tone betrayed my fear.

"Relax, Andy. It's all in the plans." He turned to look at me and repeated himself more deliberately. "It's in the plans. You can do it. I know you can. You don't think I'd give this to you if I didn't think you could do it? Do you?"

It was a rare instance in which Jack's encouragement could not penetrate my mood. It was not having the same effect that it had on the Shaws and

Robert Devereaux. I was stunned and Jack could not prop me up. He dropped me off at the Winslow house and offered some last encouragement before leaving. "Andy, you can do it. Believe me when I tell you. You can do it."

I WALKED SLOWLY, still in a daze. I threw the blueprints into my truck, wanting to distance myself from anything that reminded me of the morning. It was time to eat, so I grabbed my lunch even though I wasn't hungry.

Benjamin asked, "Well, how'd it go? What was the house like?"

I looked up in a long deliberate motion. "Beyond words Benjamin. I can't describe it. It's incredible."

More than my words, my dulled responses conveyed the impact of what I had just seen. Benjamin replied simply, "Shit! That big huh?"

"Benjamin, have you ever been awe-struck?"

"Well, I'm not sure what you mean."

"I've been trying to put it into words. And this is all I can come up with. Have you ever been to the Grand Canyon?"

"Yes. About ten years ago I took a Harley trip through those parts. Spectacular."

"Yeah, spectacular. You know what I thought when I first saw it? I thought of the other visitors that stood at the edge of the canyon's rim, gazing in awe at this natural wonder. But I thought, these people looked at it as objective observers. It had no personal significance and therefore, they weren't awe-struck. Then I tried to imagine what it was like for the first settlers crossing the American southwest to stand at the same spot. I had to believe they were awe-struck because the canyon meant something personal to them. They had to cross it. So for them, while beautiful, the canyon must have filled them with terror. I would try to imagine what they were thinking. 'It's too big.' 'It's impossible to cross.' 'It's an insurmountable challenge.' 'Our adventure is over.' All of these are similar to the thoughts that I felt today. I was awe-struck."

Again, all that Benjamin offered was, "Shiiit."

The others gathered around to eat their lunch and hear my report. I was embarrassed that they were seeing me so clearly knocked off balance, but I continued. I couldn't help myself. I described the morning's walk-through as everyone ate their lunch and listened attentively. "Guys, this'll be the most incredible house any of us has ever worked on. I can't begin to describe how big it is."

Riley smirked, "That's what we like to hear. We're ready for it Andy. You've got a crew here that will do you proud."

"I'm telling you," I said, as I pointed all around. "This place is tiny compared to the Shaw house. And it's not only huge. It's got turrets, tall cylindrical turrets on either side of the front door. They're more than fifty feet tall." I could feel their dimensions growing in my mind.

When lunch was over and everyone went back to work, I tried to focus. But as much as I tried, I couldn't. I took care of mundane tasks, but my attention kept getting pulled back to the drawings lying in the seat of my truck.

WHEN I GOT HOME that evening, Sharon was waiting for me. We had planned to go out to dinner, but I just wanted to look at the drawings and think this job over. Smiling as she always did, she anxiously asked, "How was the new job? Are you gonna be running two jobs now?"

I mumbled that it went "okay" and went straight into the bedroom to lay the blueprints out on the bed. Sharon laid down on the bed next to them and looked up at me slyly. "Why are we in here? Did you have something in mind?"

I chuckled, but couldn't be distracted. As if she hadn't said anything, I said, "Look at this! Even these blueprints are a colossal project!"

She leaned over and watched as I turned through the pages. I was mesmerized. Where the Winslow job had fifteen pages of architectural drawings, each two and a half by three feet, the Shaw house had fifty-four. In addition, the Shaw house had a complete set of structural, mechanical, electrical and plumbing drawings as well as one-hundred-fifty sheets detailing various specific features in the architecture and a three-hundred-page book of specifications. The detail was incredible: ceiling plans for the house's many wooden beamed, coffered, vaulted, barreled and trayed ceilings; wall elevations for wainscoting, crown mold, sconces, switches and outlets. There were twenty-four different types of windows, sixteen different types of doors, seventeen different types of door hardware.

Where the Winslow house stretched for two hundred and twelve feet, the Shaw house stretched for two hundred-forty and then turned to stretch for another one hundred-twelve. Where the Winslow house was primarily one floor with a basement, the Shaw had two floors with a basement and full attic. And most of the ceiling heights were well above the standard eight feet, many reaching to twice that.

The Winslow house had forty-five windows and forty exterior doors. The Shaw house had one hundred forty windows and forty-two exterior doors. It had seven bedrooms, six bathrooms, three half-baths, seven fireplaces, an indoor pool, an indoor gym, seventeen heating and air conditioning zones, four car garage and a separate servant's quarters. The house encompassed twenty-nine thousand square feet of area, with nineteen thousand of that constituting finished living space. The attic alone was three thousand square feet!

And finally, there was the site. The Winslow house sat on a fifteen-acre lot. From the driveway, I could see houses in all directions. But the Shaw house sat on one hundred and eighty acres. The driveway was a third of a mile long, shielding the house from view of the road. In all directions, there were only woods and stone walls. There was nothing minor about any aspect of this project. I knew that I was taking charge of a project that few carpenters would ever realize and most would only dream about.

"For cryin' out loud," I said, "They've even detailed how the boards in the hardwood floors are laid out! Look at this one, it's herringboned! They've spec'd everything right down to the plank patterns! Nothing on this job's gonna be simple!"

With that, I made a decision. I was talking to myself, but I had to say it. "I can't do this. This is over my head. I don't have the skills. I don't have the knowledge. I don't have the experience. I'll blow the costs. I'll make a mistake. Worst case, someone's gonna get hurt. I have to tell Jack to get someone else."

Sharon looked surprised now. I had never expressed such self-defeating fear before and she didn't know how to react. I had always displayed such confidence. Over the past months, I had been feeling more and more competent at work. But now I was showing a new side. I had talked about this new job over the past couple of days, but only in passing. I never let on that it was a big deal. I hadn't known it was such a big deal.

Sharon tried to calm me down, build up my confidence, but I was beaten.

I wasn't prepared for what I had just seen. I had ignored the drawings when Jack first showed them to us. I hadn't known it was such a big deal. I picked up the phone and dialed.

"Jack?"

"Hey Stuff, what a house, huh? I'm still thinking about it."

"Yeah, so am I," I said. "I've been thinking about it since you dropped me off. I don't know how to say this any other way except to just say it. I quit. I'll finish up Winslow if you want, but Shaw is out of my league. I can't do it."

Jack was calm, "Andy, I wouldn't ask you to do this if I didn't have faith in you. It's all in the plans. There's a team of architects and structural engineers you can call anytime you need them. I saw the way Bill and Lucy looked at you. They liked you. You can do it!" He paused. "And if that architect gives you any trouble, I'll personally kick his ass. Don't ya think I can do that?" He was laughing and I tried hard to crack a smile. "Just relax, take a deep breath, go out to dinner with your lady and we'll talk about it again tomorrow. I'm sure after you sleep on it, you'll see that you can do it. I know you can."

I hung up and just stared at the plans.

"What did he say?" asked Sharon.

"He thinks I can do it. Geez, he has more confidence in me than I do! Does he really know something that I don't?"

I was becoming despondent and Sharon started to rub my shoulders. It helped, as fatigue started to take over my body. I stared down at the mass of paper on my bed. I knew that Jack was able to get me to do things that I myself thought impossible. He poured his confidence into me, encouraging and praising what I was doing. That's what drew me to him and created this tremendous loyalty I felt for him. But this was different. Whereas in the past I felt I was capable of living up to his expectations, this time I felt no such confidence. I would have to place my complete trust in his assessment; ignoring my own doubts. As I thought about that, I realized that I believed more in Jack's estimation of my own abilities than I did. Would that be enough to get me through this?

Sharon and I went out to dinner and caught a movie. But my mind kept turning things over. As it did, I came to see that something else was driving me as well, not just faith in Jack's assessment, but deeper instincts of ambition and pride. This was an extraordinary opportunity! Ready or not, I would never see a chance like this again. In fact, very few contractors would be offered a chance like this. To walk away would violate everything that compelled me to come to Connecticut and work for Jack in the first place. I couldn't just quit. I'd regret it for the rest of my life. And then it hit me, it wasn't *my* regret I was worried about, it was disappointing Jack. How could I look him in the eye and tell him I quit? I couldn't. I realized his assessment of me had become too important and it drove me to be the man he expected me to be, whether I believed I was that man or not. First thing in the morning, I called Jack and forced the words out quickly. "I'll do it. I'll build the Shaw house."

"Good, good," was Jack's response. "I know you can do it. Didn't I tell you that a good night's sleep would do the trick?" I shook my head as he continued, "I told Bill that we'd take over in one month. So you have until April to learn all you can about that house. Do you think that is enough time?"

"I guess it will have to be." I knew my answer was laced with sarcastic frustration but, what could I say? Things had started and all I could do was go along. It had begun.

MY DECISION TO DO the Shaw house fueled my desire to finish the Winslow House. Like a conductor, I orchestrated successive waves of subcontractors through the many regions of the home. I tried to avoid any lags where nothing was happening on a particular project. I didn't want to waste a moment of time.

Cabinetmakers were set to the task of installing the built-in dressers, the kitchen and bathroom cabinets and the wet bar. Tilers laid floors and walls in the bathrooms. Plumbers followed with sinks, showers, toilets and the central vacuum system. Electricians installed switches, plugs, stereo connections, cable TV outlets and kitchen appliances. Masons installed marble surrounds for the fireplaces. Marblizers used paint to mimic the marble pattern on the wooden mantel pieces around it. Painters painted and wall-papered. And I hovered over it all.

Hovering over me were the designers. Or more accurately one designer who had become Maura's favorite. Jennifer Crowley took charge of the final interior designs of the bathroom cabinets, wet bar, built-in cabinetry, kitchen and dining room ceiling as well as color schemes and wallpaper. In the guest bedroom, she designed matching custom-made bedspreads, wall paper and shower curtain. In the kitchen, she designed custom-painted tile for the back splash and fireplace surround. The chief problem I saw with Jennifer was that her office was in Columbus, Ohio. And she chose her own subcontractors to build the cabinetry and ship it to Connecticut.

The complexity that the distance created was a continuing source of frustration for me. For instance, Jennifer's office had to make drawings for the countertops and I had to describe the site conditions to her by giving her measurements and dimensions. But walls are never perfectly straight, plumb or square and this could never be communicated over the phone. The slightest gap would show dramatically. To deal with this, pieces had to be over-built, shipped to the site and trimmed to fit the irregularities of the walls.

That worked with wooden cabinetry, but some of the countertops that she had spec'd were made of marble and the crew had no proficiency in trimming marble to fit. So, while her local marble supplier cut the marble counters and shipped them by common freight to the site, I hired my local marble supplier to fit them into place. At least that was the plan.

The first piece was delivered with a crack down its center. More than the disappointment of the broken piece, what I saw most of all was a costly delay. Without the countertop, the sink and faucet could not go in, the painters could not finish the walls, and the mirror could not be installed. One missing piece backed up three trades who were ready to finish their contracts. It could at times be difficult to get tradesmen back for just one small piece of a job. They were here now, they were giving the job their all, and once they moved on, this would be low on their priority list. This delay could become a costly annoyance.

I called Jennifer's office to tell them of the crack. "No problem," said Frederic, Jennifer's assistant, said. "It's insured. We'll have another made up and ship it out ASAP."

"Okay, but I'd appreciate it if you'd put a serious rush on it. We're ready to finish up here."

The second counter arrived a week later. The truck-driver unloaded the wooden crate and, by the tinkling sounds from inside, I didn't even need to open it to know that this one was also broken. Upon further inspection, it was not just cracked. It was shattered. It would seem that freight travel and marble were not a good combination.

I called Columbus and talked to Frederic again. When I explained about the broken piece, he asked, "Are you guys handling the freight properly on your end?"

With the pressure of keeping so many trades going at once, my patience had suddenly come to an end. I had two carpenters, a cabinetmaker and the plumber standing in front of me awaiting word on what to do about the as-yet incomplete bathrooms. "We're handling the pieces just fine here," I said through gritted teeth. "The problem is in the packing, that is if the pieces can even be packed for the trip from Ohio."

"Look, are you opening them carefully? We've never had this problem before."

My response was sudden, instantaneous and forceful. My mouth began to speak before my mind told it to. In fact, it did not speak, it commanded. And there was no question of my intent or the object of my displeasure.

"Are you telling me how to do my job?" Each word was articulated clearly and slowly.

"I'm just suggesting…"

I cut him off, repeating myself with slow and deliberate intensity. "NO! Stop and answer me! ARE .. YOU .. TELLING .. ME .. HOW .. TO .. DO .. MY .. JOB?" I was showing a ferocity that I didn't know I had. I could see it reflected in the faces of the men in the room, as conversations stopped and all eyes were upon me. I could feel it in their looks, I commanded their complete and undivided attention. And I could hear it suck the energy out of Frederic.

"No, I'm…"

"I sure hope to hell you're not. Now, listen to me carefully. You *will* get your shit together out there. I've got a job to finish here, and you're causing me unnecessary delays. The marble is not arriving in one piece and I have no time to fuck around while you figure out how to do it."

"I know how to do my job."

"If you knew how to do your job, I'd have a marble counter-top right now! I don't! Do you understand the fuckin' situation? Or am I missing something here?"

"Yes, Andy. I understand."

"Good. Now we have suppliers here in Connecticut who are quite capable of delivering marble in one piece. And I have no idea why you're wasting my fucking time with this bullshit. But, I'll tell you this. You will not waste any more. In a moment we're going to hang up. And when we do, you're going to get your heads together in that office of yours and you're going to figure out how to do your job! Got it?"

"Andy, I…"

"There's no need for discussion here. I've got my job to do. You've got yours. Are you going to do it?"

There was silence, followed by a hesitant response. "Yes, Andy, we'll do ours."

"Good. Get me my fucking counter-top. Goodbye!"

I hung up. As I awoke from my fury, I looked up to see stunned faces in the room staring at me.

Dennis chuckled. "Shiiit, you sure tore that guy a new asshole!"

Freddie Carlucci whistled an approving sigh. I just stared blankly, slowly regaining control of my faculties. That outburst had come from a place deep within me. It just erupted out of me, pouring through my lips like water from a tipped pitcher. And it felt good.

JACK LAUGHED WHILE I sat in his office and told him what had happened. "Hah, I call that verbal diarrhea. Congratulations! That's a good thing. That designer needed his bell rung and you rang it. I hope he didn't get whiplash in the process."

I smiled at the imagery.

"Now tell me, did anyone else see this happen?" Jack asked.

"Yeah, I had a whole audience," I said, rolling my eyes in embarrassment.

"Good! That's good. Trust me, Andy, the news of that blow up is gonna be all over the jobsite. In fact, I'll bet it already is. You showed your teeth. I don't think you've done that yet and it needed to be done. You needed to show you have a line and that there's a price for crossing it." He paused. "Andy, you're a nice guy and everyone knows it. But now they'll show you a new level of respect because you showed that you *can* be tough. I knew you had it in you. Good. Good!"

"I doubt that, Jack," I replied. "All I showed is that I can lose my temper."

"Andy, you're missing something here. Let me ask one question, did the other guy back down?"

"Yes."

"I mean did he really back down? Will he think twice about crossing you again?"

"He probably thinks I'm an asshole."

"Who gives a shit about that? He's the asshole. He wasn't doing his job. The point is that now he will. He'll get with the program and do his job. And that, my friend, means that you did your job. Well done!"

I was not sure how to think of this just yet. Jack continued. "That designer's going to kiss your ass from now on. That is, if Jennifer even lets him near you. I suspect you're gonna get a call from Jennifer tomorrow with a solution to the countertop. In the end, Andy, you got what you wanted. You were tough but you were fair. You let him screw up twice and then you called him to the mat. Congratulations!"

"Thanks, I guess."

"Now, do you want to know what the real trick is? Are you ready for the next step? You need to be able to do that on command, convincingly. It'll keep people at attention around you, which is always good. You've made it to the first stage. Try to think about the second."

It all fit together. I'd seen how Jack had mastered that skill, shifting suddenly from calm to ferocious. And I had seen how it worked to get people to do what he wanted. And now I knew that it was calculated. He patted me on the back as he guided me to the door. His parting words were, "Andy, you done good."

I thought back to Jack's evisceration of Scott and how I thought it cruel and unnecessary. But now, I had done the same thing to Frederic. This time I could see that it was necessary. I was becoming what I thought I couldn't. Where I had always doubted my toughness, that was now changing. Was I really learning? The prospect pleased me. Where before it was often Jack's strength that coursed through me, now I could feel it come from within; it was my own.

"WE NEED TO TALK about the jobs," Jack announced in our next meeting in his office. "Have you thought about how you're gonna run the two jobs?"

"I'm still thinking things through," I said.

"Well, I've been watching you run the Winslow House and have some thoughts. Now don't take this the wrong way. You've done a first-class job. But I think you take on too much yourself. You can do that at one job," He paused and added parenthetically, "Although I think you'll burn yourself out eventually," and then continued. "But you need to delegate. You need to direct others and stop doing everything yourself."

I knew Jack was right and I had come to the same conclusion already. I'd never be able to get through the Shaw house without handing off more of the burden to others. It seemed another way to ease my fear of the project.

"Let's do an assessment of your crew and see what we need to think about," Jack continued. "First, is it time for some spring cleaning? Is there anyone who's not pulling their weight?"

Spring cleaning? I thought it a strange way to think about the crew. But he was looking at me intensely and it made me uncomfortable. The memories of firing Simon still stung. "Well," I hesitated.

"Well what?" Jack fired back.

"Well, Chet's been coming in late. It's buggin' me because I never know if I can count on him to start the day and it affects how I organize the crews."

"Fire him." Jack minced no words, just like with Simon. "Fire his lazy ass."

I nodded. I had an idea that Jack would say this as soon as I mentioned it. "Okay, Jack, I'll take care of it."

"Andy, sooner or later you're gonna have to make these decisions on your own. I'm glad to nudge you along, but if you're gonna delegate, you need people you can count on. And when a carpenter loses interest, it's time to let him go. He knows it. You need to know it. Is there anyone else?"

"No, Jack, that's all right now."

"Okay. Now, who do you trust to run things at each job when you're not there."

I had a much better feeling about this question than who to fire. "I'd like to put Riley in charge at Shaw and I think Benjamin at Winslow."

"You think? What's up with Benjamin?" Jack left no bit of apprehension alone.

"Well, Benjamin's an excellent carpenter. He does meticulous, high quality work. But he's slow as molasses. That's all."

"Well, nobody's perfect. Benjamin's good. I trust him. Start with him and watch him. If he goes too slow, we'll figure out a way to light a fire under his ass."

Jack leaned back in his chair and laughed, amused with his own comment and relaxing a bit. "Okay, you've got a couple of weeks until you start a crew over at Shaw. You'll need to buy more tools and hire more carpenters. Have you thought at all about how you'll get started at Shaw?"

"Yeah, I'm going to put them on the garage and pool wing first. That'll keep them a safe distance from Saunder's crew. We also have to jack-hammer out some concrete that was poured in the wrong place."

"Good. I like those ideas. And be sure to keep track of all the extras we have to incur from their mistakes. I've chosen Dominic Brunel to do the shingling on the roof and siding. I want Dom's men to start at the same time your crew does. I want to show Bill and Lucy that things are moving now that we're on the job. I want it to start hard, you got that?"

"Sure Jack, no problem."

"One thing that Brunel negotiated into the contract is that we buy the cedar shingles. He's afraid of laying out the cash on that big an order. I don't blame him. So, I need you to figure out how many shingles he'll need and buy them. Do it soon, this'll be a big order and will take some time to acquire." Catching himself, he added, "Oh, they have to be fire-treated. The Shaws have lived through one fire and they're pretty concerned about this. Okay?"

"Okay Jack."

I'd been writing everything down in my permanent companion, my note pad. I put my pencil back behind my ear and, looking down, realized that I'd now need to carry two pads, one for each job.

I WANTED TO FIRE Chet quickly, get it over with. I was nervous, but I resolved myself to the task, met him privately at the end of the day and simply announced it. "Chet, I'm letting you go."

"Sorry Andy, I've been bored," Chet replied apologetically. "So I haven't been putting in the effort I should've."

"Then why didn't you come tell me or just quit?" I was angry, both at him and my own naiveté.

"Hey, it's good money and I didn't wanna give that up." He was kicking the dirt around at his feet as he spoke. "You run a nice job here, Andy, and while I understand it's time for me to go, I kinda liked coming here."

I now just wanted it over with. "Well, it was good to have you here, Chet. Here's your final check. Good luck with whatever you do next."

Chet loaded his tools into the back of his El Camino and drove off. That was it. The whole encounter lasted no more than five minutes.

MY FIRST CHALLENGE with the Shaw project was to learn the drawings, every detail. I had no particular plan for how to approach them. I cross-referenced one drawing with another, but for the most part, I just studied them in whatever order they came to me. This was much too large a project for me to even have a grasp of how much there was to do. I spent hours upon hours engrossed in the pages of information. For over a week, my dining room table and floor were home to the stacks of blueprints. And as I read them, I focused on small pieces, taking them one at a time, not allowing myself to contemplate the whole job and its magnitude. It was sort of like not looking down when climbing a cliff, just focusing on the rock in front of you and the next hand-hold.

My second challenge was to learn the job site, what had actually been built and how. Once a day, I left the Winslow house to make the thirty-minute drive to the Shaw house and observe the progress of the outgoing crew. My first visit with the project manager, Kenneth, was awkward. Nearing sixty, he had been building all his life and knew more about construction than I felt I ever would. Kenneth didn't show any antagonism towards me. But I felt embarrassed that I would be his replacement. He told me about his hobby of building wooden planes and flying them. This blew me away. Airplanes! He built airplanes! I had built balsa wood airplanes when I was a boy, but building one in full scale and then actually trusting it to fly was incredible. Kenneth was generous with his time, walking me through the job. He told me that he planned to retire after this project. He had hoped that it would be his swan song, a nice way to end his career. But things had gone wrong. He told me how difficult the architects and the owners were to work with. "California," he spat, "How was I supposed to work with architects who lived on the other side of the country?" I listened but didn't offer much. "And they could never make up their minds," he complained. "We had to build everything with the contingency of taking it out or modifying it."

He showed me the roof cone that was being built, or more accurately, crafted. The rafters were two parts, beginning as pine and ending as redwood. The redwood would be exposed as outriggers jutting past the wall and creating an overhang. The frame started as a sixteen-foot-diameter half-circle and converged over an eight foot distance to a point, much like a squat ice-cream cone cut in half and lying on its side. Then, two-by-four pine was screwed to the frame in lines parallel to the perimeter. To finish it off, the carpenters had belt-sanded it to a perfect conical shape. Once built-in the room, each piece was numbered. Then, it would be dismantled and reassembled in place. Scaffolding was already erected to install it.

When I wasn't with Kenneth, I walked the job alone, admiring and noticing all the details of what was going on. Some men made wisecracks loud enough for my benefit. "Ken says we should stack the templates over there. Yeah, I'll stack 'em all right. I'll stack 'em in nicely cut pieces for kindling." Others offered suggestions and help. One carpenter pointed to some bags of insulation and said, "Those are for filling the steel beams in the main stair well. If you go to the tip of the cone, there's a hole where you can pour it in. It will keep the columns from sweating on cold days." I thanked him, grateful for any tip.

I stopped by the town offices to introduce myself to the Redding building inspector, Charles DiMaggio. He and Kenneth had been friends for years, a point that he made clear from the start. "Ken's getting a bad rap out there. He's one of the finest builders I've ever known and he doesn't deserve to be treated this way." In his words, I felt a clear statement that I was starting off on a bad footing with him. I smiled and tried to be as polite as possible, signaling the respect that Kenneth was due. It was not difficult, for I truly admired him.

MY THIRD CHALLENGE with the Shaw house was ordering materials. I had grown used to buying large orders of plywood and framing lumber. But with the Shaw House, I was in a whole new league. The roof shingles were my first major material order.

The roof on the Shaw house was enormous and complex, with many different pitches, dormers, skylights, cones, and chimneys. I approached it as a simple mathematical task. With calculator in hand, I divided the roof into sections and computed total square footage for each. I compiled the list, added a factor for waste, rechecked my math and determined a grand total of eighteen-thousand square feet of shingles. I thought it a large number but didn't fully realize just how large until I tried to get estimates.

One lumberyard said simply that it was too large an order and refused to bid. Another asked me to confirm the number several times, expressing disbelief that I was serious. One lumberyard, Gregory Lumber, came through with a price in six figures and I was stunned.

"Jack, should I go ahead and order 'em?" I was afraid to make the decision alone.

"Are you sure about your numbers?" Jack asked.

I had confidence in my calculations but was very nervous about committing to them beyond the academic exercise of creating them. A very large amount of money was at stake. Now I knew why Dominic had negotiated this out of the contract. Pushing myself, I said "Yes Jack, it's a good number based on a ten percent waste factor."

"Okay, tell them to take off ten thousand and if they accept, order 'em."

The counter-bid came out of thin air, and I felt reluctant to make the request. This was my first time negotiating a price. But the lumberyard's owner, Kevin, accepted it, explaining, "I'll cut my margins on our first order together. Any house that's big enough to take this many shingles must have plenty more wood to be ordered."

One down, many to go. The next major material order was redwood, and lots of it. Over the indoor pool, the plans called for two-by-twelve redwood trusses connected by four-by-six redwood purlins (cross-braces that connected the trusses) and covered by one-by-six tongue and groove redwood for the finished ceiling. The entire project was to be in clearheart redwood; a perfectly knot-free wood, it was extravagant and expensive.

This was only the appetizer to the main course. The more difficult challenge came in the larger-dimension redwood I needed for the porches on the house. Posts were eight-by-eight, on top of which rested eight-by-twelve lintels, on top of which rested four-by-ten rafters, on top of which rested two-by-four tongue and groove planks. Again, this would all be clearheart redwood. And this kind of an order, coupled with the massive shingle order, meant that I immediately got Kevin's undivided attention as his most important customer.

"Andy, this is a pretty serious order of lumber. I can't just go to my wholesaler for it. We need to order it from California, direct."

"Okay, just give me a price."

"Whoa, slow down there. You don't understand. First, those dimensions are going to be very green. We can't just kiln dry something that big, so they'll have a very high moisture content. That means two things. First, you may get some checking. Second, this stuff has to come by train and it can't cross the Rockies in the winter or it'll freeze and definitely check."

Talk of the Rockies and trains made me nervous. "So what're you telling me, Kevin?"

"I'm telling you that you would get the best price if you ordered everything you need at once and we commissioned a train car to get the materials here."

"Whew," I whistled. "Kevin, that's a lot of calculations. And then once it gets here, I don't know where I'd store it."

"Look Andy, this is beautiful stuff. I'll store it for you here. Just try to get close. If you're over just a little, I'll take it off your hands. But heed my warning. Don't be under or you'll have a long wait to get the remainder of what you need." Then he added, "And Andy, remember, you're effectively ordering trees. They don't come neatly in the lengths you want. You'll get at least as long as you want but you won't get exactly what you want. Over measure to be safe."

I explained the situation to Jack. "I don't know what your cash flow situation is Jack, but this is gonna be a big up-front cost."

"Talk to Kevin and get him to help us by delaying some of the billing. With this big an order, he's making a nice profit just for being middleman. He'll give us some slack. I'll try and get a little more out of Bill to help this along on my end."

Kevin agreed to slow down the bills and I spent an entire day calculating the lumber, specifying dimensions and lengths needed of each. Then I checked them again. And then I checked them a final time. The next day, I placed the order and Kevin double-checked each of my numbers. He called it in that afternoon and told me that it would arrive in four to six weeks.

THE WINSLOW HOUSE was moving along nicely. Carpenters were busy installing baseboard and door and window trim. Painters followed behind and once they finished a room, security crews installed motion detectors, infrared beams and control panels; the telephone company installed telephone jacks and communication systems; and the electricians installed the final covers for outlets and switches.

The bathroom countertop problem was resolved after my blow up at Frederic. Simply put, I never spoke to him again. As Jack predicted, Jennifer took over all interactions with me. More importantly, she decided that marble counters couldn't be shipped from Ohio to Connecticut in one piece. But instead of letting me have a local shop cut the marble, she decided to use acrylic instead. As long as the materials arrived, I didn't care what the materials were. She promised the counter within a week.

As spring was arriving, I also began organizing work on the grounds of the house. The most important project was a series of Japanese gardens to grace either side of the front entrance. This brought me into contact with Maurizio Donatella, the first subcontractor that I hired on my own. While working at Via Via, Gino introduced him as one of the finest stone masons in the area. Originally from Sardinia, Maurizio had lived in the United States for over twenty years. I liked him from the moment we met. We talked over coffee, he took me on a tour of some of his past projects and, through it all, displayed a genuine love for his craft. On my endorsement alone, Jack let me hire him.

The gardens were designed by a premier landscape architect in New York City who specialized in Japanese gardens. The plans called for a variety of complex stonework: a cut granite walk under the house's overhang; stone veneer walls forming a border on the other side; slivers of stone shards forming a simulated river weaving through the cut granite and connecting to the veneer wall. Maurizio and I met with the designers, discussed materials that were available and how they might be utilized, and began. His presence brought a new dimension to the sounds on the job. Most notably, he brought opera, which he played on his portable stereo. In fact, Maurizio adopted me as his student.

"You have to start with some easy ones," he explained. "German operas? Forget it. You must start with the Italians and these are two that can help you begin." He handed me videos of "La Bohéme" and "La Traviata" as my first assignments. "They are easy to understand."

I liked the opera, but I liked the friendship with Maurizio even more. I would seek him out for lunch whenever I could. He loved to talk and had many stories that he told with a bright smile and mischievous twinkle in his eye.

To an enraptured group of carpenters, he explained in his heavy Italian accent, "I was once working for a contractor who I thought wouldn't pay me. So I did my work, but I made an insurance policy. I built the fireplace and chimney as I was hired to do and left. And sure enough, that son-of-a-bitch didn't pay me. So I just waited. When the house sold, the owners tried to light a fire but the chimney wouldn't draw. So they called the contractor. He checked it out, looked up the flue, into the smoke chamber and everything seemed okay."

Tapping his head, he said, "But I outsmarted him. He called me up and told me that my fireplace didn't work and wanted to know what I was gonna do about it. I told him to pay me and I'd fix it. I told him I wanted cash before I did a thing. What could he do? He had no choice? He met me at the job. He paid me my money. I put a ladder up against the chimney, climbed to the top and dropped a brick down the flue."

Then he grinned a devilish grin. "When no one was looking, I mortared a pane of glass into the flue. It blocked the flow of air. But when he looked up, he could see daylight so he had no idea what was wrong."

As everyone laughed, he leaned back proudly. "I showed that son-of-a-bitch."

AS PART OF MY TUTORIAL for the Shaw House, Robert Devereaux sent me a book about an architectural firm from the turn of the century called McKim, Mead and White. He explained that the Shaw house would be in the "Shingle Style." Using the same kind of poetic language that I had grown accustomed to with William, Robert explained that, "the shingle style is a uniquely American variant of the Victorian. It was influenced by the Romanesque Revival, Colonial Revival and the Stick or Carpenter Gothic Styles."

I had no idea what he was talking about.

"What you've got to understand, Andy," Robert continued, "is that Shingle Style buildings are composed of complex shapes and united by the taut skin of shingles. So, in the case of the Shaw house, think of the eyebrow skylights as well as other features as stretches in this skin. Picture it as though someone inside the house were pushing up on the shingle skin and it is stretching and yielding under the pressure, creating a taut hump." As he was telling me this over the telephone, I could picture him animatedly straining to push his hand upward into the roof. "Hence an eyebrow!"

For more than a year, I had been the student of William Simon. Now I was the student of Robert Devereaux. Robert suggested I visit some McKim, Mead and White "structures" in Rhode Island. "Go find the Casino in Newport and the William Low House in Bristol. Notice the stretching of the shingle skin. Study the fine details in the overhang, above the windows, around the doors. This is what we want to see in this house."

I wasted no time, asking Sharon if she would like to go to Newport for the weekend. She eagerly agreed. When I told her my site-seeing plans, she laughed, "Don't you ever stop thinking about that house?"

That weekend, we drove to Newport and mixed the fun of the restaurants and mansions with the work of architectural study. I found the buildings beautiful, although the Casino was the only one I could look at closely without actually trespassing. Just as Robert had described, I saw the stretching of the shingle skin over the entire buildings. I admired the fine details in the overhang, above the windows, around the doors. Whether it was Robert's intention or not, seeing these houses inspired me to make the Shaw house an equal.

But, despite my preparations, I still felt overwhelmed as the day approached for a full crew to start at the Shaw House. I had hired a new contingent of carpenters, bought a new fleet of tools and explained my delegation of responsibilities to Riley and Benjamin.

"Does this mean more money?" was Riley's immediate response.

"I've already talked to Jack about that. He said he'd like to wait a couple of weeks and see how things work out. But if this arrangement works, he sees no reason why you shouldn't be paid more."

"That's acceptable to me," Riley replied.

"Me too," added Benjamin.

"Great," I said, relieved that money didn't become a sticking point in my plan. I asked them if they had preferences for crew members. Benjamin had none.

Riley wanted Arthur. "He's quiet, but he's one of the most knowledgeable carpenters I've ever met," he said.

I divided the crew for them and concluded the meeting with a word of warning to Riley. "We've got a problem that you need to be aware of. The other crew is union and will still be there when our crew arrives. Under no circumstances should we let any of our guys interact with any of theirs."

Riley replied dryly, "that'd be wise."

THE DAY CAME. I arrived at the Shaw House early and watched as Kenneth's crew arrived to take their positions on the west side of the house. According to plan, my crew followed later and took up positions on the east side. We would begin on the yet-to-be built wing that housed the indoor pool, indoor gym, sauna, four-car garage, servant's quarters and mechanical room. Riley had a copy of the plans and was anxious to get started. I introduced him to the new crew members I had hired to fill out the staff. He divided them into their respective roles and the noise of activity began. Saws whined, compressors hummed, nail guns popped. And over the whole din, a jackhammer, which had been delivered at the start of the day was firing away, with Mike—one of the new guys—breaking out some of the misplaced concrete. I thought this a particularly provocative act with the crew that had poured it still on the job, and I watched for any of the possible tensions I feared between my crew and the union crew sharing the same job site. But Jack wanted us to hit the job hard and we did. There was no question that there was a new crew on the job. And to me at least, there was no question which crew was working harder.

Soon, an eighteen-wheeler rumbled down the dirt driveway, leaving a tail of dust in its wake. On the flatbed was my order of roof shingles. My heart stopped at the volume of the order. It was more than I had ever seen before. With a new car-phone that Jack insisted I get installed in my truck, I called the lumberyard in a panic. "Kevin, I may have over-ordered on these shingles. What are my options if I have to return some of them?"

"Andy, I hate to tell you this but we've got another flatbed here for delivery."

I was mortified. "Can you hold them there?" I stammered. "I may have to dump them."

"Sure, Andy, I have room to hold them for a couple of weeks."

I was gripped with panic. If I had over-ordered, what would I do? I felt myself start to freeze, just as I had frozen when I first contemplated this job. But I had to deal with this. I had to find a way to free myself from this fear of making a mistake. I made a decision that I would have to treat each day as if it was possibly my last. I would do my best, make the decisions that had to be made, and if I made a serious mistake and got fired, then I would have to feel satisfied that I had done my best. It was an easier shift in my mind than I thought it would be. My survival strategy was coming together; think of the house in pieces and try to avoid imagining its magnitude, delegate more and live each day as if it were my last. I hoped this would be enough.

DOMINIC BRUNEL'S ROOFING CREW soon arrived, ready to tackle the massive pile. I met the foreman, explained the delicate situation with the other crew still on the job and asked him to begin right in front so that visible progress could be seen from the driveway. His crew erected ladders and scaffolding, pulled back the blue tarp and began running courses of shingles on the lowest part of the roof, three stories off the ground.

I loved to find any excuse to climb onto the roof and admire both their work and the magnificent view. Beyond the farm fields and forest below, I could see Long Island Sound fifteen miles away. Although the roof was higher than any roof I had been on, I felt safe because the roof structure was not made of smooth sheets of plywood, but of wooden slats with spaces between them where I could secure my feet.

"The spacing," the roofing foreman explained, "Is so the wooden shingles can dry from both sides. If they don't breathe, they'll hold moisture and rot."

"In fact," one of the crew explained, "On a dry sunny day, you should see sunlight from inside the attic of a shingle roof. If you don't, the shingles are too close together and will buckle when they get wet and expand."

One afternoon, I found the bags of insulation for filling the beams in the main stairwell. Throwing one over my shoulder, I found my way to the tarp covered ridge, straddled it with one leg on either side and inched my way out to the peak of the cone. I cut through the plastic and found the opening to pour the bag's contents. After emptying the bag, I repeated the procedure, crawling back, getting another bag and straddled my way out along the peak.

On the final bag, I finished dumping its contents just as a strong gust of wind whipped up. It lifted the tarp off the roof with me attached and I instinctively pinched my thighs. But I was airborne, separated from my physical connection to the ground. It lasted only a second, but my heart leapt in my throat. I looked down to the ground and imagined how painful, if not fatal, the fall might be. I inched my way back along the ridge, found more secure footing on a section where the roofers had pulled back the tarp, and gained a newfound respect for the height of this ridge. At least it happened on the last bag, I thought. I wasn't sure I could summon the nerve to do it again.

As I sat quietly, trying to collect my wits, I looked to my side and eyed down the line of shingles the roofers had just finished nailing off. To my shock, they weren't straight! In fact, none of the courses were straight. The crew wasn't even using a straight edge. I watched as they nailed them down freehand. Forgetting my previous panic, I climbed over to the foreman, "What's up? Those courses're crooked."

"No one's gonna be able to see 'em up here. What difference does it make?"

I looked at the foreman in firm resolve. "I want 'em straight."

"That'll take too long," he protested.

"That's not my problem, is it? Look at this house. Do you really think we're gonna accept second-rate quality?" I had no qualms about pushing him. "We have a contract and that contract calls for a quality roof. So that's what I want."

"Have it your way."

Nothing more was said. The next day, a new crew arrived on the site.

"Hey, where're the other guys?" I asked as I greeted them.

"Oh, Dom said you weren't happy with their work. So he sent us to replace them."

I hadn't thought that replacement was necessary. I simply thought they needed to slow down and do better work. But at lunch, the new roofing foreman said, "You were wise to get rid of that other crew. They're Dom's condo crew.

They work fast but their quality sucks. I'll bet Dom sent 'em because this roof is so damn big. It's like an office building." Then he shook his head, "I sure hope Dom bid this right or he's gonna take a bath. Damn, this is big!"

Mike was sitting nearby and chimed in, "Yeah, you gotta watch out for those condo crews. I've seen them do some things that'd make your hair curl. I was on this one project, right? A standard piece of shit townhouse development. Everything was fast. We wasted no time on anything that'd slow us down. We used nail guns on everything, even the trim and asphalt roofing."

The roofing foreman shook his head. "Oh, pneumatic nailing on asphalt shingles is tricky. You've gotta get the pressure just right or you'll blow right through 'em. And the stiffness of the shingle changes with the temperature so you have to keep adjusting the pressure all day."

"Well this guy didn't care about that kind of shit," Mike continued. "Just get it up. That's all he cared about. I watched him cut out the rough openings for the windows and doors with a chainsaw. It worked but it was nasty." He laughed and then continued. "But the shittiest piece of work I ever saw was when he went to sell 'em. They were rushed to completion and put on the market in late December. I think he wanted to start payin' off his loans before the new year. Anyway, three nights before they were to be shown, there was this serious cold snap. The foundation was built badly, poor drainage underneath. And to make matters worse, the cheapskate didn't wanna pay for heat until the last minute, so he shut the furnace off. With the deep frost, the water under the floor slab froze and lifted the floor and the whole center of one of the units about an inch. Everything came up, from the basement floor right to the fuckin' ridge. You could see it in every floor; the floor humped, the sheetrock cracked." He laughed again, "So what did this asshole do? He cut the lolly column off by an inch! The whole house dropped back down, the sheetrock and flooring was reworked and the unit was sold to some poor yuppie who didn't know any better. Sure enough, the new owner complained in the spring when the ice thawed and the house sank back down the inch he cut off. What an asshole!"

LUCY SHAW MADE her first visit to the jobsite, arriving in a small, unassuming Toyota. We exchanged quick hellos before she got down to business. There were some things she wanted to discuss and she was very direct. I dutifully followed her with my notepad as she led me upstairs and began walking through some of the partially framed rooms. Kenneth's crew watched as we passed.

"Okay, look at this closet here. I think it's too deep." We walked to the adjacent room. "I want you to move this wall further into this room and create less space for the closet in that room." Before I could finish writing down what she wanted, much less comment, she said she wanted to discuss some designs in the guest bedroom.

"Of course," I replied, and followed her as she was already on her way.

She stopped, smiled back at me and then continued to the guest room. Pointing to the bathroom, she said, "I'm not sure I like where this bathroom's going. I think it's too small and awkward."

"I can talk to the architects if you like," I said.

"Yes, tell them this needs to be redesigned."

"Do you have some ideas about what you might like?"

"Well, I'm not sure. But, for one thing, it uses the only window on this wall and I think I'd rather have the window in the bedroom than the bathroom."

"That makes sense. People'll spend more time in the bedroom than the bathroom so why not use the window there."

Again she smiled. "Well, this seems a simple problem for Robert. I'm sure he can work it out."

"I'll follow up on it."

We spent two hours discussing changes that she must have been mulling for weeks. Through it all, I could tell that I was scoring points. Later that afternoon, Jack confirmed my assessment. "Hey Stuff, I talked to Lucy this afternoon and she says you were a perfect gentleman."

"She's gonna be a lot more involved than Maura was. I think it must have driven her crazy to be excluded the way she was."

"I'll bet it was frustrating for Bill too. Once Kenneth's crew's out of there, be sure to build those stairs for him to see the second floor. You got that?"

"Sure Jack, I've got it."

"Have you got everything else under control there?" Jack seemed happy.

"Yup, everything's going fine here."

"Good, you got 'em fooled for another day."

BY THE SECOND WEEK, the house was showing dramatic signs of progress. Dominic's crew was adding fresh, blonde cedar shingles to an expanding section of roof. And Riley's crew had framed the walls of the garage and was ready for the second floor trusses to be put into place. They were too heavy for the men to lift, so I called in a crane to do the job. It arrived early and Riley located his carpenters to guide the pieces into place and nail them down. The entire task took only two hours and the crane then lifted a stack of plywood on top so that the crew could begin laying the decking of what would be the servant's quarters over the garage. As I watched the final drop, I glanced at the main house to see the roofers approaching a hole in the roof that would force them to stop. It awaited the eyebrow skylight that Kenneth's crew was building in the Great Room.

I realized that we would never be able to lift it by hand, given its weight and size, so I found Arthur, pointed to the roof and said, "Can you help me put the skylight in place? We need to do it now while the crane's here."

Arthur, with his usual economy of words, shrugged, "Sure."

I ran into the Great Room to find two of Kenneth's senior carpenters standing by the skylight smoking pipes and talking.

"I'm gonna install this now," I announced. The abruptness and certainty of my announcement startled us both. I was just acting on necessity and they just stood back to watch me taking measurements. "Can you tell me where you'd lift it from?"

They pointed vaguely at the top struts of the curve.

"If I cut a hole here and here and ran a strap through, would that hold?" I had marked two spots with my pencil.

"I guess so," one answered, clearly displeased with my brash entry. I needed to take advantage of the crane. And with the skylight in place, the roofers could continue their progress uninterrupted. Valuable time would be saved.

"Arthur, can you give me a hand?" From the moment I announced that the skylight was going into place to the moment we lifted it out into the sunlight was less than fifteen minutes.

Arthur cut holes where I had marked while I guided the crane into place. We attached a strap to lift it and a long rope for me to guide it. Arthur climbed to the attic to guide it into place from there. Looking up as it rose, I was suddenly aware that if Kenneth's carpenters were wrong about where to lift the frame and the piece dropped, it would be smashed. That would be hugely embarrassing and costly. I moved away from my position directly beneath it. Once the guide rope was out of my hands, Arthur took control from the attic, and I climbed up to help.

"I'll just take a taste off this side to fit it into place," Arthur said.

Feeling giddy, I asked, "Is a taste more or less than a cunt hair?"

To my surprise, Arthur laughed, something he rarely did. It was a quiet subdued laugh. "A taste is what I like to get from a cunt hair."

He leaned over the edge of the roof, spit his chewing tobacco, and then trimmed a quarter inch off the side of the frame. It fit into place and Arthur and I secured it. Below, I noticed Saunders' men watching it go in and, if I was not mistaken, they had admiration in their eyes.

THAT WAS MY FINAL MEMORY of Kenneth's crew, a fitting end to their involvement, watching the fruit of their labor get finished exactly as they had designed it to happen. The next day was their last and I felt no sentimentality at their departure. My biggest fear, a confrontation between crews, never happened, and like the long awaited release of pent up curiosity, my crew finally got the chance to tour the rest of the house. I set up an office in the study; power, a phone, a table for laying out the plans and a rack for storing them.

Our presence was now total. The roof was in transition from the blue of the tarps to the tan of the cedar shingles. The eastern wing was going up with the lightly colored, new wood that stood in stark contrast to the weathered plywood of the western side of the house. To make this older end more inviting, Mike and I cut out the holes for the windows, transforming the exterior from a large blank plywood wall into the complex texture of a real house. The window openings became like the eyes on an otherwise blank face that brought sunshine into the interior of the house, transforming it from a shadowy world of darkness and moisture to a welcoming environment of moving air and light. Masons were brought in to build the stone veneer on the house's foundation, using field stones from the many walls that laced the property.

With the many trades on the job, I reveled in the activity. I felt as though the job was alive. Every bit of energy and activity that enlivened the space brought the house closer to what it would eventually become. Sounds came from all directions. And so did questions. "Where do we put these materials? What do the plans say about this? We need to get the architect's clarification on that? When will the redwood arrive?" I found myself at the center, the hub of all this activity and I loved it. I was surprised at my ability to answer many of the architectural questions without consulting the plans. And when I couldn't, I would hike back to my office and look it up.

But there were also gaps in the plans, places where a detail had been overlooked, or separate details that did not agree with either each other or the actualities of the jobsite. And for these inevitabilities, a phone call to Los Angeles and Peter, Robert's assistant, became a regular part of my day. I sensed from Peter that my questions were a welcome change from what had apparently been infrequent and contentious calls from Kenneth. I called often, requiring Peter to come to his Los Angeles office early to accommodate the time difference between the two coasts. I asked him everything and anything I could think of, any detail, major or minor so as to establish our relationship as partners in this process. I knew that many of the questions were extremely precise, if not picky, but I was signaling to Peter that he would be kept in the loop on any architectural decisions made on the job. We began to develop a friendship over the phone, talking often.

IN MAY, ROBERT AND PETER decided that they would make their first inspection of the jobsite. Jack made a point of being at this first meeting as well. When they pulled onto the site in their rented car and got out, Peter and I shook hands quickly, laughing that we finally had a face to match with the voice. But behind us, the house was too much of a distraction for small talk. Peter and Robert began walking towards it, seemingly mesmerized by their ideas taking physical form. I felt proud for being responsible for so much change since we took over. As we walked, they discussed how their intentions for a certain detail were playing out. At other times, I would stop the walk to ask for clarification on what was to take place. They kept complimenting the progress while at the same time calling attention to how this was much better than what was happening under Kenneth.

As we walked around to the front turrets, we came upon the masons. I tapped the masonry foreman, Roland, on the shoulder and introduced him to Peter and Robert.

"I hope you like what you see here," he smiled.

But they didn't. Something was wrong. Robert was staring intently at the stone work that had begun. It only climbed to about three feet over a span of ten feet, but he was clearly concerned. We were all silent as Robert and Peter talked quietly to each other.

Finally, Robert started. "The physical elements of these stones were supposed to suggest the idea of carrying the structure."

Peter continued. "Yes, we had hoped that this would be a transition from the rich and irregular organic materials of the New England farm field to the turn-of-the-century geometry of the building."

"Yes, this is a transition," repeated Robert. "It can't look like a mosaic. It must look as though it were supporting everything, literally growing out of the ground."

They turned back to Roland and awaited a response. But Roland looked perplexed, the pride in his stonework turning to defensiveness. With a clear note of annoyance, he turned to me and asked, "What the fuck did they just say?"

I stifled a laugh, but no one else smirked.

"I think they want you to change your style," I said, looking to Robert for encouragement. "If I have this right, think of a dry-wall. The stones rest on top of each other without mortar. They're held in place by gravity. It looks natural. Would it be possible to have the walls have that effect? Can they be less smooth? Can you use stones that have a bit more irregularity to them and make them look like they've been here for a long time, stacked one on top of the other?" To sum up, I concluded, "Maybe you could think about mimicking the shape of the stone walls you took these from?"

"Yes, that's a good suggestion," Robert said.

"So you want me to do a sloppier job?" Roland asked, still annoyed.

"No," I said, trying to turn this from criticism of his work to a suggestion for a different style. "Think of doing a sidewalk of pavers. They would all lie flat, the joints would be tight and the pieces would fit together in a perfect mosaic. This should not look like a sidewalk of pavers turned on its side. It should look more like a stone wall where each stone is carried by the ones below and carrying the ones above."

"I think I see," said Roland. "You want it to look structural and you want it to look old, like a stone foundation built-in the eighteen hundreds."

"Just like it was built at the same time as these other stone walls, and maybe even by the same hand," Peter added excitedly.

Roland added, "Would you like me to keep the moss on the stones we pull out?"

"That would be great," Robert said.

"I'll give it a try. We have to acid wash this when we're done, but I can try to keep it alive."

"Great, I think we've got it. This conversation alone made the visit worth the trip."

I patted Roland on the shoulder as Robert, Peter and Jack continued the tour. Roland rolled his eyes. "If that's what he wanted, why the fuck didn't he just say so?" He shook his head and announced the now familiar refrain, "fuckin' Architects!"

BACK AT THE WINSLOW HOUSE, I found Dennis installing some final pieces of trim in the master bedroom.

"How's it going here?" I asked in an upbeat way.

"Man, we're trudgin' along."

"Trudging? That's not a good word."

"Maybe not, but it's accurate. Benjamin has us cuttin' our joints so you can't slip a piece of paper between them. And he's checking our reveals with a depth gauge. I know we're supposed to produce high quality, but there are some things that're necessary and some things that are over the top. This is over the top."

"Hmmm. Let me talk to Benjamin."

I found Benjamin in the kitchen. "Hey, we need to get you guys done and out of here. The Shaw job awaits!" I was still upbeat. "Can you lighten up on your standards and maintain a level of quality you're happy with?"

"Sure," Benjamin said slowly. "We can loosen up. I just need to know what you want from me. I erred on the side of extra detail. But, if you want to loosen up, just tell me how much."

He was looking for a definitive answer. "Benjamin, I need you out of here. These guys can give you good joinery in a reasonable amount of time. This trim's gonna be painted, so it doesn't have to be furniture quality."

"You bet. I'll take care of it," he said, showing no sign of annoyance.

I continued to walk the job, inspecting the progress. Outside, Maurizio was hard at work on his gardens. I liked to watch him work. He had a joy in building that I admired. He thought about every stone he placed. In fact, he would study an entire pile of stones and carefully choose each one for the location it would occupy. That afternoon he excitedly called me out to the garden. I was expecting a discussion of some important design issue in the blueprints when he proclaimed, "Look at my butterfly."

"Huh?" I asked.

"Look at my butterfly," Maurizio repeated excitedly, pointing to the wall.

There, in the stone veneer of the wall, was indeed a butterfly. Maurizio had split two stones to make two perfectly matched pairs of wings. Between them was a single stone to form the body. It was beautiful, a detail that reflected Maurizio's love for his work and one which could easily be overlooked by the house's future owner. I myself would not likely have noticed it unless it was pointed out. But once pointed out, it was obvious. Maurizio was truly an artisan.

BACK AT THE SHAW HOUSE, Riley's crew was moving along nicely, framing the rafters of the garage roof and the four, hipped dormers on the front (two pitched sides and a pitched front) and the three shed dormers on the back (one pitch that slopes towards the front). He was now taking a crew around the corner of the house to frame the walls of the gym and indoor pool which would connect the east servant's quarters wing to the main house. Once the pool room was framed, it would be time for the redwood truss roof.

Riley, Arthur and I met in the Great Room—now empty of its contents—to discuss this next phase. In front of us, the truss was drawn in full scale on the wall. The project involved both structural framing and finish carpentry at the same time. We needed a competent and steady hand. Arthur was clearly the most skilled finish carpenter on the crew and I knew that they had been discussing this next phase as much as I was thinking about it.

When asked, Riley didn't hesitate. "By all means, Arthur's the man for this job."

Arthur was stoic, quietly chewing his tobacco. I could never really tell if he didn't care or if he was simply not good at showing his emotions. "Arthur, you have any need for these wall drawings? Kenneth must've put a lot of time into making them."

"Shit no! Why would someone go through all that trouble? They'd be more of a pain in the ass than they're worth."

"Then how do you want to set up for building them?"

"I'll build 'em on their sides right next to the pool room. I'll build one on top of the other and we can use a crane to lift 'em into place." Arthur was using an economy of words as always, limiting his conversation only to the simple facts.

"Show me where you wanna build 'em and where you want the lumber delivered. I can have it here tomorrow." Then I added, "You know, we'll have to keep this redwood covered up or it'll turn black if it gets wet."

Arthur looked at me with a sarcastic frown. "Yes, Andy, I know."

Chastened, I continued, "Do either of you have any objection if I take charge of the second eyebrow skylight?"

Riley smiled, "Be my guest. I've been thinking about that for days and would be glad not to have to worry about it."

I felt a need to prove my carpentry skills to the crew. The second eyebrow skylight would sit over the pool roof. But this one was far larger than the one on the main house, measuring thirty-eight feet from end to end. The custom window had already been bought by Kenneth and was sitting in the living room awaiting a frame to put it in. I'd been eyeing it for days, considering how to build it. It excited me to consider the possibilities. I admired how Kenneth's work resembled an airplane cowling and hoped to do the same, bringing my early childhood hobby of balsa wood planes to such a large scale.

"Great, can I take Mike to help me?" I had grown to like Mike, he was young, energetic and what he lacked in experience, he more than made up for in enthusiasm and a desire to learn. He reminded me of myself.

"Sure," Riley replied. "He'll be flattered you picked him. He's a good choice, a bright kid."

MIKE AND I BUILT a full-scale mock-up of the pool room roof in the center of the house and then built a thirty-eight-foot arched beam to frame the top of the opening of the window. Using trigonometry and my calculator, I developed a list of thirty-nine triangular trusses that would carry the beam from above, twelve inches on center. The horizontal members would carry the ceiling inside the eyebrow. A steeply sloping member would rest on the roof of the pool and the member connecting the two would form the roof of the eyebrow. Each truss had a different set of dimensions, building from small on the edges to the largest in the center and then decreasing in size back to the smallest. For each, I calculated three dimensions, one for each member, and handed the list to Mike.

After an hour, Mike returned, frustrated.

"Andy, I can't get your plans to work. I built the members to your dimensions, but they don't fit together."

I groaned, realizing again how the precision of my engineering calculations clashed with the imprecision of wooden realities. "Okay, forget this third dimension here," I said scratching a line through the last column in my truss chart. "Just build to these two dimensions and let this third one be whatever it's gonna be."

THREE TEAMS NOW WORKED toward the same goal. Arthur's team built the trusses, stacking them one on top of another. Riley's men built the walls on which the trusses were to stand, with notches every six feet for each truss to fit into. And Mike and I built the eyebrow to sit on top of the whole structure. A deadline for the first two was set with the planned arrival of a crane.

It took only two hours to drop each truss into its resting place and the entire crew stood back to admire its beauty. Eight trusses, each twenty-four feet wide and twelve feet tall, stood at successive attention. They were beautiful ribs of wood awaiting their skin of a roof. Lacking any knots, the grain was a smooth wave of gentle color differences. The redwood had no strong lines or dark strands but rather a smooth, soft hue. And more than the color, the wood itself looked physically soft, very different from the harder look of oak or fir. The edges were gently curved, not sharp. The precision of the truss bolts gave the assembly extra beauty, creating the image much like the machine look of a truss bridge.

The next step was to build the roof in reverse. The purlins were installed to link the trusses together. Then, the ceiling of one-by-six redwood was installed, followed by insulation and then the outer roof. On top of the roof, I would install the eyebrow and the roofers would then cover the whole thing in cedar shingles. Until that final step of protection, the redwood roof had to be kept protected from any rain.

But, with the trusses in place and the final form of the roof defined, another problem emerged.

"PETER, WE'VE GOT AN ISSUE on the back of the house. It has to do with the way the pool room wing meets the main house. If you'll go to the east elevation section on drawing A.7, you'll see that it shows the pool room ridgeline meeting the main house just below the band of trim mid-way up the wall. It doesn't. It meets the house two feet higher."

"Oops," Peter chuckled. "That seems minor enough. I don't see a problem."

"Yeah, but the problem is at the lower end. As near as I can tell, someone made these drawings based on trusses that were smaller than what were actually spec'd. So, it comes higher at the top, but it also comes lower at the bottom."

"Show me. I don't understand."

"If you'll go to drawing A.6.2 and look at the southern elevation, draw the roof hang of the pool room at a level one foot lower than what is drawn."

After a moment, he said. "Oh, that's more serious."

"Yeah, and this'll screw up the runoff of the roofs, the door on the western end of the wall, the way the roof meets the gym roof on the eastern end and the way the overhang meets the main house in drawing A.7.1."

"Okay, now I'm concerned. I'm gonna need a little time to work this one out."

We discussed a few more drawings, confirming how real life contradicted what was planned, and Peter said he'd bring the matter to Robert.

Later that afternoon, he called to say that Robert was planning to fly to the northeast anyway and would come to the house that weekend. "Can you be available?"

"Sure, no problem."

"Can you see if Jack can be available too? Robert thinks this merits his attention too."

ON SATURDAY, Robert, Jack and I met at the dormant jobsite. I had the carpenters snap chalk lines where the finished pool roof would meet the house. The problem was plainly evident. They also built me a simple mockup of the roof truss tail as it would jut out from the poolroom on the other end. This showed how the detail was going to differ from that drawn. Robert just stared at the problem, throwing out suggestions. "Can we raise the trusses to fix this?"

"That'll interfere with the guest room windows," I said. "And they'll still miss the gym roof."

"Can we slide them to the north?" Robert tried again.

"That'll throw them off center with the pool room."

Robert continued to ponder the problem. It was becoming clear that there would be no simple solution. "I'll get back to you. We'll have to discuss this back in the office."

"You can't wait too long. We need to get that redwood covered so it doesn't get stained by rain."

"Is there anything you can do to buy us some time?" Robert asked.

"Will you let me start roofing from the center? Can we agree right now that those trusses stay where they are and we can finish the middle portion while you guys work out the ends?"

Jack smiled at me. I had taken charge of the conversation, giving quick answers and offering constructive suggestions for dealing with the problem. And my quick answers were giving Robert some consternation which Jack seemed to enjoy.

"Yes," Robert offered, really having no choice. "Start from the middle, we'll work out the ends. When do you need an answer?"

"I need something by the beginning of next week, or we're gonna start backing up on each other."

"Agreed. I'll have your answer by Monday."

We filled the next half hour touring the job site and the meeting came to an end. Robert suggested Jack and he go for lunch, adding, "There are some other things I'd like to discuss with you."

Jack turned to me. "Are you free for another hour or two, Stuff?"

"Sure, I've got nothing going on."

At the restaurant Robert expressed his pleasure at the progress of the job. Jack returned the praise in equal measure. It was a casual and relaxing lunch, sharing thoughts on the transition between contractors and the shifting state of mind of the Shaws.

Then Robert turned serious and said, "But there's something we need to talk about Jack. Bill's becoming uneasy with the growth in costs."

Jack's tone adjusted quickly to meet Robert's. "Well, I appreciate your concern, but trust me, this job's going along just as it ought to be."

Robert persisted. "Well Jack, you guys are doing a first-class job and I don't want to diminish that, but we need to find a way to cut costs. The budget is starting to go beyond projections."

"Whose projections? Your projections?" Jack asked. "I'll tell you something, this job was out of control before we got here. You just didn't know it yet because there was such bad management."

I pulled back and watched, unable to tell if Jack was mad or not. And I also couldn't tell if his retort was meant as a jab at Robert or Kenneth. But now I waited for him to take charge of the meeting with Robert.

"Well, Jack, we need to find a way to cut back on costs and you can help us or not. But if you want to talk about management, I can show you where your contract holds you responsible for that mistake on the pool roof."

My heart began to race. This was the architect's mistake, not ours! There was no way we could be held responsible for the problem unless we were expected to cross check all the drawings before the house was built. That would have been impossible.

But Jack just ignored the threat. "Robert, this job's on budget. I can appreciate that Bill's getting a little nervous right now. The money's flowing, that's true. And a lot more will flow before this is done. But if he wants the house you designed, then he's gonna have to spend some money to get it. We went through the same thing in Nantucket. I don't know what your arrangement is with Bill. And I don't know what your estimates were before things got started, but I'm not gonna be held by them. I didn't agree to that."

"Jack, are we supposed to exercise no cost control over your work? Is that what you're suggesting?"

"I'm not suggestin' anything. All I know is my contract is with Bill. It's not with you. If Bill has a problem with how I'm runnin' the job, then he can come and tell me. Until I hear that, I'll proceed as if he's happy. If you think my costs are too high, I'm not really concerned. Maybe your projections were too low? Maybe your percentage is what needs to be cut? Did you ever think about that?"

Robert was now annoyed. "Jack, our percentage is right in line with AIA standards. There's no problem there."

"Good, if my numbers are good and your numbers are in line with AIA standards, then things are going along as they should be." He paused and began again, "Robert, I hear your concern. The house is expensive and Bill's nervous. So that makes you nervous because you gave him some numbers that may be missed. Relax. Bill's no fool. He knows he's got to pay for quality. And you've designed a first-class house. Right now, there're naturally going to be some expenses. It's always expensive to change contractors mid-stream. But in the end, he's gonna get a house that he'll be happy with. And that's what's most important. It may cost him more, but he's not losing any more sleep over his contractor. And in the end, the customer will always forget a high price before he forgets poor quality."

Robert nodded and acquiesced. We finished our lunch talking about other things.

After Robert left, Jack turned to me in the parking lot and erupted. "Did you see that bullshit? Robert's squirmin' cause his cost estimates are off. That's no surprise. What do architects know about costing a job? I'll tell you what they fuckin' know. Nothing! There's no way I'm gonna be held to his price estimates. I'd lose my shirt."

"But what about his comment that we could be held liable for this mistake on the pool roof?"

"Bullshit. That's an empty threat. I'll bury his ass if he thinks he can pull that off. He was just tryin' to bait me. I wasn't gonna fall for it. He thinks he can yank me around? Well, I've got news for him. He can't! I have an understanding with Bill. Do you know what that means? Robert doesn't run this project for Bill. I do. And if push comes to shove, Robert is expendable, we're not. I know that. Bill knows that. The only one who doesn't know that is Robert. But if he pulls that shit again, he'll sure as hell find out!"

PETER FAXED THE POOL ROOF solution to Jack's office on Monday. It was a simple set of drawings that showed how the roof would step up at the ends, bringing it in line with their original locations. It was a clean detail, I thought; an elegant solution that no one would see as a cover-up. Work could proceed uninterrupted.

The pool roof was completed and the eyebrow was finished and disassembled for reassembly in its final resting spot. On the ground, I fed the pieces to the crew in the order they were needed. As the frame was completed, I looked with pride at its curving shape. It looked like an airplane cowling, just like Kenneth's eyebrow did. The carpenters put in a few final bolts and nails to secure it in place. I had prepared for this moment by having my camera ready.

"Hey everyone, move towards the center and stand on the frame. I want to take a picture."

The guys cautiously stepped onto the frame. But Arthur was reluctant. Slowly he put one foot on, then another until the entire crew was balanced two stories off the ground, atop a row of trusses that cantilevered off the roof. I snapped the picture, intending it as a rival for Jack's picture of pickup trucks on the first floor deck of the Rogers house. Clearly, this was a comparable feat.

As the crew climbed back down to return to their other work, a car pulled into the driveway. I watched out of the corner of my eye as two men got out. They made their way around the house and walked toward me.

"You Andy?" the taller of the two asked.

Still trying to direct Mike in some final steps in the eyebrow, I answered, "Yeah, that's me. What can I do for you?"

"We're lookin' for work and were wondering if you could use more help." The taller one again doing the talking. The shorter one seemed reluctant.

"How'd you hear that?"

"Some of your guys told us. We just drove out from Colorado."

The shorter one, now seemed very uncomfortable. "Come on. He's really busy now. Don't bother him."

"Are you too busy to talk now? Should we come back later?" the taller one asked.

"No, I can talk. This is pretty much set."

I called out some final instructions to Mike and then turned to the two men before me. "So you came out from Colorado? How many other guys're out there lookin' for work?" I meant this as a joke but neither of the two men laughed.

"I'm not sure. Times're tough out there. And no one's building anything like this."

"What're your names?" I asked.

"I'm Herman and," pointing to the shorter man, "this is Walt."

Herman was balding on top with short blond hair on the sides. He had blue eyes and spoke politely and clearly. Walt was rougher, had several days growth on his face, wore his hair in a pony tail and wrapped a bandana around his brow.

"And who do you know on the job?"

"We both know Riley and Dennis pretty well. We've worked with 'em on a couple of jobs and I went to high school with Dennis."

"So you know carpentry?"

Walt now spoke, "We've been around for a long time. This is one impressive bit of work ya got going here. I've never done work quite like this, but I assure you we can handle it."

I had not planned on hiring more men but liked the idea of increasing the size of the crew. There was a lot of work to be done. And, I felt, these guys from Colorado were more experienced than what I had seen of the local carpenters. "Lemme think it over. Can you come back tomorrow around this time?" As a formality I got strong endorsements from Riley and Dennis.

Jack left it to me to decide. "It's your crew," was all he said.

The next day, they were hired.

I JOKED WITH JACK that this job gave me both the source of my frustration and a way for me to work it out. If a subcontractor was being uncooperative, a material order was wrong or late, or the architects were making changes, I could grab my tool belt and "go pound nails" to work out my frustrations.

And, while I was satisfied with the progress at the Shaw house, Benjamin was still exacting very strict controls on the work at the Winslow House and they were squeezing productivity.

"Benjamin, I need you out of here," I said emphatically. "The painters are right behind you and they're soon going to catch you. And then I need to arrange the floor finishers to come in. That means you need to give me a date when you'll be out. What's your estimate?"

"Well," he said, deep in thought while kicking a nearby sawhorse, "I think we could have this wrapped up in three weeks."

Without hesitation, I replied, "not good enough. This needs to be done in two."

Ever pragmatic, he answered, "Andy, I can have this done anytime you want. It all depends on the level of quality you want."

I was unequivocal. "Benjamin, I want you out in two weeks. I'll plan on letting the painters have the whole house on June first and then giving the house to the floor finishers on June sixth."

"If that's what you want, Andy, that's what you'll have." There was no defensiveness in Benjamin's reply. He stated it as a simple fact. The date was set. And with it, so was the level of Benjamin's quality.

The crew finished on time and my plan to turn the house over to the floor finishers was met. It was mid-summer and the house was nearing completion. Barry Sutton wrapped up the grading of the topsoil and spreading grass seed. A generator was installed for backup power in case of a blackout. And Maurizio put the finishing touches on the Japanese gardens. Aside from a small punch list, the house was complete. The carpenters could now rejoin the rest of the crew on the Shaw house.

BENJAMIN AND HIS CREW merged with the Shaw job easily. The crews were divided up and I had them working in four groups in four different areas of the house. All had the same objective—get the house dried in.

One crew installed windows where the roof was complete. I preceded them by marking precise centers where the windows would go. Many of them were part of a long string of windows, necessitating precise distances between them and precise heights to set them. I used a builder's level to measure the height of each rough sill plate to make sure that windows would be shimmed to the same exact height.

Another crew built a covered walkway just outside the indoor pool; starting with the eight-by-eight redwood posts that had arrived from California and building the redwood roof on top of them.

A third crew installed the strapping that would support the final shingles on the garage.

And the fourth team built the redwood roof overhang on the eastern wing. Four-by-eight redwood outriggers were attached to the ends of the rafters. Roof vents were slid between them—pieces of clear redwood with four screened holes, each measuring an inch and a half in diameter. These allowed air to travel under the cedar shingles and help them dry after a rain. Trimming this assembly, a two-by-ten redwood fascia board ran along the outer edge of the roof. And over it all was attached two-by-four tongue and groove redwood to complete the detail. The first corner of this assembly was built as a test. It was beautiful, but…

"Riley, those're wrong," It sounded more blunt than I intended. But the vent pattern was wrong. Rather than the four circles forming a square, they formed a rectangle. It was different from the vents that the Saunders' crew had built on parts of the main house already.

"Huh, what're you talkin' about?" he said defensively.

"Come here," I led him around to a part of the house already completed. "See this pattern, you're supposed to drill those holes in a square."

"Fuck! Goddammit! I'll rip it out." Riley was angry.

"No, wait," I said, surprised at Riley's disproportionate reaction. "This is the furthest corner of the house. It's a minor mistake." Then I said with authoritative finality, "It would be a waste of labor and materials to rip it out and do it again. Leave it." I knew that this was suggesting a compromise in the plans, but the job needed to keep moving. Recounting something I had heard once on the Rogers' house, "The ancient Greeks would always build a flaw into their sculptures so they wouldn't offend the gods. This'll be our nod to the gods."

Riley had trouble suppressing his anger. He stormed off, an edge to his step that showed he was still angry. I wondered if he was more affected by the project than I had originally thought.

His crew wrapped up the overhang detail on the east wing, allowing the roofers to devote larger crews to the project. With each square foot of shingles installed, more roof was covered, more space was dried in and the shingle pile was drawing down. The shingles waiting at Gregory's lumberyard had weighed heavily on my mind every day that they sat there. I monitored the rate of shingle consumption daily. And it was slowly becoming clear that my numbers were not off. With enormous relief, I finally calculated that I would not be responsible for selling a large amount of roof shingles on the Fairfield County market and called Kevin to tell him the news.

"That's too bad, Andy," he laughed. "The price of shingles has been going up and I could have unloaded these for a tidy profit!"

AFTER THE FLOOR was finished at the Winslow house, I brought a small crew back for the punch list. Before entering the house, everyone took off his shoes at the front door. The jobsite was no longer a place where the carpenters were leaving their marks, but rather a place where their desire was to leave no marks at all.

Painters were putting finishing touches on the walls and baseboard. Electricians put final outlet and switch plates on the walls. Carpenters installed brass towel bars, curtain rods, door hardware and other finishing touches in each room. The rooms were a pleasure. They smelled of drying paint and stain. The wooden floors were smooth on my stocking feet and shiny, glistening really. The carpeted floors were soft rich pile. The cabinets smelled of fresh wood. Sounds carried with an echo. The eight-foot solid doors, in particular, made a deep click as their latches caught against the brand new brass strike plates. With that click, the room was complete both physically and, for me, mentally. It was released from my consciousness, liberating much-needed attention for other tasks.

Some special finishing tasks were completed personally by me. If Maura wanted a particularly heavy painting hung, I took care of it, being sure to hit a stud or top plate with the hanging bracket. In many locations, blocking was added just for this contingency; in the center of walls or fireplaces for pictures, around windows for curtain rods, in bathrooms for towel bars.

One project lay dormant until I worked up the nerve to finish it. This one Jack told me specifically to supervise. A curved alcove had been specially built-in the dining room to display an ancient, three-foot tall bronze Buddha from China. Waiting in the space was a stand built by the cabinet makers on which it would sit. Carefully, Benjamin and I opened the packing crate, revealing the finely detailed Buddha within. I did not know how old it was but, judging by both the decay in the back of the statue and the cost of the alcove, I was sure it was very old and perhaps even priceless.

Looking at Benjamin, I conveyed the import of our task. "If we drop this thing, we pick up our tools, go to our cars and just start driving, got that?"

Benjamin nodded, "No shit."

Dimensions, measurements and positioning were checked and rechecked. When we were sure that we were set, we lifted the Buddha carefully into place.

"Move it a little to the left. Okay, now a little forward." We were afraid to finally let go and place our trust in the stand. When we finally judged our positioning to be correct, we slowly released our aching fingers. It fit perfectly, sitting regally in the alcove.

A string of light fixtures surrounded the space to illuminate the seated figure and I wanted to see the final effect. I pulled the bulbs out of their boxes and put each in place. With a flick of the switch, the bulbs flashed in one bright moment and went out.

I called the electrician who sternly explained, "Andy, never touch halogen bulbs with your fingers. The oil from your skin burns 'em out when they're turned on. You should've known better than that! Did you burn out all twenty of them?" the electrician asked, emphasizing the magnitude of the mistake.

"Yes, all of them," I said sheepishly.

"Nice job. I'll fix it."

FOLLOWING A THOROUGH CLEANING, the Winslow house was officially complete in September. Before we could hand over the keys, the building inspector had to issue a "Certificate of Occupancy" or "CO." I walked with him as he checked the electrical outlets to make sure they worked, flushed the toilets to make sure they drained properly, turned up the thermostats to make sure that the heating and air conditioning system was responsive and searched for any unfinished business that the owner might not see. And then it was done.

After the building inspector left, I stood alone, mesmerized at both the CO in my hand and the house that stood around me. I marveled at what I had built and all that I had learned and experienced in bringing it to reality. On the Rogers house, I learned how to be a carpenter, how to use tools, apply certain tricks and build pieces of the house. But on the Winslow house, I learned how the entire house was put together. Beginning at the first stage of the foundation, I learned how each successive step built on the one before. I learned the order that the house was constructed, piece-by-piece, guided by the vision of the architect. I learned how to be a builder.

As I stood in the halls, I was alone and yet felt completely connected. The house was a part of me and I was a part of it. I didn't want to leave, preferring instead to just walk, stroll, wander and continue the feeling of accomplishment that this place poured into me. For an hour, I drifted along, noting every visible and invisible aspect of the structure, each flooding me with memories and feelings of the time that had passed; the concrete foundation, wooden structure, overhang, tree in the middle, insulation, sheetrock, everything!

I was startled back into consciousness by Jack's voice. "Hey, Stuff, is that the CO you're holding in your hand there?" Jack, suddenly present, was standing at the front door.

"Sure is! Well it's the hand written form," I said. "The official certificate will be typed up this afternoon. But we passed without a hitch."

"That's good news. Good. I'll pick it up and give it to Maura and Randy with the keys tonight. I know they're thrilled with the job." He looked around the room, "The place looks fantastic. Just fantastic." Then he turned to me and added, "You done good, Stuff. You've come a long way."

More than at any other time, I stood taller from Jack's praise. It fed my confidence, my self-esteem, adding to the joy I had been feeling for the past hour. "Thanks Jack, I feel pretty good right now. It was hard."

Turning serious, he said, "You still need to delegate more, Andy. Or you're never gonna get through this. You'll go crazy."

"Well, I've tried. It's hard when the person you delegate to, like Benjamin, is so hard to keep in line."

"I was getting nervous about his pace too. But you got him moving. What'd you say, 'get in gear or I'll fire your ass?'" Jack laughed.

I smiled. "I don't wanna fire Benjamin. He may be slow, but I trust him."

"You've said a mouthful there my friend. Trust is the most important thing in this business. That's what I've been trying to tell you." He smiled at me. "Andy, I know there're parts of this job that must be a difficult transition from the clean professional world you came from. But, I'll tell ya, I'm proud of ya." His words were said with great emphasis and I drank them in. His overt praise meant as much to me as finishing the house itself. I had come here to work for Jack and rise to the challenge of doing something I didn't know how to do. And now, I could feel gratified that I had in fact done both.

Jack continued, "I'm sure there are people who don't understand what you're doing here right now; your parents, your friends. I know what it's like to buck the path that's been set for you. I've done the same. Did you know that my father wanted me to go into the military? He had it all arranged when I was young. He sent me to military academy and had me on track to graduate from West Point. It was all set. That was the path I was supposed to take. But, when I had one semester to go, I quit. I decided I was living someone else's life and I quit. What do ya think of that?"

I couldn't imagine coming so close and walking away. I'd at least finish and then decide what to do. And I also couldn't imagine him at West Point; in a military uniform, taking orders from someone else. It completely contradicted the image I had been developing of him.

"My father never understood that. So, he quit me. I opened a gas station where I could build race cars. It was what I wanted to do. My father never once came to see me race. He thought it was beneath me. Then I started building houses, and he still wouldn't come see what I was doing. When he was in the hospital, dying, he called me to his bedside and told me that he was proud of me." Then, with a depth of emotion I'd never seen him reveal before, he said, "That son of a bitch waited until the very end to tell me that I'd done good. It was worth it to hear it, but goddamn it!" He stopped, trailing off into his own thoughts.

"Andy, you've come a long way. Some may try to tell you it's a mistake, and they may have your best interests at heart. But only you know what you need to do with your life. And if what you're doing is true and real, you'll do it well. And that's what's in your best interests."

He looked straight at me now, making his grand conclusion. "If I'd followed what my father originally wanted me to do, I'd have his endorsement but I wouldn't have my self-respect. In the end, I got both. All along, I think he respected what I was doing. He just didn't wanna admit it. Even though he told me I was wrong, I knew I was right. Stick by your idea of what's right, Andy. Believe me when I tell you; that's what success is. And in the end people will respect you because you respected yourself."

I nodded silently, feeling as though speaking would trivialize what he was conveying. I just basked in the emotion that Jack had poured out.

"Stuff, I have something here for you." He reached into his pocket and pulled out an envelope.

I looked at it and knew right away it was a bonus. I had hoped for this. Actually I had expected this. It seemed only fair. Jack's time on the job had dwindled to nearly nothing over the time I had been here. And he couldn't have done that if I hadn't taken on more myself, going from his representative on the job to his supervisor. I had anticipated a check as big as ten or twenty thousand dollars on the assumption that his profit had to be well into the six figures.

He handed me the envelope and I momentarily hesitated, not knowing whether I should open it now or wait till later.

"Go ahead and open it," he said casually.

I peeled back the flap to reveal the top of the check. It was in the amount of one week's pay. I was stunned. This was much too small an amount for what I had done for him. I tried to hide my disappointment but I suddenly felt the weight of the job slamming down on me.

"Is something wrong?" Jack asked.

I continued to look down at the envelope, tucking the check safely back inside. Softly I said, "I was expecting more than this." I was trying to suppress the deep disappointment, the feeling of betrayal that was inside me.

Jack said nothing. He just stood there as I looked down at the envelope lost in my emotions. But I didn't need to look up to know the emotion I would face from him. It was unnerving how fast we had gone from the euphoria of basking in our accomplishment to the tension of being at odds. The silence forced me to look up. And as I did, I was met with a look of anger I had never seen directed at me before. His eyes were narrowed and he was sternly staring at me, his skin flushed red. I braced.

Through gritted teeth he growled, "Well, how about if I just take that check back and tell you to go fuck yourself?"

"I put a lot into this house Jack," I said defensively. "I worked my ass off and I'm beat. This is disappointing."

"You expected more money for what you did? Correct me if I'm wrong here, but I'm under no obligation to give you a fucking thing. I paid you already, remember? This is generosity! And this is how you accept it? You know what I call this? Ungrateful, that's what I'd call this little act. Fuckin' ungrateful."

I briefly considered handing him the check back out of principle. But I knew that would only inflame him. I wished he hadn't given me anything. Too small an amount was worse than nothing at all.

Jack's voice was firm but strained. "Remember when Gary demanded that bonus for covering the windows in the rain? You were pissed. You said it was wrong to demand a bonus. Remember that? Well, that's what you're doing right now."

I turned to face him squarely and tried my best to stand erect. "I think that Gary has a different relationship with you than I do." I suddenly felt foolish at the word relationship. It was so suddenly clear that this was business for him. How many times had I heard it from him? Never trust anyone. I corrected myself. "Jack, our initial contract was for me to be your eyes and ears on this job. I only started there. I just kept on taking more until I was running this job. You don't even need to be here."

Jack just stared at me. His body was rigid and his frame leaned forward menacingly. I was completely unnerved. I wasn't really sure he wouldn't take a swing at me. I could tell it was taking great self-control for him not to.

He snarled, "This is what you're gonna do. You're gonna take that check and put it in your fuckin' pocket. Then I'm gonna get in my fuckin' car and drive away. And you're gonna think about everything I've done for you, you ungrateful son-of-a-bitch."

I put the check in my pocket. He turned, got in his car and drove away.

I climbed into my truck to head back to the Shaw house. But instead, I left the key dormant in the ignition. I sat and pondered what just happened. There had always been this tension with Jack. I had grown used to his ability to do that, to shift radically from one emotion to the other, keeping me and others off balance. But this was different. This was the most extreme he had ever gone with me. It forced me to reflect on whether I saw our relationship correctly. He always alternated between pulling me in and pushing me out. Sometimes he referred to the company as "us" or "ours." Other times it was "me" or "mine." How much would he really let me in? Maybe that was why his fight with Neil was so violent and so final. I could always sense Neil's frustration at not being closer to his father. And I could understand his anger at my seemingly getting closer than he could. Jack never hid that from him, which in itself, seemed rather callous.

I pondered what Jack and I were looking for from each other. I had felt our relationship was somewhat akin to that of a father and son. But was that reciprocated? Surely, I had felt his guiding hand like a father. But I had to recognize that he was not my father. He was a businessman, one who, by his own admission, trusted no one. And one who could be fairly cold in his business dealings; how he'd treated Neil or Max and Olaf, his threat about Red having a very unfortunate accident. I was only here because I hadn't screwed up yet; because I served his purposes. I had been taking over his business, running it for him. But now I felt that I was being taken advantage of. I felt foolish at having taken on increasing responsibilities and not once discussing those responsibilities and the appropriate compensation for each. I thought back to the Rogers house and how Neil had been running it, Jack only showing up to walk Mr. Rogers through. I recalled Neil's final words in his fight with Jack. "You never come to the job. I did everything." I assumed he was exaggerating his claim, with Jack's control taking place behind the scenes or before I got there. But now I believed that I was wrong. Jack got what he wanted. He always got what he wanted. He got his son to run one job and then fired him when he demanded fairness. I should be under no illusions that I would not get fired just as easily. I now knew where I stood with him. And more importantly, I had to decide if I wanted to stay with him. I knew I didn't want to make a hasty decision; the Shaw job was too important to me. But I had to give serious thought to how I would deal with Jack in the future. Things had to be different. They already *were* different.

JACK AND I DIDN'T TALK more about the confrontation, but our interactions were chilled. We discussed decisions, but there was less warmth. To me it seemed that this was more honest. I still loved the building; on that level I was a hopeless idealist. But I no longer idealized my relationship with Jack. I now understood it with crystal clarity. I now knew this was a business relationship. He would still give me suggestions as before, try to teach me, but I now saw these lessons as what they were; an investment in his business, helping him to make more money. It was in his own interests to train me, keep me on top of things.

It puzzled me why Jack had not simply fired me when we had our fight. I had openly confronted him much as Neil had. But I realized that Jack needed me more than he needed Neil. The Rogers house was almost done when they had their fight and Jack had been doubting Neil's capabilities for a while. Perhaps he even felt more comfortable knowing that I was in the wings. He had alternatives to Neil. He had me. I felt some regret with the realization that I had been so naïve, that I may have hastened Neil's departure.

But this situation was different. The Shaw house was barely half done, and Jack had no alternatives. I was fairly sure that he did not have a trusting relationship with anyone else on the crew, but even if he did, I really couldn't see any of these tough carpenters working with the Shaws the way that I did. The Shaws and the Winslows liked me, were comfortable with me and would surely be unhappy if I were fired. The mere fact that Jack allowed me to do the walk throughs was testament to the extent to which he relied on me, he needed me. On the whole, the job was running smoothly and he needed me to keep it running that way. Only a bad businessman would disrupt that and Jack was not a bad businessman. Now I had to think like a businessman. I had to decide how I was going to handle this new situation.

As a businessman, I began to see more clearly how my role on the job had evolved from what it had once been. Or more accurately, how *I* had evolved. I began to see that my task was not to build the house, per se. It was to manage the many relationships that made the building process proceed. Just as I had begun to gain greater clarity on my relationship with Jack, I could see that I was learning how to manage relationships in order to do my job. In fact, it was this more than anything else that helped me conquer my fear of this project. I didn't know how to do everything in building this house. But I did know how to talk to people. I realized that it was through me that all of the people involved in making the Shaw house a reality could communicate with each other. With equal clarity I could talk to and understand the distinct wants, needs and languages of the multi-millionaire owner, professional architect, carpenter, plumber, mason or laborer. I was the binding thread in this intricate web of relationships, and beyond my relationship with Jack, I parsed my energies in four primary directions: the crew, the owners, the architects and the subcontractors.

THE CREW. In managing the crew, I learned to focus on maintaining morale, eliminating deadwood, and hiring fresh blood. I hired for competence as well as satisfaction and harmony. I fired for the same. Were people getting along? Were they feeling engaged by the tasks they were given? And were they doing their job? I strived for a sense of satisfaction among the crew. Firing people was my most difficult yet most important challenge. And through the months I would repeat it many times. While my core crew remained the same, I was constantly bringing new people into the jobsite and getting rid of others.

My laborer Ron, for example, met his end on an early Monday morning. Recommended by Benjamin months earlier, his job was to move materials, keep the jobsite clean and load the dumpster. It took the crew anywhere between five and ten days to fill the thirty cubic yard steel box. It was a regular routine. But Ron had not been measuring up. He was inattentive to what he was doing, preferring instead to spend his time chatting with whomever he could find.

One morning, the truck from Danbury Carting arrived to swap the full dumpster for an empty one. From my desk, I listened for the loud harmonic ring as the empty steel container hit the ground. I was busy calculating the order of siding shingles and clapboard, another enormous order—nearly three thousand square feet of clapboard and seven thousand square feet of shingles. In the background, the low whine of the truck's pulley began dragging the full dumpster onto the flatbed. All was going as it had always gone. But then it suddenly stopped.

I waited to hear what should have happened next, a resumption of the whine as the dumpster was fully secured to the flatbed. But instead, I heard the driver cursing. "What the fuck! Who's gonna clean up this crap, because it sure as shit ain't gonna be me!"

I walked to the front door to view the scene. The dumpster door had swung open, dropping a full third of its contents onto the ground. Next to the pile, Ron and the driver were engaged in an animated discussion. I sighed, walked slowly out to the two and asked what happened. Ron looked at the ground as the driver turned his anger towards me.

"Well, I think you can see for yourself. He didn't lock the door and half of your garbage is on the ground instead of on its way to the dump." Pointing at his watch, "I've got a schedule to keep. I can't wait around while dip-shit here picks all this up." He was pointing at Ron.

"Not your problem," I said. "Let's get this door closed and get you outta here. We'll load these scraps into the new dumpster."

Surprised by my willingness to lend a hand, the driver softened his tone as all three of us began pushing scraps aside until the door was free to swing closed. It took only a few minutes. The dumpster was loaded up, the driver left and Ron and I were alone.

Pointing to the ground, I said, "Load this shit into the new dumpster." I turned and walked away.

Since Benjamin recommended him in the first place, I felt an obligation to let him know that I planned to fire Ron.

"No problem, Andy. In point of fact, I thought you might make the decision several days ago. I think he sees the writing on the wall too."

And that was it. It was all part of the jobsite rule of survival. People accepted getting fired. It was all part of the world they lived in. This time, the actual act was easy. I told Jack I was firing Ron. He didn't even ask why, wrote a final check and I gave it to Ron the next day. He thanked me for the job and apologized for the mistake with the dumpster. I wondered if he thought this one act had brought about his end, but felt no need to explain otherwise. I disliked the sudden finality of these decisions. I would simply decide to let someone go and that would be it. No warning, no chance for him to adjust to the expectations I had for him.

Once, I tried to change that with a carpenter whose work had become careless. I told George that if he didn't shape up in one week, he would be fired. To my disappointment, the week passed with no change in his quality. None! So, I gave him his final check, which he accepted with gratitude and left. Later, Benjamin told me that George interpreted the warning simply as a signal that he was to be fired in a week. He made no attempt to change. He saw the decision as inevitable. And in his acceptance, I found discouragement. I was trying to find a balance between my notions of fairness and what seemed to be standard practice. My attempts seemed misplaced.

While I met with little resistance on some occasions, others were not so easy. I still struggled with every firing decision and the act of carrying it out. Luke, a twenty-four year old laborer, would test my growing understanding of jobsite survival. He would not be the last. Luke had grown up with wealth but had not been able to make much of himself. His father kept a close eye on his life and provided support when Luke could not make ends meet for his wife and new baby. For several weeks, he had been pushing to move up to carpenter and was becoming increasingly belligerent about not getting what he wanted. I simply did not need another carpenter and I was not sure he had the ability. Also, I didn't like the way he demanded his promotion.

On one particularly difficult day, I was taking a breather when I heard shouting upstairs and went to see what was happening. I found Walt pacing with Arthur between him and Luke. Walt explained that he needed a load of two-by-sixes and told Luke to get them. Luke told him in return to "go fetch his own fuckin' wood." According to Arthur, Walt flew into a rage, grabbed a scrap of lumber and lunged at him before he stepped in between them.

Luke didn't challenge the explanation. "I was just sick of being his lackey," he said. I was tired and in no mood for Luke's insubordination, especially against Walt, someone who could make anyone nervous.

I told Luke I wanted to speak to him alone. I decided that it was time for us to clear the air. He'd been getting more and more disgruntled and I'd heard that he was talking me down around the job site. I walked Luke to a spot fifty feet from the house so that no one could hear us and began.

"Let's get this out in the open. Do you have a problem with your job?"

"No," he said, staring at the ground.

"Really?" I said sarcastically, "Do you have a problem with me?"

Again, "no" was his reply, still looking down.

"Luke, we're here all alone. Just you and me. If you've got something to say then let's just get this out right now. Because I think you've got an attitude problem." I felt pushed into being so direct. I had a lot on my mind and I had no patience. The laborer job needed very few skills. Keep the site clean, get lumber when it's needed, that's it. I could replace him in a day.

But Luke just kept looking down, saying nothing.

I laid it on the line, "Your job is to do what the carpenters want. If you can't handle that, if you've got a problem with that, then maybe it's time for you to leave."

"You firing me?" Luke spat back, looking up at me for the first time.

With little thought, I shot back, "Yeah! Pack your shit and hit the road. I'll mail you your last check."

"You can't fire me."

"No? Well I just did. Pack up and get off the job."

Luke closed the distance between us, putting his face right in front of mine. "I'm gonna kick the living shit out of you."

I had not given much thought to this decision to fire Luke, and didn't expect this response. And this surely was not what I wanted to happen. Surprised by his reaction, I was dismissive, "Yeah, right, get off the job."

But he remained firm, yelling again, "I'm gonna kick the living shit outta you."

"Then take your shot right now." I was surprised at my words. I was never one to pick a fight. But I couldn't back down.

Luke yelled again, "Next time I see you off this jobsite, I'm going to kick the fuckin' shit outta you."

"Get the fuck off the job," I said as he turned to grab his things.

The exchange was loud enough for everyone to hear and it was the kind of confrontation that I was not used to. I held my composure until Luke finally left. But once he was gone, I found a place to be alone. I felt horrible. This was exactly the kind of nightmare I had envisioned when firing someone. And I questioned my judgment in letting my emotions drive my decision. This was someone's livelihood. Had I taken it away too lightly? Was Luke's anger justified? Or, was I simply too thin-skinned to do this? It shook my confidence in hiring and firing people, something that was now a critical part of my job.

It wasn't until I had fired fifteen people in twelve months—I kept a running tally as each exacted its own personal toll on my psyche—that I began to see things differently. I had a revelation on the latter three of that tally, all finding their end on the same day. One carpenter had made a costly mistake on the master bedroom porch; one of many. I caught a second carpenter leaving the port-a-potty while finishing the last of his whiskey nip bottle. The third had been coming in late and his effort on the job was weak. Some of the carpenters had complained when teamed up with him.

Within fifteen minutes, all three were given their final paycheck and told to leave. Despite my justification, I was still filled with doubts. Three people entered the field of the unemployed and three at once was too much. I was despondent and invited Benjamin for a beer after work.

With a full mug in front of me, I poured out my feelings. "Benjamin, I don't know how many more times I can do this. I don't even know if I did the right thing. I didn't listen to any of their excuses. I just fired those guys."

"Yeah, and you know what they say about excuses—they're just like assholes. Everyone's got one and they *all* stink." He laughed.

But I didn't smile. I shook my head and said, "This sucks, Benjamin. These firings are tearing me apart."

Benjamin's demeanor sobered. "Andy, you had to do it. Those guys weren't carrying their weight."

"But now they're outta work. I can't help thinking about that. They've gotta go home to a wife, girlfriend, landlord, bank and explain that they won't be bringing home a paycheck."

Benjamin, in his usual gift for the practical, agreed, "Yup, that's true. Some people are outta work today. They're not gettin' a paycheck. But this is happening at other jobsites around the state too. It's not your fault."

"So you mean I have no choice in the matter? No say? I'm simply carryin' out what needs to be carried out?"

"Well, sort of."

"That doesn't make me feel better. I made the decision to fire these people. If I decided not to, they'd still be employed. I wonder if the other guys live in fear that I'm gonna fire them?"

"Now wait a minute, Andy," cautioned Benjamin. "You're makin' it sound like your decisions were arbitrary. Were they?"

"No."

"Right, you made these decisions for a reason. Don't ya think the guys that got fired know that? And," he paused, "Don't you think the guys that're still on the job know that too?"

"Yeah, I guess so. But I wonder what they see. With George, I tried to give him a chance, and he saw my efforts as a final decision to fire him. What do they see?"

"They see someone who's trying to hold a high standard of work. Stop thinkin' about the guys you fired and start thinkin' about the guys you still employ. They're the ones that deserve your attention. They knew those guys had to go and they're glad you did it. If you didn't do it, they'd wonder if they should slack off too. By firing people you don't want, you're making a statement to those you do want. The guys that are left feel better about what they're doing and the job they're working on. And they have more respect for you for doin' it."

Benjamin's lecture was a turning point, a watershed in my thinking about what I was doing and why. The pain of telling someone that he was fired would always be difficult, but the pain lingered less if I focused not on who left but on who stayed. My notions of building a crew took on new meaning. The idea of one stable and permanent crew was dispelled. The idea of a constantly evolving crew replaced it. It came down to what Jack had been saying all along—be careful to trust people.

THE OWNERS. Where my relationship with the crew was in constant contention, my relationship with the owners was more of a friendship. Lucy was a regular visitor to the site and we became friends. Sometimes, she would come to the job just to admire what was happening. Other times, she had a clear objective. In either case, I was her personal guide, explaining every step, where it was leading and allowing her to introduce her own opinion on that direction. She wasn't afraid to make decisions. She would see something happening and ask me what the plan was. I would explain where things were going and she would suggest some adjustments. I would explain the pros and cons, never holding back from a direct opinion. She was equally direct in her decisions.

Usually the crew noticed her as she walked through, saying hello with a smile. But she became such a regular visitor that other times she was overlooked. One day, the two of us walked into the Great Room while some carpenters were working on scaffolding overhead. Just as we entered, Arthur turned to Dick and asked, "Would you take a cunt hair off that?" I blushed and made a loud cough to announce our presence. Lucy didn't react.

Sometimes, she would arrive with her twelve-year-old daughter in tow and I wondered what the girl saw. Did she recognize the magnitude of what was happening or did she simply say to her friends that her parents were building "a house?" Even Lucy seemed unfazed by the scale of the project and was always amused at the attraction the house held for others. Once, the Goodyear blimp made a very deliberate and obvious turn overhead to gawk at the colossus below. At other times, people would drive onto the jobsite in complete defiance of the "no-trespassing" sign at the gate. Lucy laughed these intrusions off. This was one area where Bill and Lucy differed.

"This is my house," Bill said excitedly. "They have no right to come inside my house. Do I ask to come into their living room? No!" He made no mistake about it, "tell them all to leave!" One day I was carrying out his orders and asking yet another sightseer to leave when the intruder introduced himself as an editor of *Progressive Architecture*. I called Bill for clarification on his no-trespassing rule.

"Throw him off the job. I don't care who he is. I want him off the job. If he wants to look, he can call me. But frankly, I don't care if he's carrying a check from *Publisher's Clearinghouse*. I don't want anyone in my house."

This was a very personal task, building someone's house. And I liked making Bill and Lucy happy by building what they wanted. I learned to appreciate the satisfaction Jack described at fulfilling a promise to a client. My job was to help them get the house they wanted. I beamed when Bill made his first trip to the second floor on the stairs that we built for him. We walked through the rooms he had never seen before. He asked lots of questions about what would go where and how the room might feel. As with Lucy, I was direct in giving my reactions, explaining the pros and cons. Always, I included what I interpreted to be the architect's intention and generally found myself defending the architect's plans. If any final changes were made by the Shaws, I would run them by Peter first to allow him the chance to argue against it.

Playing intermediary between the architects and the owners was becoming more important as the house moved closer to completion. Once, we walked through the developing space of the master bathroom and Bill matter-of-factly talked through the different features in the room. As he was walking out of the bathroom, he said, "we walk through the doors right here and…"

I stopped him. "No Bill, there're no doors here."

"No doors? There are no doors to my bathroom?"

"Nope. The plans call for an open hallway."

Bill became animated, "Well, we have to have doors. Don't you think we should have doors? We're supposed to have doors!"

"Well," I offered in mock embarrassment. "I'd prefer to have them myself."

Lucy laughed, "I think we should have them. Not for me. I don't care. But I think we should have them for other people."

"Well that settles it," Bill concluded. "We need doors."

I relayed the decision to Peter who replied in two days with a new set of details.

These kinds of events slowly privileged my position with the Shaws. I was becoming a friend. One day, over lunch, I asked Bill and Lucy how they had picked Robert Devereaux to be their architect. Bill smiled as he explained, "That was a difficult choice. You can't just simply ask firms to give you full house drawings and pick the best one. We asked for concepts. But, we knew we had to pick on personality. This would be a long relationship. So, when we interviewed each architect, we invited him to our home in Weston. After we discussed concepts and credentials, we walked through the house. We really love that house. So after the tour, we asked each one which was their favorite room and why. If their answer agreed with ours, then we knew we had a match. Robert was the only one that got it right."

"And once chosen, how'd you tell Robert what to do?"

"Well," Lucy explained, "we gave only vague guidelines. We told them that we wanted to be able to see sunlight in the front and back of each room. And we wanted it to be stately, but not garish or opulent. We wanted a country-house, a house you could live in and put your feet up in. We rejected five designs before they finally got it right."

They seemed satisfied that Robert had delivered on their expectations and were excited to see it becoming a reality. Some parts were turning out as they had anticipated, others were a surprise. They would never fully know until it was finished.

THE ARCHITECTS. The architects and I maintained an on-going partnership, limited in closeness by the telephone, but tied ever more tightly by necessity; they needed me to keep them informed of job site conditions and I needed them to give continued guidance on gaps in the plans. I talked with Peter nearly every day, and Robert through him. I would transmit to Peter both reports on the progress that had taken place and questions about future progress.

Some of my questions involved glaring errors. "Should we follow the porch roof detail in ceiling drawing E.6 or the detail in roof drawing E.5? One shows the roof jutting out one foot from the turrets. The other shows it flush." These often got quick answers, some of which resolved the issue, some of which did not. If not, I would follow-up with another question given the ramifications of the first answer. "But if we make it jut out, then the roof will not line up with the deck below. Is that what you want?"

Sometimes my questions left Peter at a loss. "I'll check this and get back to you."

Other times I would probe for the real intent behind the drawings. "Should the tongue and groove in the exterior overhang on drawing D.4 line up with the tongue and groove on the finished ceiling in the hallway on drawing D.8? Since they're adjacent to each other, should we think of them as a continuous ceiling interrupted by the exterior wall?" These questions pleased Peter. A pause on the other end of the phone was followed by "Good question." Peter provided answers and quizzed me about the look of his designs as they were completed. But it eventually became clear that the builder/architect relationship was, by definition, contentious. As the job progressed, I needed their involvement in more immediate ways but their delays would cause backups in the entire process.

For example, for months I had been asking for a finalized exterior door "schedule"—a list of the designs for each of the house's forty-two exterior doors and four garage doors. Their absence would hold up the siding and the final drying in of the house. But Robert was hung up on making a final decision. Each day I would call, each day I would get the same answer. "We're working on it."

Finally, in early August, the door schedule was sent and I collected bids for custom production in pine, oak and mahogany, each coming in respectively higher prices. I told Peter the general price differences—Jack never wanted me to reveal numbers with the architects—adding that if there were any doors to be painted, pine would be the wise choice. He assured me that they would all be stained and told me to order mahogany. I placed the order and a month later, received word that the doors were set to arrive in two weeks. Now, we moved to the next question.

"I need to know the stain colors. If we don't finish them when they get to the job, they'll absorb moisture and move," I explained emphatically. "We're having a warm, damp fall and I can't leave these doors unprotected."

Peter hesitated again and, as with the original schedule, it became a question for every phone call—"What's the finish decision on the doors?" And again, the answer was always, "We're working on it."

Finally, as the doors were one day from delivery, Peter announced triumphantly, "Andy we've made a decision. We'll fax you the paint colors this afternoon."

"Paint?"

"Yeah, paint, what's up?"

"Peter, I told you I could've saved a lot of money if we'd gone with pine instead of mahogany. You told me to get mahogany and now you want me to paint 'em? That's crazy!" I was angry, both at the constant delays and the wasteful decision.

"Sorry, Andy. I know it doesn't sound quite right, but that's the decision. Even though they're painted, mahogany's a much better door than pine, won't you agree?"

"Yeah, they're better. But Peter, that's crazy. These're beautiful doors. We can't paint 'em?"

"You will." And that was how Peter left it.

But I did not. For the first time, I went over his head to have the decision reversed. I called Bill at his office, something I didn't often do.

"Bill, this is Andy."

"Hey Andy, how's my house going?" Bill replied chipperly.

"It's going well except we have a little situation that I think you might want to weigh in on."

"What's up?"

"I've ordered the exterior doors. On Robert's instruction, I ordered mahogany rather than pine. Now, he's telling me to paint 'em. That mahogany cost you an extra forty grand. If I knew they'd be painted I would've ordered pine. You have any opinion on this?"

"That doesn't make sense, does it? I mean, isn't mahogany a beautiful wood?"

"Yeah it is. It doesn't make a whole lot of sense to me."

"What's their reason?"

"I'll be damned if I know." This was an unusual statement for me as I normally interpreted and defended the architect's decisions to Bill.

"Then don't do it," he announced. "Tell them to give you a finish that lets us see the wood. That doesn't make sense."

"I'll take care of it." I said, satisfied that rationality had prevailed, or at least *my* rationality.

Peter sighed when I told him the news. "I had a feeling you were gonna do that."

THE SUBCONTRACTORS. Of all four relationships, I loved orchestrating the subcontractors the most. The process of collecting competitive bids, choosing the winner, timing their involvement and assuring a quality product was a matter of constant oversight and orchestration. I loved the activity they created; the noise, the questions, the rapid progress that many hands brought each day. I always liked to have as many on the job at one time as possible. With each extra trade came one more bit of life to the job. And with each extra trade, my role as coordinator became all the more important. The house was changing all around *me*.

But these were independent crews and I had limited control in getting them to fit with my schedule and that of the other crews. The roofing, for example, required coordination with the masons who flashed the chimneys, as well as the carpenters who put in eight eyebrow bathroom vents, a lead-coated copper kitchen vent, two eyebrow skylights, and a series of thirty-two standard skylights.

The masons, a constant presence on the job, worked on hundreds of square feet of stone veneer along the base of the home, as well as the stone walls that had been disrupted by the construction site. Roland, the owner and foreman of the masonry company, was often joined by his father Alan, working side by side with his crew. Alan, with his white hair and gregarious laugh liked to call me "smiley." Their presence created some complications with the Colorado guys.

First, the masons were mostly native Italian, used to their Italian ways. One custom was having beer—one beer Roland assured me—during lunch. The Colorado guys also liked their beer, often bragging about drinking as much as a case of beer each after work. The tiny local liquor store had increased their stock of beer just to accommodate their nightly purchase. I could not tell Roland how to run his crew, and the beer had no effect on their work. But I would not entertain the notion of my crew drinking on the job. I justified it by the simple fact that masons did not work with dangerous power tools, just heavy rocks.

The second problem emerged when one of the masons told Walt how much they were being paid; a violation of one of Jack's cardinal rules. Riley brought out the crew's complaint by asking why they could get paid that much to "stack rocks." I again took the comment as more of a complaint than a serious request and let the matter die.

After the masons finished the veneer, the carpenters had to finish the myriad of detail work on the exterior. Porches were built, windows were slid into place, extensive trim framed banks of windows, custom made vents were constructed on the gable ends, and various decorative trim details were added. None of the work was simple; all of it was redwood, much of it was in large dimensions. Beyond the standard two-inch-thick stock, there was four-, six-, eight-, ten- and even twelve-inch-thick stock. For a while, the four bays in the garage were nearly filled with redwood lumber.

And then the siding began. Cedar clapboard was applied up to ten feet off the ground and cedar shingles finished the rest of the wall. On Jack's instructions—and to the annoyance of the sider—I set up a builder's level and shot the height of the first course of clapboard all the way around the perimeter of the house to make sure that the siding contractor ended at the same height where he began. Jack and I both imagined the nightmare of his courses not meeting.

As the siding proceeded, it brought the house closer to the rich look of the Shingle Style as I had learned it. One fancy detail that the architects added late and gave them great satisfaction was running the courses in an undulating wave on the east and west facing walls. This was similar to a detail that I had seen at the Casino in Newport and Peter explained, "The waves faced the two oceans."

The house had enough space for dozens of contractors. And the complexity of these projects required that they get started early. Freddie Carlucci's crew was back from the Winslow job to do the plumbing. The house's kitchen, laundry room, six full baths and three half baths kept him and his sons very busy. As a last minute idea, Jack decided, in consultation with the Shaws and the local fire marshal, to install an outdoor fire hydrant and connect it to the indoor pool since there were no hydrants within a mile of the house. And finally, he had to run the piping for the air handlers and humidifiers in the HVAC system (heating, ventilation and air conditioning). The job was the only item on Freddie's schedule for months.

The Shaw house had a four-pipe HVAC system that could run hot and · cold to any zone at any time. The standard two-pipe system could only run hot or cold at any given time and the homeowner had to decide when to switch from one to the other. Further complicating the project, this house had seventeen zones, each with a humidifier and an electrostatic air filter. So the piping and ductwork for each zone needed dedicated piping all the way back to the boilers and condensers. Beyond the seventeen standard zones, there was an additional set of heating coils on the north side of the house that would activate when external thermostats detected sudden drops in outside temperatures. Finally, a commercial timing box was installed to automatically adjust the temperature in the various zones to offset sudden shifts.

The electricians had their challenges as well. It was decided that there would be no telephone poles on the property. So a trench was dug along the entire length of the driveway, a third of a mile. The house had an eight-hundred amp service, much larger than the average home, so the main wiring was fairly thick. Six-inch pipe was buried with pull boxes every two hundred feet and nylon rope stretched from box to box. The task of pulling the wire itself involved lots of grease, a strong motor and patience to make sure the rope didn't snap. Once inside, the main power passed through an automatic transfer switch that would shift power to an eighty-kilowatt generator in case of a power failure. Next, the power was split into one of eight breaker boxes distributed throughout the house.

Given the artistry of the designs on the surrounds, hearths, mantels and veneers of the house's seven fireplaces, I knew Maurizio Donatella was the man for the job. Each surround was made of marble or slate, splayed out to a picture frame and made of at least fourteen pieces of precisely cut stone. Two fireplaces offered even more complex challenges. In the Great Room and the living room, the chimneys were veneered with fieldstone from floor to ceiling—twenty feet in the first case and fourteen feet in the second. As with the external veneer, these stones were gathered from the property and laid in a structural fashion like the exterior veneer. Adding further complexity, these two fireplaces had a very heavy piece of cut granite as the mantel that would span from one side to the other, ten feet in the Great Room and eight feet in the living room. And finally, each fireplace had a stone arch that would span the distance over the fireplace and carry the veneer above. As Maurizio worked, he again played opera. When the plumbers set up nearby with their rap music, he hastily packed up his materials to work in another part of the house.

The garage doors were a custom design and contracted to a local commercial door manufacturer. But, I had to acquire the specially-milled wood veneer that I had delivered to the manufacturer for application. This kind of complexity was becoming a common element of my job, one that cemented my relationship with my various lumberyards.

As with the Winslow house, my wood orders fell into two categories. The first was the standard lumber or material order: two-by-fours, two-by-sixes, plywood, and nails. These were handled by Philip Morgan at Ridgefield Supply. I never ordered lumber by the piece, always by the pallet or "cube." This made me very popular at the lumberyard, becoming known as the contractor with the deep pockets. If I asked for something, it was loaded into my truck while I tended to business with Philip or the owner of the yard. Any request that might have been dismissed had it come from another contractor was taken seriously from me. The other category was the more unusual and challenging types of materials: half inch by half inch copper mesh screen, brass rods for custom made light fixtures, twenty-four different types of windows, sixteen different types of doors, seventeen different types of door hardware and on and on. These became a source of humor between us but without the common orders, Philip wouldn't have found it so amusing.

The second category was the specialty lumber, which I bought from Kevin at Gregory Lumber. Kevin acquired the large dimension redwood, cedar roof and siding shingles, cedar clapboard, and veneer plywoods. He also provided me with the many types of hardwoods and softwoods that went into the final finished spaces. I ordered maple, cherry, mahogany, teak, red cedar, aromatic cedar, walnut, southern yellow pine, sugar pine, red oak and white oak. The sites and smells of the lumber yard was a pleasure each time I made an order.

Not all sub-contracting decisions were carefully planned out. One day, Robert was on-site when the lightning rods were being installed on all the chimneys. He was instantly offended by the copper rod protruding from the top of the chimney and the braided copper cable running down the outside of the brickwork. Work was halted while Robert made an impassioned plea for Bill to provide the additional cost of running the cables inside the flue rather than outside. The request—and cost—was granted.

In the fields, Barry Sutton set up shop, devoting almost all of his resources to this one job; the septic field, oil tank, and outdoor pool as well as backfilling the foundation and grading parts of the property where the tennis court was to be built. When these jobs didn't occupy his time, he screened the rocks out of the topsoil that had been scraped off the property before the foundation was dug—he finally got what he asked for at the Winslow House. By the time he was done, he had created a large and valuable pile of topsoil had the Shaws wished to sell it. Despite the sizeable amount of money involved in his contract, he unwisely tried to make more. He was caught when I noticed that he would sometimes run two machines at once. Since he couldn't possibly operate both simultaneously, this meant that one sat idling while he worked with the other. An excavator bills for work based on man-hours, the task and machine-hours. The latter is based on a clock that keeps track of the time the machine is in operation. Barry had leased too much equipment and was trying to get them to pay off by running them simultaneously. When I figured out the trick, Barry explained that he just wasn't paying attention. Jack was angry but controlled at the news and talked to Barry himself. By the end of the week, Barry's machine inventory was reduced to one and when the heavy grading was done, he and Jack parted ways. A landscaper from Westport completed the landscaping.

Amidst all this activity, Charles DiMaggio, the building inspector, made frequent visits to check on progress. At first he scrutinized the job; a remnant I thought of his bad feelings about my taking his friend's place. But as time went on, just like inspectors for the Winslow House, he sometimes never got out of his car, driving around the site and then leaving. But when he wanted to walk through the house, I would give him a personal tour. When he wanted a change, I dutifully took care of it. Most of the time, these were minor issues. One issue that he paid particular attention to was fire protection. He talked about it constantly. He was pleased with our decision to add the fire hydrant and fire proof roof shingles. He was also persistent about two continuous fire resistant walls that ran from the basement all the way to the ridge with no gaps in between. Charles got quite animated at the need for fire blocking in all pass through walls. Since the house was balloon framed, the second floor deck didn't fill the space between the exterior wall studs. Air and fire could pass unobstructed from one floor to the next. Charles wanted blocks put in to stop that flow.

All of the subcontractors formed a community, working towards the same goal. To keep things moving smoothly, I spent most of my waking hours thinking about the house. I kept my note pad with me at all times, writing down things that needed to be done, materials that needed to be acquired. I drank lots of coffee and would often spend my day in constant motion, being called to the roof fifty feet up, the basement twenty feet down, or the east or west ends divided by two hundred forty feet of hallways.

AS I MANAGED all these relationships, I was feeling more in control of the job, more confident in my abilities than I had ever felt. I had taken on the responsibilities of picking and managing the subcontractors, working with the architects and the owners, and hiring and firing carpenters. Jack did not force them upon me. I had gradually taken them for myself. And the more I took, the more I developed my own sense of what I could do and who I was.

With this realization, an idea began to grow in my head. Since I had come to Connecticut, I had learned to manage all my relationships in building these houses except one. I had not managed my relationship with Jack. He had been managing me, stroking me, building me up. This was not based on the father-son benevolence that I first thought. It was business. It was money. Jack had been communicating in that way every time he gave me a raise. Money had been his way of showing approval and appreciation. And I hadn't seen that. I appreciated the raises, but never really considered the significance of the money until we had our fight over the bonus. As long as he paid me with salary and raises, I would continue to be his subordinate.

But, whether Jack acknowledged it or not, I was his partner. I was running the jobs. I had taken the responsibilities and I was the builder. And with this realization came a second. As in all my other responsibilities and roles, I needed to tell him that I was his partner. I decided that rather than wait for a bonus after the job was done, I was going to ask for a cut of the profits before.

I began to do some calculations. I wanted a fair cut but all financial matters were strictly Jack's domain. I had no idea about his arrangement with Bill or the final costs on the house. But I prepared my argument nonetheless, knowing that it would come down to how confident I acted in asking for a percentage. I had to be able to stand my ground and not repeat the disaster with the Winslow bonus. If I got anywhere around fifty thousand dollars, I'd be ecstatic. To build my confidence in asking for such a large sum, I kept reminding myself that this was a business deal, nothing more.

I met with Jack in his office, and after talking of progress on the job, I made my bold pronouncement, "Jack, I wanna negotiate a piece of the profits for the Shaw job." My heart was racing. I had no idea how he was going to react and my nerves were on edge as doubts fought their way into my mind. Was I out of my mind? No, I told myself, I was merely standing up for what's fair. I had taken complete control of the Shaw job and deserved to at least be heard.

"I see," said Jack, leaning back in his chair and staring directly at me. "Not satisfied with my bonus policy, huh?" I didn't want to go there and I didn't want this discussion connected in any way to that fiasco. "So what makes you think you deserve a part of the profits? We have a deal on compensation already, don't we?"

I pressed on, cautiously trying to read whether I was getting into trouble with each step. I maintained my façade of confidence and proceeded. "As I see it, my responsibilities in this job have been growing to the point that I think I deserve more than hourly compensation."

"Your idealism giving way to the profit motive?" He asked.

"I'm just asking for what's fair," I replied.

Pulling himself up to his desk, he leaned towards me and sternly asked, "Answer me this, why should I give you anything? Why should I give you one goddamned penny? We had an arrangement. Why should I agree to change it now?"

Despite my gut telling me to back down, I remained firm in the face of his edginess. "Well, in my view, the arrangement's already changed. I started as your overseer but now I'm your supervisor in every sense of the word. I'm in complete control of the Shaw job."

"Ah, so you don't think you need me anymore." He leaned back into his chair again, crossing his arms.

I couldn't read him, but didn't want to waver. I kept telling myself that this was just business. "No. That's not what I'm saying. I'm saying that you've got your role and I've got mine. And I think my role lets you not worry about what's happening on the job. It frees you up to make money in your other business." I added with finality, "We're partners."

He added sarcastically, "Oh yeah? And what's my role?"

"I know I couldn't have handled some of the tough things that have happened on these jobs. You've guided me through a lot of stuff. I couldn't have dealt with Red or Ace Construction the way you did. Shit, I didn't even see Ace's scheme coming. And I'm not even sure I could handle Robert or Bill the way you can. That bullshit over the pool roof." I shook my head. "I was ready to blow up when Robert said he could charge us for that." I stopped, choosing my words carefully. "But Jack, I'm learning. I'm learning from you, from the subs, from everyone. And I am becoming more of the builder that I wasn't when I started here. I feel part of something here. And I want that to continue. And I think the compensation should now reflect that."

"Really," Jack said, amused at my self-assessment. "Tell me what you're thinking. What amount of money do you think would reflect that?"

I began my logic, not wanting to just blurt out a number without justification. "Well, as near as I can figure it, this house is going to cost around five million." Jack remained stoic. We were now entering uncharted territory. I was guessing and he knew it. "And the percentage for a time and materials contractor has to be around ten or fifteen percent."

"That's generous," Jack quickly replied. He leaned back in his chair, put his hands behind his head and stared at the ceiling.

"And Saunders walked away with probably a tenth of that." Jack rocked his head back and forth. I began to feel like he was playing with me. But I continued. "So, figuring conservatively, the profit on this job is three maybe four hundred thousand dollars."

"Nice try," he said sarcastically, "But you're forgetting office expenses, accountants, lawyers. Then you have to figure in my salary. I don't draw a paycheck from this job until it's done. And then sometimes I have to front money until Bill comes up with it. What's that worth?"

The numbers were getting murky. My heart was pounding in my chest. I had a number in mind when I entered the room, but I was losing confidence in it.

"Well, even if we're talking around two hundred thousand dollars, I'd like to propose that my share be around a quarter of that. So, it would seem that fifty thousand dollars would be fair."

"I see." He just sat there thinking. I couldn't read whether he was annoyed or seriously contemplating my proposal.

"And what if I don't give you anything?"

"Well, I don't know. I hadn't thought about that. I'm just asking for what's fair."

"Fair? I think you've got an inflated idea of what's fair. You're not worth fifty thousand dollars."

"Are you saying you don't need me?"

The bold statement stirred his attention. He calmly sat upright. His demeanor changed. Was he softening? I couldn't tell but it was an opening.

"Jack, look at me." I was now the one leaning forward, engaging his gaze, looking him right in the eyes, hiding the nervousness that was behind my own. "On the job, I am you. I am your representative in every way possible. When Bill and Lucy talk to me, it is as though they are talking to you. I know you know that. And I know that that means a lot to you." The momentum of what I was saying propelled me forward. My outward confidence surprised me. "Jack, that tells me that you trust me. And I know you don't trust anyone. I know that's worth a lot to you. Now we're simply putting a dollar amount on that. What's your trust worth?"

I was cornering him much as someone might corner a dangerous animal. I wanted to win the argument and I wanted to make my case solidly. But I didn't want to get him angry. I could see his back was up. He was losing ground. I was taking it away from him. I kept telling myself, this is only business.

He nodded his head, "Okay. I see your point." He sat silently, playing with a pencil on his desk. "What if I offered you thirty thousand?"

"Forty."

"Thirty-five."

"That's acceptable." It happened quickly. Outwardly, I was maintaining a serious demeanor to match Jack's, despite the mix of fear and excitement that coursed through my veins.

"Then it's a deal." He reached out his hand and we shook.

"I think you gave in too easily," he said. "Why didn't you push for more?"

"Well, I wasn't sure I was going to get anything. And I have to admit I was a little nervous after our fight over the Winslow bonus."

"Yeah that," Jack sighed.

"I'm just asking for what's fair. That's all. It's just business." I would have sworn I saw the crack of a smile although he did his best to conceal it.

That evening I pondered over what had happened, what insight I had gotten into Jack's way of seeing the world. I felt that he respected my willingness to face him, look him in the eye and ask for what I wanted, what was fair. In responding to the Winslow bonus, I didn't do that. I looked down, to the side, anywhere but straight at him. And I had offended him, rejecting what he saw as a gift. To him, that bonus was beyond our agreed arrangement. And therefore, he was under no obligation to give it to me and I had no right to demand more. That was his logic. It was just business. And today, I had dealt with him in a business fashion. We had negotiated a new contract. And I negotiated from a position of strength. I still needed him, but I now knew that he also needed me. Negotiating the bonus on this house was a culmination of my maturing in my relationship with Jack. I was never his son. I was no longer his subordinate. I was his partner. I had earned it. And I could now see that Jack would never just give me that. I had to take it when I was ready. That was the only way.

THE DAY AFTER our new agreement, a subcontractor did not show up as promised and it sent me into a rage. As I picked up the phone to urge him back to the site, I felt a sharp pain in my stomach, nearly doubling me over. I sat down and waited for it to pass. Then I called a doctor to set up an examination.

The doctor asked me, "is your job stressful?"

"Yes."

"How much coffee do you drink?"

"A lot."

Do you exert yourself during the day?"

"Continuously."

"Outside?"

"Always."

"Are your eating habits balanced?"

"No, I sneak meals when I can."

With each successive answer, I knew that I was spelling out an unhealthy lifestyle. The doctor just shook his head, "Andy, you seem like an intelligent man. Do I really need to tell you that something has to give here? Eliminate stress, eliminate coffee, relax more during the day and eat right. There's no ulcer here…yet. If you continue on this path, there likely will be."

I opted for the only things I could control. I would cut back on coffee, pay more attention to eating right, and manage my relationship with Jack better. The job would remain the same. There was little I could do about that. It would always be a source of stress.

But, while the job gave me plenty of stress, it also brought me enormous pleasure. I would often stay late and walk through the silent job alone. There was never any particular order or direction to my walks. With notepad under my arm, I simply began to meander, and as I walked, I saw everything, every bit of growth. My logical purpose was to inspect the house, make sure that nothing got overlooked; no problem remained unsolved. But my romantic purpose was to appreciate the beauty of what was transforming around me. In my head, a vision of what the house would eventually become was firmly formed. It was the result of what the drawings directed and it was the product of what was built before. With each additional piece of wood, stone or steel, previous decisions decided subsequent decisions. There was a logic and order to it. A certain trim detail on one end of the house meant that other trim had to match it or have a sound reason why it should not. The house was coming alive and I loved watching it happen, helping it happen, feeling it happen. These walks were a form of meditation for me, a chance to cement my relationship with the house.

On one late summer day, I began my walk as usual. I had planned to meet Sharon for dinner at five o'clock and I had half an hour before I had to leave. And so I began. I admired the effect of a new wall that defined the final shape of the dining room. I stopped to admire the grain and texture of a wooden threshold in the sunroom, a windowsill in the study, a piece of trim in the servant's quarters. Normally, during the workday, I would watch a carpenter's work and remark with sincere appreciation, "Doesn't that look nice," or "Impressive bit of carpentry there." But now, in this solitary walk-through, that appreciation needn't be articulated and therefore, took on a deeper, more personal importance. I admired the house in all its facets without trying to understand or explain what I was feeling.

If something was out of place, out of level or out-of-plumb, it caught my attention. Inside and outside, I scrutinized every line, every shape. My eye noticed everything that had changed since I last saw it. I sighted my eye on everything to make sure that parts that were supposed to align, did. The eaves of three dormers over the garage had to line up from one to the next to the next. When I climbed onto the roof to sight them, they did not. So, I marked it down in my notepad for the carpenters to fix. I measured the distance between windows to make sure they were perfectly consistent and I measured their combined placement with respect to the room to make sure they were perfectly centered. Outlets had to be centered on windows, switches had to be consistently distanced from where the door trim would be. Details that were visible from a window had to be even more perfect than these expectations. I looked out the guest room window and didn't like the way the shingles were coursing over the eyebrow skylight. I had already told the roofers to restart twice before. Maybe this time they'll get it right, I thought.

I was looking at hollow stud walls but I saw the final rooms. I saw the finished walls, the light fixtures, the trim. I marked in my notebook where blocking needed to be placed to accommodate sheetrock edges, ductwork, plumbing or future locations of curtain rods, towel racks, artwork or light fixtures. I noticed a piece of wood that would interfere with some work that the plumber would shortly be doing and I marked it down for removal.

As I walked, it occurred to me that the easiest way to get the sheetrock to the second floor would be through the master bedroom porch. So, I made a note to "leave out middle windows in master bedroom porch" in my notepad. In the main stairwell, I noticed that the first flight of stair treads didn't line up with the second flight so I took out a black marker and wrote directly on the risers how much each had to be padded to create the desired result. In the sunroom, I marked where additional blocking was necessary for the built-in speakers.

I became lost in the walk-through. It was euphoric, just me alone with the house. But I was not alone. I felt the house as a participant with me. I knew every inch of it, what it used to be, what it was now and what it would become. Each turn revealed something new yet also something that I had nurtured, encouraged and therefore expected. I loved the process I was a part of. I loved watching the house grow. And I loved working with the men who made it grow. I moved through the house, but I was not fully aware of how. I just moved without an active thought of where I was going. Time and space blurred. When I came back to where I began, I looked at my watch to find that two hours had passed. I was late, but I was also stunned. Only an instant had passed since I began the walk. But time had somehow been transformed. It stood still as I lost myself in the house. And in losing myself, I had found myself. At that time, at that moment, I was where I was meant to be. I was doing what I was meant to be doing. Everything fit together. I had never felt such certainty before. I was in love. I had found my calling.

"JACK, I'VE DECIDED to hire Aqua Pools for the indoor pool." I expected no reaction other than a simple nod. This pool was to be built of freestanding concrete walls within the enclosed space of the pool room and beneath the redwood truss ceiling; custom work, but nothing outrageous.

But Jack raised his eyebrow. "Aqua Pools? You sure?"

I was surprised. I had negotiated three bids, compared the quality and reputations of each, considered the personalities of the representative of each company and worked the prices down. "Aqua's bid has come down to a competitive price, and they seem to have the most experience in one-of-a-kind pools," I explained. But Jack remained silent. So, I kept talking. "They originally spec'd eight-inch side walls and I had to ask them to change to twelve-inch walls to match the architect's drawings. They still seemed like the best choice." Jack was still silent. "Aqua's salesman, Sean Hawley, said it was unnecessary but that they would make the change to accommodate the architects."

Finally Jack spoke, still lost in his thoughts. "Twelve-inch walls, huh? Architects making engineering specifications? That's trouble. It only costs more money and usually for no sound reason." He then refocused, "But Aqua? Are you sure?"

"Jack, they seem like the best choice to me." I had made this choice just as I had made the others. And I figured I had done well so far. My work with the other subcontractors was going well.

"Well, if that's what you wanna do, I'll stand behind your judgment." And Jack stood aside to let me make the decision.

Aqua's engineer, Tommy, and the crew arrived on schedule. They took extra precautions to protect the redwood ceiling by hanging plastic over the entire room. They built a wire mesh basket where the pool would stand, and using a high-pressure hose, shot the concrete into the basket. There were no forms. The concrete stuck where it was shot and was troweled in place to a smooth finish. They were done in a week and the pool looked great, except for one problem. The walls were only eight inches thick despite an extra charge of two thousand dollars for twelve-inch walls.

I now had a problem. These walls had to carry a suspended concrete deck that would be poured over them and the architects felt that twelve inches was necessary to carry the load. An extra four inches couldn't be shot onto the inside of the pool without making it smaller and it couldn't be shot onto the outside because there wasn't enough space to do it properly. Even if there was, Tommy said he couldn't guarantee a good bond between the two layers. He ran some calculations, and I asked the structural engineers to confirm them. Both agreed that eight-inch walls were adequate for the structural load. So I called Jack to hold back two thousand dollars from Aqua's bill.

"Andy, I've already paid it. I thought the pool was done, isn't it?"

"No problem, Jack. I'll take care of it."

"If you say so," Jack sounded unconvinced.

Sean Hawley came to the site to discuss the issue. "Sean, you could pay back the two thousand dollars, or your crew can build me a concrete bearing wall I need on the eastern end of the pool." It seemed a reasonable solution to me, an easy way to resolve the issue through barter.

Sean promised to check on it and get back to me. But after two weeks of repeated calls, I hadn't gotten an answer. I began to feel that I was being given the run-around. In the meantime, Riley had begun building the forms for the suspended pool deck. With his past experience as a concrete foreman, this was going to be right up his alley. It was a blessing really, as this was a tricky piece of work. Forms were built on stilts both along side and inside the pool. For a week, Riley directed the construction of the form work. And for that week, I kept pressing Aqua for an answer—build the wall or pay the money. Sean kept saying he would get back to me. Finally, Riley reached a point where he could no longer wait. So, I bought the materials myself and let Riley build the wall. His masonry skills were rusty and the wall was not perfect, but it would soon be covered over and it would do the job.

The deck pour was an impressive bit of teamwork under Riley's direction. Walt climbed under the forms to make sure that there would be no "blowouts"—a truly dangerous job with wet concrete being poured over his head in a tight crawl space. The rest of the crew, all of them, mucked around in the concrete, pushing it as Riley directed. I remembered back to Red's direction of the Winslow basement floor and thought that Riley showed just as much competence in what I knew was a stressful task. The pour went without a hitch and finished in just under three hours. It was completed around ten thirty and the guys took a break for the rest of the morning while Riley pulled them as needed for troweling the mix as it set up.

With the pool done, I wanted to get money back for the pool walls.

"Oh that'll be a bit of a delicate matter now," Sean explained. "We'll have to get billing involved and that requires our owner's approval. He's very busy."

"Look Sean, I've tried to be reasonable here. I tried to find a simple way out but you dragged your heels. Now, all I'm asking is for you to pay back money for something you didn't do. Tell me where I'm missing something here?"

"Andy, you're making perfect sense. And I'm sorry it's come to this. But, I have to get my boss involved now, and that's something I've been trying to avoid."

I was beginning to doubt everything Sean told me. I just wanted this resolved. In the grand scheme of the job, it was a minor sum. But it was the principle of the matter. Aqua was keeping money for something they didn't do.

Weeks passed with Sean promising action "any day now." Then, without any warning, he called from his car phone to say that he, Tommy and the owner were on their way down the driveway, concluding, "Andy, we'll settle this issue today."

I looked out the window to see Sean's now familiar pickup truck with the Aqua logo on the side. It was followed by a clean, black Porsche. As they parked in the courtyard, I watched Sean and Tommy get out of the pickup truck. And out of the Porsche stepped a well-dressed man in his mid-thirties looking as if he was on vacation rather than working. In the passenger seat was a woman who remained seated.

"I'll be right back, Baby, this'll only take a minute," the well-dressed man said as he winked at her.

Riley was walking by and I stopped him. "Riley will you stick around for a minute? I'm gonna have a talk with this guy and I'd like some reinforcement." I knew my age could be a liability at certain times on this job and this looked to be one of them. Riley had a very seasoned look, one that I hoped I could borrow for credibility.

"Hi Andy, this is Nick DiMartino, the owner of Aqua Pools," announced Sean. I extended my hand. Nick shook it but didn't look at me. He was looking around the room at the redwood ceiling, the pool, and the concrete deck that now rested on its walls, hiding them from view.

I nodded hello to Sean and Tommy as Nick started the conversation abruptly. "So, what's your problem? Everything looks fine to me."

Surprised at his brashness, I started slow and direct, "There *is* something to talk about here. We paid for twelve inch walls and these are only eight inches thick."

"What? They look fine to me," Nick replied, now looking directly at me, the two of us facing each other on the pool deck. Since it was only four feet wide, Riley stood behind me while Sean and Tommy stood behind Nick.

Tommy spoke up, "Well actually Nick, they really are only eight inches thick."

Nick spun around, pointing his finger at Tommy, "You shut the fuck up! When I want your opinion I'll ask for it. And right now, I don't fuckin' want it." He finished the invective but stared at Tommy for a few seconds as

I watched in amazement. Then he turned back and glared at me.

"The walls are eight inches thick," I repeated, trying to sound calm while my heart began pounding. "The contract clearly states that they're supposed to be twelve inches thick, but they're only eight."

"Oh really, so what's this shit about you wantin' us to build you some concrete walls. Was that in the contract?"

"It was an offer to settle this easily. Your guys had cement, block and a crew here and I needed a wall. It seemed a simple exchange and a simple solution. But, it doesn't matter now. We built the wall. It's done. The pool is done. You were paid for something you didn't do."

"So are you saying that this pool isn't done right?" He raised his voice. "Are you saying that we did something wrong?"

Nick was trying to manipulate me, force me to follow along on his agenda for this meeting. I knew this routine well from my dealings with Jack and was determined not to take the bait. "The pool is fine. The walls are less than what was spec'd but they'll carry the load. Everything is fine, except that you owe us two thousand dollars that we paid for something we didn't get."

Nick smiled sarcastically, "Yeah right, and you're gonna give that money back to the owners?"

"What we do with the money is none of your business. What is your business is paying us back for something you didn't do."

"*I'll* tell you what my fuckin' business is. And as far as I'm concerned, you've given me no goddamned reason to pay you one fuckin' dime."

He stared at me and I stared back in disbelief. This was bizarre. He was simply trying to steal from me. I wanted to handle this myself but knew I was getting nowhere.

"Fine," I said in exasperation. "This isn't my money, it's my boss's. I'll let you work it out with him."

"Fine," Nick repeated with finality, "You talk to your boss. We'll see if he can explain things a whole lot better than you can, ya dumb-shit." He turned and walked out.

I was shaking. I didn't speak. I didn't move. Sean and Tommy turned without looking at me. Riley and I stood alone in the poolroom as they drove off.

"Well, that was interesting," Riley said. "I don't think the word 'asshole' quite sums up how to describe that guy."

I smiled and tried to laugh, but I was furious. "Thanks for the moral support, Riley. I have a phone call to make." I walked off.

"Jack, I need to talk to you about Aqua Pools." My voice was unsteady, my speech rapid.

"Andy calm down. What's up? You sound all-a-flutter," Jack was laughing. "Has someone given you some shit? You need me to take care of it?"

I hated eating this small amount of crow after negotiating our new deal. "Yeah, I guess I need some help. I've got a situation like what happened with Ace." It was my way of reminding him of what I said when we made our deal. And this was one of those times that I still needed him "I just had a talk with the owner of Aqua Pools. Well, I'm not sure I'd call it a talk." I recounted the story and Jack listened patiently. When I was done, he was firm and reassuring.

"Okay Andy, put it out of your mind. There's nothing more for you to worry about. This is my problem now. And believe you me, I'll take care of it." We hung up and I put on my tool belt to work off the anxiety that was consuming me.

Later that afternoon, I got a call from Sean. "Andy, did you talk to your boss about what happened today?" he asked tentatively.

Still feeling raw, I replied "Of course I did. I said I would, and I did."

"Well," he said, sounding contrite, "I'll be down this afternoon to settle up with you. I'm sorry if we caused you any problems. Bye." I stood for a moment holding the phone. The nervous energy that had been bottled up inside me now exploded in a loud laugh. I quickly dialed Jack's number.

"Jack, you wouldn't believe what just happened! Sean from Aqua called to say he'd come by the job to settle our account. What'd you say to him?"

"Hah!" Jack exclaimed. "You bet your ass they're gonna settle up. No one fucks with us and gets away with it."

"But, how'd you do it? What'd you say?"

"Andy," Jack's voice was now serious, "Listen to what I'm gonna tell ya. This is some serious shit. Have you ever heard of *the family*?"

I paused. Where was this going? "I think so," I said cautiously.

"Well, Nick is in the family. And I happen to know some people who are higher up in the family. And so, I talked to those people, who talked to Nick and told him that he should treat Andy right or he'll find himself in a pine box."

Silence hung on the phone. I didn't know what to say. Part of me didn't believe what I was being told and part of me didn't want to hear what I was being told. But what could explain the rapid turn around by Aqua? I recalled that summer day when Jack assured me that Red would not burn the Winslow house or he would "meet with a very unfortunate accident."

Jack asked, "Do you understand what I'm tellin' ya?"

"Yeah Jack, I think I do."

"Andy, I'm telling you this because I want to protect you. I had reservations about Aqua from the beginning. I knew Nick had an attitude problem. In fact, even his own relatives don't like him. I had a feeling something like this would happen, but I hoped it wouldn't. It wasn't your fault." Then he started to laugh, "Do I take good care of you or what? I'll bet this really put a crimp in his little vacation with his lady friend, don't you?"

"Thanks, Jack. I appreciate the help." I couldn't muster the same laugh. I wasn't sure what else to say. The situation was over. I wanted it put behind me. I hung up the phone and got back to work. I had to admit that having Jack available when I needed him allowed me to concentrate on the process of the job; building the house. Jack would have to be my "gorilla in the closet," I thought. I opened the door when he was needed to get a difficult problem resolved. At this moment I really didn't want to know how, just that it got done.

WHERE I WAS JACK on the job, my crew was the extension of me. And I worked hard to keep them satisfied and attentive to the house, particularly the guys I began to refer to as "the Colorado guys." Feeling that they would be happier knowing that their trips home were a formal part of the routine of the job, I organized what was previously a random schedule of trips into a regimented procedure.

And I tried to get to know them better. They had only one social activity, so I drank with them after work a couple of times. Whenever I did this, I woke up as hung over as they were. They told me of buying a case of beer each every night and I never would have believed it had I not witnessed their capacity to drink at a bar. But at the bar, I learned more of their unusual, even outlaw, lives.

Walt had been married four times by the age of forty-six. He had a temper that was fearsome and had spent time in prison for beating up his stepfather. I was slightly on edge whenever I worked with him. He was polite when I faced him, but I was sure he acted otherwise behind my back. He seemed capable of violence while at the same time could be amusing and strangely charming. He was unique in his outlook on life, abiding by rules that I neither understood nor liked. Walt bragged, for instance, about not having a Social Security number.

"How'd you do that?" I asked in naive amazement.

"They never asked me and I never applied," he replied proudly. He boasted at having filled out three tax returns in his life. Each time, he used fake identities and each time he received a refund check. Walt liked to talk about his going to the brothel in Danbury. He even bragged about once using his wife's credit card to pay for the services. Whether it was related or not, his wife had just announced she was leaving him. He took it in stride, deciding that he would pick a new wife who was more neatly trimmed "where I liked to snack."

Herman had a degree in geology but said he couldn't make a living at it. So he took up carpentry. He liked the brothel too. In fact, he fancied himself a connoisseur of prostitutes. "Whenever you get into a city," he would explain, "you ask taxi drivers. They know where the best girls are." Once he hired one, he explained, "the biggest challenge and the biggest turn-on is to make a hooker come." In general, Herman was a quiet man. On more personal matters, he was very private. He had a scar on his forehead, more like a crease or a dent. When I asked him what it was, he found an excuse to leave the table. Riley just looked over to me and shook his head. "Don't ask."

Dennis had five daughters. The youngest was five and the oldest had just entered college. He kept pictures of them in his wallet and talked affectionately and lovingly of them. But Walt painted a different picture, telling how he once witnessed Dennis' daughters throwing stones at him while he was in a drunken stupor, yelling "Daddy's an asshole." The other guys teased him about this, and Dennis showed anger for the first time that I had known him. He spent the rest of the evening brooding in the corner.

Arthur, usually so quiet on the job, got more talkative as he drank. Or more accurately, he got more argumentative. Riley explained, "Every time he gets drunk, he gets angry. At the core of it, he just wants his tribe's land back. He's still angry at the white man." Arthur had an overriding sense that he was being taken advantage of. He would talk about how Jack did not deserve the crew or the work that they were doing. "He's just riding off our backs," he groused, quick to add the inclusive, "yours and ours." I would defend Jack, pointing out that there was no way that anyone of us could land a job like this and it was a testament to his "earning his bones." I would also lightly chastise Arthur for his lack of tact in dealing with Jack. "You can't tell him that if he paid you on contract, he'd see what you can really do. That's the same as telling him that you're ripping him off." Then, trying to offer the positive, "You need to work with him. If you do, he'll give you what you want." Arthur would nod and change the subject to some other way in which he was getting screwed.

Riley was the most controlled of the crew. He did his share of drinking but revealed fewer deep secrets when he was drunk. He talked about his work with large construction firms like Bechtel. He had been a concrete foreman, running big jobs in the Colorado area. He missed the work and the responsibility that came with it. I tried to ask subtle questions, looking for clues as to why he had left that work. The only answer I could surmise, without Riley coming right out and admitting it, was that his drinking had become a problem. But he did what was necessary to make things work out. He, of all the crew, was the most balanced. He spoke for the crew when there was an issue to be aired and did it well. He even started dating a local woman, having separated from his wife back in Colorado.

Benjamin would come drinking, too. While he lived in his own apartment with his girlfriend, he hung out with the Colorado guys a lot. Benjamin liked to elaborate his philosophies on life; burying money in mason jars rather than going to the bank, not buying car insurance.

"But what," I asked, "would you do if you were pulled over by the police?"

As in all his comments, he spoke in a calm controlled and thoughtful manner. "Well that happened just a few months ago. I was arrested for drinking and driving and for operating a vehicle without insurance." I listened intently thinking this was a felony and would involve jail time. But Benjamin casually explained, "I came to a meeting of the minds with several people that were important to my case." He offered no more explanation than that. He settled back, proud of accomplishments that were contrary to anything I knew about how society worked.

I learned all this by socializing with them. But try as I might to get to know them better, something was happening. I was beginning to feel more distant from them and that distance was growing. First, their drinking was getting worse. I could see it in their manner as they came to the job in the morning. They would walk slowly, their eyes bloodshot, sometimes even wearing sunglasses before the sun rose. One day, Dennis was sporting a black eye. "Nothing serious," Riley explained. "We just needed to clear the air last night." What did that mean, "clear the air"? I tried to picture the scene, but I couldn't. The more I saw, the more I found their lives to be completely foreign to me. They worked, they made money, they sent that money home and they drank. The only disruptions in that routine, as far as I could tell were their occasional trips back home to visit with family.

They moved out of the flophouse in Brewster and rented an apartment together. While I thought this was good for their personal well-being, I saw a solidification of them as a powerful bloc in the crew. They thought and acted as a group, a group that began competing with me. I was slowly becoming aware of the power struggle this created.

One morning, I arrived at work to find the Colorado guys waiting for me. Riley approached with a request. "Andy, the guys've been talking. We've been working here for over a year and we're makin' good money. But, our weekends're wasted. We don't wanna go out and find other jobs, so we'd like to know if we can work weekends."

I wanted to help if it would raise morale and keep productivity and commitment up. But I explained that I'd be sticking my neck out for them. As I expected, Jack was resistant to the idea. After I pressed, he agreed with the stipulation, "They're your responsibility, Andy. You'll need to keep an eye on them." I was prepared for the stipulation, but didn't like it. I looked forward to my weekends off, and I didn't want to have to worry about the job when I wasn't looking. But I wanted to trust them and give them a try with this new arrangement.

The guys were pleased with the news. Riley thanked me for talking to Jack and we worked out a plan where, each Friday, we would meet as a group to discuss specific projects for them to do over the weekend and outcomes that I could expect to see on Monday. These quickly became negotiation sessions with me laying out what I wanted, and the crew either agreeing, or more often, trying to scale back my expectations.

With these meetings, the distance between the crew and I grew a little more. We had now become, in a small way, adversaries. I was "management" and they were "labor." I wanted more production and they wanted less. It became a contest and I lamented a loss in the camaraderie that I thought we had. Or did we? It was becoming clear to me that the bond I saw with them was as illusory as the bond I saw with Jack. This was business too. They wanted money. That's all they were here for. Jack saw it. And now, so did I. But there was something else here, something more sinister. I saw no way for a contractual solution to this problem. I felt that I was on an unavoidable path towards a clash with the crew. Or more accurately, this part of the crew, as the job was increasingly dividing the Colorado guys who worked continuously from everyone else who worked only during the week.

Soon, Monday morning would reveal unmet expectations set on Friday. There would always be excuses—"we ran into complications," "we got a late start," "we ran out of materials," or simply "we underestimated how hard the job would be." I would voice my displeasure but, in many ways, felt in a weak position to counter these arguments.

Weeks after I agreed to the weekend work, I arrived on the site to find the crew waiting for me again. They had talked the night before and wanted to revisit an old issue.

"We want Jack to pay us on a contract basis," Riley announced.

"I know how Jack's gonna respond," I said. "You remember how he reacted at the party when you first brought it up." I wanted to help them. I wanted to increase their motivation and commitment on the job.

In discussing it with Jack, I asked, "Wouldn't it align their incentives with ours?"

Jack was adamant, "No way! They're employees, not subcontractors and not partners. If we get into this, everything'll change. Think about your little encounter with Nick DiMartino. That's what you can expect with these guys on a regular basis."

"Don't you think I can work with 'em? Maybe with a contractual relationship, they'll work harder."

"Bullshit! No way!" he repeated, "once money comes into the picture, people change. These guys would sell their own mother to make a buck, believe me when I tell you. They have no allegiance to you or to me. They just wanna make money. Think about it, if this is so good for us, why do they want it? I'll tell you why, because they smell an opportunity." He narrowed his eyes, and asked me, "Are you sure you're getting all you can out of these guys? Keep an eye on 'em. Something's starting to smell fishy here."

The guys were disappointed with the answer. I thought it would end there, but a fundamental change occurred with the news. They started coming in late. At first it was just a few minutes; minutes that hung like hours since they made up such a large and important part of the crew. Then one day, all five of them came in two hours late. The time was unbearable. I took the lateness personally, as a statement that I had no control over them and therefore, limited control over the job. I filled the time by putting on my tool belt and doing some work in the main hallway. With each board I cut, and each nail I hammered, I grew more angry and more frustrated.

I realized that I had lost control of the job. And, feeling the fool, I knew that I had done it. I had handed it over. I willingly hired them all, knowing that they were friends. I tried to hold everyone together by being cooperative and considerate. I worked hard to build a relationship with them that was respectful and trusting. They had been my teachers and I respected them. But now, I was feeling very much taken advantage of. It had been building for weeks and I hadn't seen it. But, now it was in my face. They were making a statement that I couldn't ignore.

When they finally arrived, they didn't walk in. They strutted in, joking with each other, laughing as if nothing were wrong. I was furious. I glared at them as they passed by me. "Have a nice sleep did we?"

They said nothing, casually put on their tool belts and sauntered off to their respective jobs. I was livid; and I was scared. There was a lot of work still to be done, and the way things had now become, I feared for the future progress of the job. It was genuine fear—this project might be in trouble and it was up to me to fix it.

ONCE AGAIN, I FELT NAÏVE, like a child being taken advantage of by much more seasoned and experienced men. It was time to do something. As I was losing a grip on the crew, I felt that I was losing a grip on everything. I felt isolated, alone and lost.

That evening Jack took the news in stride. "Andy, relax, you're getting too wrapped up in this. There's nothing we can't fix."

I felt torn. I needed to hear these reassuring words from Jack but I also wanted to stand on my own two feet and take care of this situation. It was, I felt, my responsibility in our business relationship. "Jack, this is my problem. I'll fix it."

Jack nodded in acknowledgment. "What's your plan?"

"I don't know yet. Can you just let me work it out?"

"Well, this is my job too," Jack said. "I'd like to say that I can just stand back and let this go, but I can't."

I was bouncing between competing emotions of need and independence. "Well, I have to weed out some of the Colorado guys, that much is clear. They have too much power."

"Uh huh," Jack nodded, as if he knew that already. "Can you identify anyone in particular that's the cause of the problem?"

"I'm not sure. They act as a group."

"Let's try it the other way. Is there anyone you think shouldn't go?"

I thought about it. "Well, I'm not sure if any of them will work out if I start getting rid of some of them."

Jack nodded. "That's a good observation. You'll have to move carefully and react if things start to get ugly." Then he paused again. "Is there no one that's worth keeping?"

Realizing an ulterior motive, I asked, "What's up, Jack?"

"Well, now may not be the right time to talk about this, but I have another project lined up. Before you told me about this situation, I was going to ask you who you might recommend to run it." He quickly backtracked, "and please understand, I'd have you do it, but I don't want to load too much onto your plate. You've got your hands full with the Shaw house."

I felt a twinge of jealousy that someone else would be running an S&S job. But Jack was right. There was no way I could take anything else on. The Winslow/Shaw combination had been very difficult. Now Shaw alone was proving an enormous challenge. One more job would put me over the edge. From a business perspective, this was the right decision. And also from a business perspective, another point was eminently clear. Jack was minimizing his dependence on me to run his company. Whether by design or just by consequence, my role in the company was being diminished. There was nothing I could do about it.

"If I were to pick someone to run a crew on another job," I said, "my answer would have to be Riley."

"Okay. That makes sense. So, how do we get rid of the other guys without losing Riley?"

"Wait a minute! I'm not saying we need to get rid of everyone. For example, I don't think Benjamin would line up with the Colorado guys."

"Do you know this?"

"No, I haven't asked him."

"Ask him!" Jack's voice was firm. "You need allies. I think you're right. I think Benjamin could be your ally. Get him before you do anything, before the others guys get to him first."

"Okay Jack. I will. I'll talk to Benjamin first. I think we should talk to Riley first too. Those are the two most important guys."

"Anyone else?"

I sighed. "I wish we could keep Arthur."

Jack pounced. "Him? I don't trust him. There's a lot going on inside that head of his. He may not say much, but he's always thinking."

"I know that's the way he seems. But I see something else. He's a great carpenter, one of the best I've ever seen." I sighed in resignation, "But, you're right, I can't be absolutely sure I trust him. He's a bitter man. And I think it'll be worse when the other guys go. He has to go too. It's the only way I'll regain control of this job."

"Now you're talking like a contractor."

I let out a weak smile. There was a lot of unpleasant work to do. "Do you want me to tell Riley about the other job?"

"No. Tell Riley to call me. I'll talk to him. Have him do it tomorrow. At the same time, talk to Benjamin. Then what?"

"Jack, that's as far as I can plan out right now. After those first steps, can you just let me play it by ear? Like I said, this is my mess. And I'll clean it up."

"Okay, I'll give you some room. You're the boss," Jack replied. Then broadening his smile, he added, "Just don't fuck it up!"

As I drove home, I thought about how things had changed. And I couldn't see how they'd ever be the same again. I felt betrayed and it hurt. I was surprised at how complete the break had become. I had lost trust in them and once lost, I couldn't get it back.

I BEGAN WORK THE NEXT DAY by asking Benjamin, "Can we take a walk?"

"Sure," he said, "lead the way."

We walked to a remote part of the house. The sounds of work could be heard from distant quarters. Once alone, I began in a grave tone. "Benjamin, I'm gonna need to make some changes around here and I want to know if I can count on you when I make 'em." I could hear Jack in my words, in my voice. My firmness and conviction sounded as though they were coming from him. In this darkest moment, I found that once again I had to rely on Jack as my source of strength.

Benjamin nodded knowingly. "I've been wondering how this'd play out. I knew somethin' was gonna happen. It was just a matter of when. What do you need from me? I'm with you."

There was no equivocation in Benjamin's response and it put me at ease. "Good. Good. I'm getting rid of the Colorado guys. I'm doing it one by one, and I'm figuring out the reasons as I go, but I wanna make sure that you're feeling secure and can maintain the morale of the rest of the guys." I paused, looking him straight in the eyes, "As I do this, I need to rely on you to help me keep this job alive. Can I count on you to do that? To be my right hand man?"

Benjamin extended his hand and I grasped it. As we held firm, Benjamin said, "You can count on me."

"Thanks. I needed to hear that. I need to tell you something else. I'm going to try to keep Riley but I'm going to put him on another job. I don't think he'll work with me after the others are gone. But I want to keep you with me." Looking Benjamin straight in the eye, I added, "Benjamin, there's no one I trust more than you on this job." These words sounded like the exact words that Jack might use on me. And I said them with an honesty and a purpose that conveyed the effect I wanted. Benjamin seemed impressed, nodding his head in reply.

After a moment's pause, Benjamin spoke hesitantly, "Andy, honestly..." He stopped. Starting again, he said, "Okay here goes. Look I don't want to tell you how to do your job. And I'll follow your lead on this. But, you don't..." He stopped again, having difficulty saying what he wanted to say. This was rare for Benjamin, always one to speak his mind.

"What is it?" I asked. "Tell me."

"It seems to me that you don't need an excuse to fire these guys. For one thing, you already have one. They fucked up when they came in so late last week. And for another, it's *your* goddamned job. If you want 'em out, tell 'em to get out. It's really no more complicated than that."

"Benjamin, for one thing, if I was gonna fire 'em for being late, I should've fired 'em at that moment. But since I waited, I feel like I've lost the moral justification."

"Bullshit! Moral justification? You want 'em off the job? Get 'em off the fuckin' job."

"Remember when we talked about firing people and what was most important; thinking about the people that're left behind? Well that's what I'm thinking about right now. I need to do this so I can look both you and the rest of the crew straight in the eye and say, 'I'll treat you fairly just as I've treated everyone fairly.' And I need to do it in a way that I can look myself in the mirror tomorrow. It's who I am and it's the kind of crew I want left behind when this is done. I need to try to stick to that."

Benjamin laughed, "Andy, you're too honorable for this business. I admire it, but you're too nice." He looked out the window, thinking for a moment, then he looked down at his feet. He seemed pained. "I really hesitate to do this…" He was shuffling his feet, kicking a stone on the floor. "No one likes a snitch. But, if you want an excuse to start this whole shebang off, I have one for ya."

He raised his head to look me in the eyes. "Check the blocking in the west wall of the guest bedroom. There, you'll find something that shouldn't be there. I won't tell you whose it is and I won't tell you who put it there. But let me just say that there are people on this job who don't like what's happening either. I'll say no more. I've said enough already. But, there's my first bit of support."

"Thanks." We shook hands one more time. A slow firm grasp, eyes locked on each other's.

Benjamin's words helped. He had announced that he was going to stand by me in whatever I did. And, it seemed, others were ready for a change as well. Once in the guestroom, it took no time to find what I was looking for. On one of the wall blocks was a zip lock bag full of pot. I put it in my pocket and hunted down Riley.

"RILEY, JACK AND I HAVE a proposal for you. Can we talk in my office?"

"Sure Andy, what's up?"

We walked to what was to become the study, but was for now my temporary office.

"Jack wants you to call him. He's lining up another job and he asked me who I think would make a good foreman. I said you." I wanted to impress upon him that *I* was giving him something, something for which he might feel a sense of obligation in return, an obligation that might help me as I got rid of the rest of the guys.

"Well, thanks Andy. I'm flattered you'd say that about me."

"Jack would like you to call him to discuss the details. He's at his office right now. I told him you'd call. Use my phone."

It was a brief call. When Riley hung up, I asked, "So what'd you tell him? Am I losing a carpenter?"

"Yes, I guess you are," Riley was scratching his head. "Jack and I are gonna iron out the details tonight over a drink. Next week he wants me to see the job and he says it may get started as early as next month, which will mean I'll need to be on site before then."

I extended my hand. "It's been good working with ya. I wanna thank you for all the help you've given me with this job. And I hope I can count on you for the final weeks before you go."

"No problem. Of course."

Riley seemed to be standing straighter, or maybe it was my hope. He was moving up the ranks at S&S Custom Builders. I felt a need to confide in him about what my next steps would be. But I wasn't sure how much I trusted him. Riley lived with the other guys and getting rid of them would have serious implications for his life. I pulled the bag of pot out of my pocket. "I found this on the job. I'm gonna have to do something." I knew this was a gamble. For all I knew, it belonged to Riley.

Riley looked at the bag and then looked up at me. No emotion was revealed in his face. He said, "I understand."

TWO DAYS PASSED. Arthur and Walt had gone west to visit family and the crew dwindled in size. Dennis was now one of the senior carpenters and I assigned him to frame in the closets in the servant's quarters. But, later in the day, I found him walking around the main house, tapping in some nails on the header of the pantry doorway.

"Hey, Dennis, what's up? You need more materials?"

"No, Andy, that's going fine. I'm just checkin' out some past work here. It's been botherin' me."

"Well, what is it? I think everything's going fine so far."

"No, Andy, it's not." His words were urgent and certain.

Narrowing my eyes, I said, "Explain."

"Look here, and here, and over here. We're not using enough nails. These jambs're gonna twist and peel. When they do, the doors won't fit anymore. And then look at these headers. We're not using enough nails here either. The frame's not strong enough. It's gonna move. This house is too big. The wind is gonna push it hard and this framing is just not strong enough. We need to go back and put more nails in." His eyes were darting around the house, looking everywhere, everywhere but directly at me.

I looked at the headers and jambs, all with a full contingent of nails holding them together. I looked over at a steel post that led to the ridge and was reminded of the extraordinary steel infrastructure that had been designed by the structural engineers. Surely if there was a house to challenge on its structure, this was not it.

Then, I adjusted my positioning to get a better look at Dennis' eyes. Each time he looked around, I adjusted. He seemed unaware of what I was doing. I was catching glimpses, bits and pieces of a pair of eyes that were bloodshot, although that was not unusual for these guys. Their many nights of drinking had made them seem almost permanently bloodshot—one of them even remarked just how white my eyes seemed in comparison. But, more than bloodshot, they were unfocused, glazed. The pupils were dilated and Dennis was not fixing his gaze on any one place for more than a moment.

My heart began to race. My stomach began to churn when I announced, "Dennis, you're stoned!" I felt sure but I was startled almost as much as he was that I had made the accusation.

Dennis, for the first time, looked straight at me. He looked as though he had just been shocked awake by a splash of ice water. Now, there was no question that his eyes were glazed and unfocused. I could see it clearly.

"Andy, no I'm not! I would never get stoned on the job."

"Dennis, don't bullshit me. I know what it looks like and you're stoned."

I articulated these last words slowly. They were sure and unequivocal.

"Andy, you're wrong." Dennis was sounding pained. "I'm not stoned. Maybe I'm tired and that's what you're seeing, but I'm not stoned."

"Dennis, you're fired." Again, the words startled me as I said them.

"No Andy. I'm not stoned. I'm not!"

"Dennis, you are. I'm sorry, but you are. I can see it. It's obvious."

"But…but…but my wife, my kids. I need this money. I need to keep bringing in this money." The shift in Dennis' defense validated my suspicion. I caught him. But, it also stung. I liked him.

"Dennis, I'm sorry. I'm sorry to have to do this. But I have to. You're stoned and you're fired." I wanted to console him. But what was I thinking? He was experienced. He knew how this world worked. "Come by tomorrow morning and I'll have your last check. Pack up your tools, and call it a day." And I walked off. Soon after, I saw Dennis' car departing down the driveway.

I finished the day by myself, keeping busy at different projects, but my mind kept drifting back to Dennis. As the rest of the crew left, they did so with more reserve than usual, each glancing over at me as I reviewed some paperwork near the front door, expressing emotions that I was in no shape to interpret. I just wanted the ordeal over. I felt alone. I told myself that I just had to endure one more week and things would get better. I called Jack from the empty jobsite. My voice was calm but somber. "Jack, I need a check for five hundred fifty dollars for Dennis. I fired him today."

Jack responded with equal sobriety. "You've got it. It'll be at the front door when you come by."

The next morning, Dennis came to the job an hour after everyone else started. I was relieved, not wanting to do this as everyone was arriving. He got out of the car. I met him half way up the front steps, rough concrete awaiting a fieldstone veneer. I was going to make this brief.

Dennis opened, "Andy, you're wrong. You're making a mistake."

"Dennis, there's nothing more to discuss. Here's your check. Good luck." We shook hands but the act lacked warmth. Dennis got in his car. He stared back at me as he made a three-point turn, shaking his head in disapproval as he did. As he drove down the driveway, all I could think was, it was done. I put another advertisement in the paper looking for carpenters.

AT THE END OF THE DAY following Dennis' departure, I packed up my papers and prepared to leave when Herman approached me. "Andy, can I talk to you?"

"Sure, what's up?" I was braced for a confrontation over Dennis.

"Well, I need to talk about something important. But I don't have a ride. Can I get a ride from you and tell Riley he can leave without me?"

I became even more cautious and tentative. Do I want to be alone with him? Actually, he was the least intimidating of the bunch. "Okay," I said.

Herman went outside for a minute and returned. We were alone on the jobsite. "Lemme begin by saying, I'm quitting."

I exhaled. The statement was not what I expected. But once the surprise passed, my first emotion was strangely, resentment. I took it personally that Herman had decided that he no longer wanted to work for me. Quickly getting my emotions back in check, I felt the relief of another one going. "Okay," I repeated slowly. "Why?"

"Andy, I can see the writing on the wall. Everyone can. You're pissed about that day we were late and you're getting even."

I winced. "It's not that simple."

"Well, it is. At least I think it is. There's something you should know about carpenters. That's what I wanna talk to you about. Carpenters are transient. Well, most of the ones I've known are. We get bored. We get tired. We know we wanna move on, but we sometimes can't get the energy to do it. This is a nice job. It's a great place to work. The projects are fantastic. Lets face it, no one's building houses like this. We all know that once this job ends, there'll be few like it again." Herman smiled. "Andy, I'm tired and so are some of the other guys. It's time for us to move on. You seem poised to make us do it, but you seem to be struggling. Dennis gave you a bit of a rough time yesterday, but he knew you were right."

I felt anger well up inside me. "Dennis knew I caught him and still put me through that?"

"Andy, don't sweat it. This job's a good thing and it's hard to give up. It was time for Dennis to go, and now it's time for me to go too. I can wait for you to do it. But, I'll save us both the trouble. You're learning. I can see you're learning."

I felt I was being condescended to. "Thanks, Herman. What do you think I'm learning?"

"Andy, you're a good guy, a smart guy. That has gotten you through this job. You've learned how to build a house, at least the technical side. Now you're learning the human side. That's the harder part and I know a lot of guys who've never mastered it. You need to know both sides to do this work well. For one thing, you need to be tougher, more aware of the motivations of the people that work for you. Not everyone is driven by the desire to leave a mark, to build a mansion. Some people just wanna make money, some people just want security." He narrowed his eyes. "And some people just wanna fuck with you. And the motivations change. Someone who's with you today will be against you tomorrow. People change. You've got to be less concerned with becoming friends with us and keep alert to when that happens."

"So, what motivated you guys?"

"Well, I can't speak for everyone. But I think we were all still into this until a couple of weeks ago. We were giving you and Jack good, hard work. But, we just got bored and frustrated with being so far from home and living in a dump. Remember that day Dennis had that black eye? I think that may have been the beginning of the end. It's just too hard living so close to all these guys. When one guy gets bored, it infects us all."

I wanted to believe that I hadn't been taken advantage of all along. Whether this was true or not, I appreciated hearing that something positive was happening, that in some way I was becoming better at what I was doing. "Thanks, Herman. Thanks for being honest with me."

"You're welcome. I guess I just wanted you to know that."

We shook hands, I closed up the jobsite and drove Herman home. We talked about his plans to go back to Colorado and find work for the ski season in one of the mountain towns. He said that he felt more at home there anyway and wasn't sure he could endure another New England winter. I dropped him off at the curb and said goodbye.

"TWO DOWN, TWO TO GO," was how Jack reacted to the news as we sat in his office.

He was upbeat in contrast to my intense mood. I felt like I couldn't relax until this was over with. I replied, "Yeah, now for the other two. Walt's comin' back the day after tomorrow and Arthur's comin' back next Monday."

"Do you know what you're gonna do?"

"Well, Walt has to go first, before Arthur gets back. That'd be easier." I paused, "Do you think he might come around after he sees that Dennis and Herman are gone?"

Jack stared back at me from across his desk. "I don't think that's what we agreed to, is it?"

"Well, I said I'd play it by ear, and I'm just trying to consider the situation now that it's changed."

"I'd say you're balking. What's up?"

"Oh I don't know. Maybe all this firing is getting to me." My energy was tailing off. I was becoming more despondent with every word.

Jack asked, "Are you afraid to fire Walt?"

Jack's question was like an electric shock. I was afraid to admit it, but he was right. Walt had spent time in prison for beating up his stepfather. Of all the guys, Walt was the most aggressive, the most unpredictable. I was embarrassed to admit it but I looked up and said, "Yeah Jack, I am."

"That's all you needed to say. I'll take care of it."

I should have been ashamed, but I wasn't. I needed Walt gone and I didn't think I could do it. Once again, I needed Jack to act as my gorilla in the closet.

WHEN WALT RETURNED to the job, I felt obvious, transparent, thinking there was no way he didn't know what had happened, why it happened and what was going to happen. He made jokes—"Well, pretty soon there'll be nobody left workin' here"—as he went about his business, in a manner more lackadaisical than usual. Around ten o'clock, Jack paid a visit to the job, something that was rare enough by now to arouse suspicion. He joked and cajoled his way through each of the crew on the site. I walked with him, not knowing what he had in mind, how it was going to happen.

Walt was the last to be visited, working alone on the far western end of the second floor master bedroom suite. He saw Jack and me approaching and put down his hammer.

"Well, Jack, what a pleasant surprise." There was a sarcastic edge to his voice; a suppressed energy waiting to be released.

"Walt," Jack said as he nodded. "How're things going?"

"Good, Jack, good."

"You keeping busy?"

"You know how it is. I just got back. I'm getting' into the rhythm."

The small talk had a tone that suggested both men knew what was happening, that each was sizing the other up. They were posturing and I thought it looked like Walt was considering a physical confrontation with Jack. With each passing moment, I was feeling more uncomfortable.

Jack leaned forward in a provocative manner, escalating the posturing, "Well, Walt, I've been thinking about making some changes around here. And one of those changes is that we won't be needing your services any more. You're fired." He was standing firmly on both feet, his large frame an imposing barrier between Walt and me. Reaching into his pocket, Jack pulled out an envelope. "Here's your last check. Collect your gear and beat it." It was sudden and direct. There was a firmness, a meanness in the announcement.

Walt glared at Jack, his frame rising to meet his. Here it comes I thought. I considered the possibilities if it turned violent. But Walt didn't say anything. His glare turned to a smirk. He shrugged his shoulders, picked up his tools and started for the door. His path took him right past me and I braced. I watched him through every step that brought him closer to me. As he approached, he stopped in front of me, looked me in the eyes and said, "I knew I had to go. I just wish you had the balls to do it yourself." And he walked off.

I was cut to the core. It was a perfectly delivered blow. Nothing he could have said would have more effectively emasculated me. But I needed this done and I needed Jack to do it. It wasn't perfect, but given the circumstances, it was the best option, the best I could do.

THE CHANGES I HAD ENVISIONED a week before were coming to pass. I was taking back control of the job. The Colorado guys were going and I was getting calls from people in response to the advertisement. The phone was ringing regularly, tying up my time and keeping me close to my office. I would ask people the usual questions about experience, tools, and a car. With each call, I wrote down their name and said I would get back to them. Call after call, I would begin, "Shaw's residence," to which I heard, "I'm calling about the ad…"

Then one call began differently, "Andy, this is Arthur."

I took a moment to regroup from my morning routine of questions. I had never spoken to Arthur on the phone before, much less from New Mexico, where his wife lived. "Hi Arthur, what's up?"

"Well, I might ask you the same thing. I've been talkin' to Riley and it looks like you're making some changes out there."

Here we go, I thought. If it had to be over the phone, so be it. "Yeah, I guess you could say that. Dennis, Herman and Walt are gone."

"I need to ask you a straight out question," he said. "Am I gone too?"

I was going to work into it slowly. "Well, Arthur, I think you're by far the best carpenter on the crew."

Arthur cut me off, "Then why's Riley gonna be the foreman on Jack's next job?"

"I think Riley's better at managing the overall aspects of a job. He's a better and more experienced foreman. I think you're better at the mechanics of carpentry."

There was silence on the other end. Then, he said, "Would it do me any good to tell you that you're wrong? That you've got the wrong guy?"

"No Arthur. The decision's made."

"And has it been made about me too? Should I even bother to come back?"

"Well Arthur, what do you think?" I wanted Arthur to see it my way. He wasn't going to like working here without his friends. "Like I said, I think you're the best carpenter on the job, but I also think you haven't been happy here. And now with Riley moving on to another job and becoming a supervisor, are you really gonna want to come back?"

Again, there was silence. I heard Arthur spit. He was chewing tobacco as always. "No, Andy, I guess not. I think I'll throw in the towel."

"I understand."

"I'll arrange for Riley to ship my stuff. It's only a few tools anyway. Riley tells me he's gonna keep the apartment and Debbie's moving in. My stuff wouldn't fit anyway." He chuckled.

I laughed. "You don't think Debbie'll like the way you've decorated?"

"Naw, I guess not."

"Good luck, Arthur," I said.

"Thanks, Andy," Arthur sounded awkward. "Take it easy."

"WELL, STUFF, HOW'S THE JOB goin' these days?" Jack's remark sounded harshly glib given all that had just happened. I was feeling tired and drained from the blood letting of the last weeks. But it was over and I was thankful for that.

"Okay, I guess." I said, trying to sound upbeat.

"Hey, you done good. Cheer up. You had some shit to deal with and you dealt with it. You rose to the challenge and pulled it off."

I was trying to feel proud of what happened. Walt's remark still stung, and I was in the process of reinvigorating a crew that had been decimated. Activity on the job was noticeably slower than usual.

"I don't know how the search for new people's going, but I have someone for you to meet. His name is Frank. He's an experienced foreman and a good guy."

I was quick to jump on the latter half of that sentence. "A good guy? Is that his qualification? My whole perspective on hiring is different now. A guy can be the best carpenter in the world, but if he and I don't click, if I don't trust him, I'm not hiring him."

"Good! Good!" Jack was emphatic. "You're learning an important lesson! I've told you before and I'll tell you again, trust is everything in this business. Think about it this way. You want two things in the people that work for you. You want people who know their job and you want people you can trust. If they don't have either, that's easy. Fire their ass. If they have both, you can't ask for more. Keep 'em. But few people have both. So you're usually going to have to hire people who have either one or the other. The question is, which do you pick?"

I waited for him to continue, knowing that most such questions were rhetorical. He would answer them.

"You pick the one you trust. You can't teach trust. You can teach carpentry but you can't teach trust. Remember that. You can have the best tradesmen in the world, but if they fuck you just once, you're out of business. Surround yourself with people you trust and you'll never go wrong." He paused. "And I think you're starting to get that. You're learning to use your gut. That's the only way to tell if you can trust someone. No resume, no long list of jobs, no sweet-talking is going to tell you shit. You have to feel it."

"Yeah, Jack, I've come to realize that. But I wonder sometimes where you draw the line on that." I looked up at him. "Do you realize that I'm the only one who works for you who hasn't gotten fired? I've watched all these people get fired by you, even Neil. I sometimes wonder if I'm just an inch away from getting it too."

"Andy, that's nonsense. Neil had it coming. He needed to grow up. And what about our agreement to give you part of the profits? Doesn't that make you feel more secure?"

"Yeah Jack. I guess so." I paused, the energy and therefore my inhibitions seeming to fall away. "Do you know I've lived every day prepared to get fired? If I didn't accept that, I'd freeze. It's the only way I can make decisions. I figure that if I do my best today, and I make a mistake and get fired, I can feel satisfied that I gave it my best shot. I can walk away with my head held high." I hadn't expected to say any of this. When I walked in the door to Jack's office, I had planned to talk strategy. But it was pouring out. I couldn't stop it. The events of the past week, following all that had happened with Jack since our fight over the bonus, had worn me out.

Jack looked concerned. It was a look I had never really seen on his face before. "That's a hell of a way to live, Andy."

"Well, it's the only way I could. I've been living every day like it was my last. Otherwise, I wouldn't be able to make the decisions I've needed to make. The consequences are too severe. I'd be crippled."

"Isn't that true in everything anyone does? At least anything worthwhile, anything that involves risk? Doesn't it require forgetting about the consequences and taking the leap?" He thought for a moment. "Andy, look at your success. You followed your dream, Ya done it well." He leaned back in his chair and added, "and you're now being rewarded for it."

"So you're saying that if I take a chance and follow my dreams, the money will come."

Jack guffawed, "That's bullshit! Anyone who expects to get paid for what they love is a fool and an idealist. You're lucky that you love something that people wanna pay for. Remember, if you want the money to come, you have to ask who has the gold and what you need to do to get it."

"And you want the gold?"

He looked at me seriously, "You bet your fuckin' ass I do. Andy, listen to what I'm gonna tell ya. Everyone needs money. You need to put food on the table and a roof over your head. You can't eat your idealism, you can't drive it, and you can't get a girl with it. Show me two idealistic men, one with money and the other without and I'll tell you which one's gettin' laid." Jack let out a loud laugh. "Andy, you're a good guy. Don't sell that short. That's one of the reasons why you're a success. But I'm not payin' for your being a nice guy or for your idealism. I'm paying for your strong work ethic, your trust worthiness and most importantly, the results those traits provide."

I ABSORBED EVERYTHING as I drove home that evening, the events of the past week, his words. I was surrounded by people whose primary motivation was money. With Jack, the crew, the subs, I had mistakenly believed that friendship and a passion for building was the dominant element of our interaction. And in each case, I was wrong. Now my defenses were down. My idealism was under fire. And it was changing me. I was being hardened, tempered. It had been happening for a while, I just hadn't put my finger on it.

But there was still something unformed in me. I was learning from Jack. I wanted to emulate him, but there were still limits on how far I would go to do that. I wondered if it was only a matter of time before this piece of my training was complete. I thought about how cruel his tongue lashing of Scott was; how I never thought I would possess that fierceness. And then, I tore into Frederic over the countertop at the Winslow house. And where he trusted no one, I was now adopting that same hesitancy. It was born out of his tutelage but drilled deep into me by the school of my own experiences. Maybe I was becoming Jack.

Later that night, I talked it over with Sharon. "Do you think I'm too romantic?"

"Andy," she smirked, "I could always use more romance."

"No, that's not what I mean. Am I too idealistic?"

"Where's this coming from?"

I told her about the conversation with Jack, concluding, "Would you still want to be with me if I was poor and idealistic?"

She laughed, "Well I can't speak for all women. For some, money's very important." Rolling her eyes, she added, "especially here in Fairfield County. But that's not the way all women think."

"So money's unimportant to you?" I asked incredulously.

"Well I don't know about that," she said. "But, I think money can tell you something about a person. I remember when I met you, my first thought was that we wouldn't have anything in common because you were just a carpenter."

I was surprised. I had no idea she had any reservations when we met. It reminded me of my experiences on Nantucket, reinforcing the disconnect between how people now saw me and how I saw myself.

"But then I got to see that you weren't *just* a carpenter. You had a passion for it. That's different. Someone can have money, even a lot of it, and have no passion for what they're doing. Boring! I think that's what drew me to you; your passion. That's what I found," she stopped herself, "that's what I find attractive about you."

She thought for a second, "I can't be with someone who doesn't have a passion for something. But I agree with Jack. That could mean that I'd be with someone who's poor. Someone can have passion and not make money. I hope I could live with that but I guess I'll never know until I come to that bridge."

I frowned, and she added, "But I'm not looking to find that bridge right now. I'm very happy crossing this one!"

I smiled and she laughed, "Now, stop all this and kiss me. Money's not an issue with us. Just be who you are and everything'll be fine. You think too much!"

I laughed, "I've heard that before."

Was it just passion that made the difference? No, I thought, it was more. Maybe passion got me to take the chance to leave my job in Boston and grow to learn about building. But I was feeling something more now. I carried myself with a quiet confidence that I had never experienced before, sure of myself in any social setting. I felt secure when I went to dinner parties with Sharon, talked with my friends and family, everywhere. When people asked me what I did, I was no longer hesitant and defensive as I was in Nantucket. I answered, "I'm a builder." The answer was not just what I did. It was who I was. I wasn't becoming Jack, I had become a builder.

TO HELP REBUILD THE CREW, Jack arranged for Frank to meet with me on the jobsite. It occurred to me that this may be more of Jack shoring up the crew with people he knew, people that might give him alternatives to relying totally on me. But I let that fear go. There was nothing I could do about it. I would still live my day as if it were my last.

I interviewed Frank the way I interviewed all carpenters; with a renewed strength. I would put people on the spot much the way Jack did. This was *my* jobsite and I would tolerate no challenges to my dominance.

When I was talking with Frank, I challenged him. "Frank, how do you feel about working for someone as young as me?"

"No problem."

"No, I want you to give it more thought than that. I don't want some bullshit interview answer. You've been around this business a lot longer than I have. How do you feel about me being your boss?" I was surprised at my own bluntness, but I didn't care if I sounded harsh. This was my job and I was going to make damn sure I had a crew I felt safe with.

Frank backed up, startled by my bluntness as well. "Andy, I think we can work together. I don't want your job. The shit you have to deal with, the owners, the architects. No thanks! I like to build. I'll leave all that other crap to you, gladly."

I was the same way with other potential hires. Having a car and tools merely got them in the door. Similarly, references and experience only got them a chance to meet with me. Once I faced them, I would test them to see if I wanted them.

With Mark, a young go-getter, I finished an amicable interview with, "Okay, now tell me something." I looked him dead in the eyes. "It's one o'clock in the afternoon and I smell alcohol on your breath. Are we gonna have a problem with that?" The question was sudden and direct and it gave me a dizzying feeling of power to deliver it, knocking him off balance. It reminded me of my first phone call with Jack and how curt he was. I could see now that he was establishing the tone of the relationship; he was the boss. And I was now doing the same.

Mark looked stunned and embarrassed. He stammered, "No Andy. No problem at all. I'm unemployed right now and met up with a buddy for lunch. We had a beer, that's it. I take my work seriously and would never drink around power tools."

I remained stern. "Good then, we'll see you tomorrow."

One by one, I replenished the crew. It took just over a week to get rid of the Colorado guys. It took another week to get replacements. And now things were back to the full level of activity. Construction never stopped while I made my changes. It simply dipped into a lull. Subcontractors never left the job and some of my crew continued to work. Lucy didn't notice the slowdown. So to someone who wasn't in tune with the specifics of what was happening, things seemed the same. But everything was indeed different. The new crew made for new work habits, new stories, and new language. They spoke with fewer obscenities, lived more balanced lives and brought a new vitality to the jobsite. I felt more comfortable with them and they highlighted for me how different I was from the old crew.

But beyond the crew, *I* was also different. I was confident in my place at the center. I did not assert myself as the leader on the job. I assumed it quietly. I walked and spoke with an intensity and control that expected people to listen. They were to act according to my expectations. I would accept nothing less. Just as Jack dominated the mood in a room, I was now exerting the same power, the same strength. I would not lose control of the crew again. This new crew was *mine* in a way that the old crew never was. I had handpicked each member because I trusted that I could get along with them, talk to them, lead them.

Frank joined Benjamin as my new foreman. He was even tempered, mixing his instruction with joking barbs to keep things moving. One day when the crew was tying up one loose end outside, he complained, "You guys're movin' too slow." Pointing skyward towards some circling turkey vultures, he added, "Look, even the buzzards can't tell if you're moving. They're thinking, lunch!"

Mark was a member of a local ministry and was "born again." Words like "salvation," "mercy," and "Jesus" found their way into his conversation easily. On his first day on the job, he had a terrible case of gas. "From the Mexican food I had the night before," he sheepishly explained. But, showing no mercy, Frank permanently labeled him "Beans."

Franz and Tony were two brothers from Germany and they talked of their travels in the United States. At times, I had to translate between Benjamin, with his rich southern drawl, and Franz and Tony, with their German accents. This became a continuing joke on the job, with the guys referring to them as, "Franz and Hans." They watched one day as I took Lucy on one of her walk-throughs and expressed their dismay at the personal service.

"How can you spend such time with her?" Franz asked. "She must be a difficult client. Anyone who builds a house like this must be a difficult client."

When I explained that I enjoyed working with her and that she had good ideas for design issues in the house, he dismissed the possibility. "A woman? If you tell me she can pick colors or wallpaper, I'll believe it. But I can't believe she can design the structure."

This set the crew on the lunchtime topic of difficult clients. "Beans" told of a tile job he did for an engineer. "Can you believe this guy took out a micrometer and measured the grout joints of every single tile? I'll tell ya, I wanted to take the Lord's name in vain that day."

Mike was quick to reply, "Yeah, but the worst are lawyers. Never take a job with a lawyer. Every time I do, I got screwed. They never pay. It's really strange. Do they do this just because they think they can?"

"Everyone tries to screw you out of money!" replied Frank. "You've got to always be prepared for it. I had this guy once that came home every day and found something that he wanted fixed. First it was a windowsill, then it was a crooked shingle. Every day it was something new. I kept fixing them until one day, I realized this was never going to end. So I found a way to get him off my back." His talk was animated and everyone waited anxiously for the explanation. "I put up a rake board that had this big fuckin' knot in it. When he came home from work, it caught his eye immediately and that became his issue of the day. He told me to fix it. I said okay but just left it. And each day he came home, this goddamned knot—sorry for the language, Beans—was his issue. He became obsessed, but I left it right there. One day the knot fell out and I thought he was gonna have a coronary. This big black hole just staring down at him like some kind of evil eye. But he stopped harassing me with new issues. That knot was all he could think about and that knot let me do the rest of my work."

THE LAST SLOT TO FILL WAS LABORER, I decided to broaden my pool of applicants and placed an ad that read, "Laborer wanted, male or female, must have own car, call Andy." Patty was the first to call and we arranged for an interview. She was a college student and single mother who wanted to work outside for a few months. When she arrived, I watched as she nervously navigated the plank that straddled a deep hole at the front steps.

I led her all over the house and asked her to lift some two-by-tens to give her a sense of how strenuous the job could be. She walked every plank, lifted every weight with determination. As we were finishing up, I glanced at her long pink fingernails. "I'll cut them tonight if I get the job." I liked her commitment and hired her. This raised an eyebrow from Jack and amusement from the crew.

But it was *my* crew. I was glad for the new stories and the new personalities they provided. They were like a breath of fresh air; an air that reinvigorated me. In this new atmosphere, I cemented the important lesson that I was learning on the Shaw house. House building was about people. While I learned the intricacies and management of wood working, masonry, electrical, plumbing and the multitude of other trades that contributed to the final building, only now did I fully appreciate how it happened, the product of so many working towards one end. The most important task of house building was creating a world where all these people would come together to create something grand. I was building a house, but I was also building a community that made it so. And that community required a strong center. That center was me.

IN THE WINTER MONTHS, the crew moved along more smoothly than the year before. I had arranged the project into two sequential pieces. The second floor was completed first. Then it was insulated and plastered while the crew completed the framing of the first floor. The crew then moved back to the second floor to do the finish work while the first floor was finished. Since each floor alone was far bigger than most homes, I had the leverage to tell subs to split their work to fit my plan and avoid the lag time that we had at the Winslow house. I felt proud that I was able to organize the job so that the crew could find comfort in one of the increasing number of plastered rooms kept very warm by the propane heaters. I also noticed that my propane bills were much lower despite the significantly larger space. Less heat was simply flying out the roof.

As the crew made the crucial transition from rough to finish carpentry, they changed their tools and refined their attention to detail. Saws were fitted with blades that had more teeth, lighter trim hammers replaced those used for framing, drills were brought out for predrilling nail holes, and four, six and eight penny finish nails replaced ten and twelve penny sinkers in our tool belts. And this new arsenal of tools was turned towards the details of baseboard, window and door trim, wainscoting, fireplace mantels, and importantly in this house, wood ceilings.

As I assigned a particular room's finish carpentry to one team, I was scrutinizing the plans for the next. Some plans still lacked specific details, for which I would get clarification from the architects. Then I would order the materials and have them carried into their assigned room. When a crew finished one project, I would escort them to the waiting project, the plans and the materials already in place.

I watched closely for the specific skills and talents of each carpenter and tried to match each with a suitable project. Franz and Tony worked extremely well together so I never broke them up. They got some of the more challenging projects. In particular, they were given the study in the first floor of one of the turrets, easily one of the most expensive rooms in the house. It was round on one end and adorned entirely in cherry. The coffered ceiling was built with beams that radiated like spokes from the center towards the curved outside wall. Between the spokes were another set of beams that connected them, creating the many coffered spaces, each one a beautifully constructed recessed panel of woodwork. The fireplace mantel, baseboard, window and door trim, and the cabinetry, also made of cherry, required Franz and Tony's careful hand in fashioning the many angles and curves of the space.

Dick was most efficient and detailed when he worked on his own. I assigned him the walk-in cedar closet. Located in the far western end of the second floor, the room was twenty feet by fifteen feet, as big as most average bedrooms. First, we installed plywood over the entire room. And, since this was one room that did not have a flooring layout design in the blueprints, I had taken the liberty of designing a serpentine pattern of red cedar. With the plywood and floor in place, Dick set up in the closet and didn't leave for two weeks, applying a layer of half-inch thick aromatic cedar strips over the entire space. He would emerge only to have morning break and afternoon lunch with the crew. When he was finished, the crew gave him a standing ovation. In his impromptu acceptance speech, he explained that no one would be happier than his wife. She could no longer take the smell of cedar on his skin and had banished him to the guest room for the previous two nights.

The crew approached their finish work with a level of detail that was a compromise between Benjamin's unrealistic standards of quality and my pressure to maintain a reasonable time frame. Frank played adjudicator, keeping things in check. If things got too slow, he would pick them up by stressing that everyone had to keep me happy. When things went too fast, he would point out how unhappy Benjamin would be if quality suffered. Everyone was engrossed in his work and appreciative of that done by others. During breaks, lunch or after work, people would often wander the rooms to admire what else was happening on the job. The progress was fantastically beautiful.

And we were all learning together about reaching levels of detail we had never reached before. To keep precisely straight lines, Benjamin had instructed the crew to put away their cotton string lines and use fishing line instead. Banks of windows with a common twenty-five foot sill, or ceilings with beams that criss-crossed from one end of the room to the other were as straight as lasers. The attention to detail went well beyond that in the drawings.

For example, the complex wall plans left many dead spaces closed in. I directed the crew to build trap doors for access to the crawl spaces. I justified the doors on the grounds that access to the space behind the walls could prove useful for future repairs and changes. In reality, I both hated the idea of wasted space and loved the idea of creating secret passages to get to them. Wherever there were hollow spots, I found a way to create access to them, or better yet among them. I was a creating a secret world within the house.

Later, when a truckload of maple was ordered for door and window trim, Mark excitedly showed me a piece of tiger eye in the load—a wild squirrelly pattern that happens occasionally in maple. I instructed the laborers to consolidate all tiger eye for the entry foyer fireplace mantel.

There was a culture of pride and detail that influenced every decision, every action on the job. Joints were tight and lines were straight, level and plumb. Wood was hand-selected for each application. Things were going exactly as I wanted them to.

TO FILL THE MANY subcontracts that remained on the house, I spent much of my time soliciting bids, describing what I needed, comparing the competing bids, negotiating final prices and then selecting the subcontractor.

Part of the task of selecting a sub was visiting some of their other projects to assess their quality. It was time consuming. And adding to the time, I often had to go back and ask for addenda when two bids were based on different information. An important part of this process was making sure I was comparing apples to apples.

One of the biggest contracts went to the cabinet-maker, Coastal Woodworking. I took competing bids, but had decided to stick with the cabinet-maker that Kenneth recommended when we first met. In fact, Kenneth had already collected a preliminary bid from Coastal. He said that their quality was the best in the area and that they were one of the few that he trusted to handle such a large job. I liked the owner, Terry Kuhn. He was extremely professional and competent. And, something I had learned to appreciate after the Aqua Pools fiasco, he negotiated the contract and he oversaw the design, construction and installation of the cabinetry. He would be the one that I dealt with from beginning to end. He would "own" the project. There would be no middleman like Sean Hawley. And, to my great delight, Terry's crew picked up on the level of detail being pushed at the job by my carpentry crew. For example, when they built a bank of cabinets for the cedar closet, they made each row of drawer faces out of the same piece of wood so that the grain ran continuously from one drawer face to the next. Whether the owner noticed or not, we didn't care. People loved what they were creating.

The flooring contract was a difficult bid to let out. The architects had drawn the layout for nearly every piece of wood in every room. The plans called for variations in width, variations in species, specific borders, shifting patterns, herringbone, and sills. The drawings were complex and adding to that complexity, Lucy had decided to design the sunroom herself, specifying a checkerboard pattern of alternating dark walnut and light maple squares running on a diagonal across the room. Peter approved the design but only after he and Robert were given an opportunity to draw up plans. A second unusual complication involved laying, sanding, staining and finishing the floor in one closet so that a temporary wall could be installed above it. As the closet was across from Bill's study, this allowed him the future option of taking the wall out and turning the room into a secretary's office.

One subcontractor said that he could not do the floor patterns that the architects had drawn but provided a bid based on straight flooring anyway. "This is just too valuable a contract to let go without a fight," he explained while I told him that I couldn't accept the bid. Others said they couldn't bid outright, but would do it on time and materials. I wouldn't accept that either. When I finally had competing bids, I had the hardest time understanding what they were offering given the complexity of the contracts. It took two weeks to finally sort through the bids, make sure they were offering the same service and let the bid out.

I counted a strangely high number of inspectors coming to the site, many of whom lacked any particular agenda: the Health Department, Planning & Zoning, the Fire Department and the nearby water company. I suspected that Charles DiMaggio was tipping them off that this was a place worth visiting. More tourists! But these could not be told to leave.

ONE MAJOR CONTRACT LEFT to be completed was the tile work. I approached Val Gianini, the contractor who had done the tile work at the Winslow house. A friend of Maurizio Donatella's, Val's quality was excellent but he lacked the self-confidence to take on such a big project. Inviting him to visit the house, I could make no headway in convincing him to submit a bid. There were six full baths, three half baths, a laundry room, kitchen backsplash and the indoor pool deck to be tiled.

It was the pool and master bath that pushed him over the edge. The entire pool deck was to be covered with ten-by-ten, handmade tiles from Mexico; very expensive. And the master bathroom was to be an exquisite array of marble—the floor, the walls up to three feet, the Jacuzzi surround and, most dramatically, the curved countertop that ran around the same turret wall as the study below; again very expensive. Val kept shaking his head as he walked, letting out occasional sighs that eventually turned into groans.

"Andy, this is too much. I can't do this. It's too much," he protested repeatedly.

"Val, you can do it. I'll work with you. I'll buy all the tile. I'll pay for it. All I want you to do is lay it. You can do it. And think of the money you'll make. This is more than fifteen standard house contracts all in one. You'll have work to last a crew for more than a month. You won't have to go out and get any more work. Call up some of your friends to help."

"Oh, Andy, it's too much," he kept repeating.

"Please, Val, I'm begging you, just gimme a bid. Don't just turn it down. Gimme a bid. What's it worth to you?"

But Val wouldn't budge. He turned the job down, forcing me to negotiate with three other subcontractors. I knew none of them and, after reviewing samples of their work, felt I saw similar quality and could make no distinction in their character. They were all adequate. I settled on the lowest bid, wishing I had more information to make my choice, but it was my last interior bid and I wanted it done.

Ross Fischer was given the contract. As with Michael Lapre, I didn't like him personally, but thought I could trust him to do the work. Ross excitedly accepted and, on the agreed date arrived with his crew of four tile men, one of whom, to my frustrated surprise, was Val. I said hello to everyone and showed them the tiles already delivered to the garage. I then left it to Ross to disperse his crew. When they were set up, I found Val working alone in the servant's quarter's bathroom and challenged him.

"Val! What's going on here?"

"Oh, hi, Andy. I'm working for Ross."

"I can see that! Why would you turn down the job for yourself and then take it with someone else?"

"Oh, Andy," Val said sheepishly. "This was too much for me to do. Ross is better at taking this risk than me."

"Don't you realize that he's simply taking money that would have been yours? He's gonna profit off your work when you could have kept it all for yourself!"

"Andy, this is the way I feel most comfortable. Please don't make me feel bad."

"If that's the way you want it, that's fine with me." I relented with a smile. "In the end, I got the guy I wanted. I know the job's in good hands."

In the ensuing days, Ross would begin by telling the crew where to work and then leave for another job. Those few times he did stay, he spent on his car phone. I came to the aggravating realization that Ross was a broker. He bid on jobs and hired other men to do them. He did no tile work himself. He found people like Val, people who were afraid to take a risk and took it for them. Then he skimmed some of the profits. I didn't like it. I saw Ross as little more than needless overhead. He was a leech, a parasite.

I resolved to make the best of the situation. Tile work proceeded and

Ross submitted bills for work as it was completed. Jack wrote checks and I handed them to Ross. Everything was going fine. The bathrooms were beautiful. But then, one morning, I arrived to find the tile men packing up their tools.

"Whoa, what's going on here?" I couldn't afford to have the crew leave to do another job. I needed them to stay on schedule. The finish date was too close!

Val announced, "We're leaving, Andy."

"What do you mean you're leaving? You can't leave. I don't care what other jobs Ross has going. You've got to stay here and finish this one."

"We'd love to Andy, but Ross hasn't paid us," Val replied.

The comment stopped me long enough to realize that they were extremely upset. One of them, Billy, said, "Andy, I've got house payments, and a wife and kids. I need this money. What the fuck's going on?" He was close to tears.

"Wait a minute," I was trying to catch up. I hadn't even finished my coffee. "Ross hasn't paid you...anything?"

"Nothing," Val said. "He says you haven't paid him so he can't pay us."

I felt a genuine and deep anger. I was being called a liar and a cheat. I was about to explode, but there was no one to vent at. These guys were in the same predicament as I was. I took a deep breath and began in a very controlled tone. "Val, that's not the way I do business. You know that from the Winslow job, from Maurizio. This is a first class project and I don't pull that kind of shit. Ross has been paid three payments so far. Believe me when I tell you. I've paid him nearly five thousand dollars."

Billy lost control. "Oh shit! Oh shit! Now we're screwed. Ross is never gonna give us that money. He's fucking us! He's keeping the money for himself!"

Val, in a more calm and resigned tone, said, "No, I'll bet he's paying his other contractors with the money from this job. We might see the money from one of his next jobs, if we stay with him." He was shaking his head. "I suspected this. He must be behind and trying to play catch up."

"Look," I said, still trying to collect the rapidly forming thoughts in my head. "Screw Ross! From here on, I'll pay you directly. I need this job done. I need you to do it. And you need money. We're all in the same boat."

Billy cried. "We can't do that! We can't cut Ross out!"

"You don't need to worry about Ross. Leave that to me. I'll take care of him. I'll put a stop on the last check. If I can, I'll pay you that one too. But don't go. What've you got to lose? You can leave and have nothing. You can stay with Ross and take the chance that this'll happen again. Or, you can join me and be sure that you'll get paid. And you get to keep his profit."

The guys looked at one another and asked for privacy to caucus. I walked to the garage while they talked among themselves. Val was the strong one, trying to convince the others to stay. I waited patiently, thankful that Val was here and that he was a friend. He waved me back.

"Okay, we'll stay," he announced. "But we need a payment soon." This sounded like a plea rather than a statement. I agreed to find them something.

They pulled their tools out of the truck while I called Jack to explain. Jack said it was too late to stop the last check so I asked for a small advance. "If we give them a little something, they'll know we're for real and they'll trust us more than they trust Ross. And, I think I'll trust them more if I can get them beholden to me a little."

"Good thinking. A small check'll be on my door."

That afternoon Ross arrived to inspect the work. I stayed at my desk and waited for him to approach me, the fury inside me growing to a controlled rage. Ross stormed into the study, my office. "You can't do this! You can't steal my crew!"

I stood slowly erect and faced him squarely. "As near as I can tell Ross, they're not your crew if you don't pay 'em."

"They're my crew. They're mine. I'll pay them when I decide to pay them. You have no business getting involved in how I run my company."

I leaned towards him. "I do when it affects the way I run my company. They were about to walk off my job this morning. That means that the way you run your business *is* now my business." I glared at Ross, holding back none of my loathing for him.

"I don't give a shit. You still can't do that. We have a contract."

Prepared for this, I replied. "No, we don't. I never signed anything."

Ross stopped. Eyeing me suspiciously, he said, "What?"

I had struck the blow I wanted. He was in such a rush to get started, he had forgotten to get the contract from me. In the past, a handshake was often good enough so I hadn't thought anything of this omission. But now that the contract was still in my brief case, I knew I held the cards and I continued to press, "No, I never did. I wondered why you didn't ask me for the signed bid but I feel comfortable with that oversight right now."

Ross was flustered. "I'll have to check my records Andy. Fine, go ahead and pay my crew. They'll get the money from me, too. This'll all work out in the end."

"Glad to hear that. It's all just business, right. I've got something to get done here and this seemed the best way to do it. Nothing personal." I paused and glared at him. "But if you get in the way of my finishing this job, I will brush you aside without so much as a thought." I let the silence hang until he turned and left. I had finally faced the "crooked contractor" that Jack warned me about so long ago; and today I had emerged the victor.

That evening I explained to Jack what had happened, and he couldn't hold back his praise, "That's my boy! Great job!"

Val, Billy and the two other tilers were relieved to get the advance check and promised to deliver the job as promised. It seemed as though the arrangement had become what I wanted it to be in the first place. Val and I worked closely, arranging the tile work to be completed in a methodical fashion. They wrapped up their work on time. I would never hear how they settled things with Ross, whether he had ever paid them the money they were owed. But, since they were able to keep Ross's profits in the checks I had given them, I hoped that they came out ahead.

WHILE VAL AND I were wrapping up the tile indoors, work was being completed outdoors. Barry Sutton had already finished blading off the final grades outside the house and pulled his equipment off the job. The outdoor pool was finished without any problems by a competitor of Aqua Pools, Water Environments. The tennis court was installed to the east of the house. And with the advent of spring, Bill and Lucy hired a landscape architect named Nelson Maybury of Princeton, New Jersey, to do the final outdoor designs.

Nelson taught at the School of Architecture at Princeton University, had published several books and was difficult to acquire for private projects. He designed a variety of elements around the house and took care of contracting the work from Princeton. To make things easier, I provided oversight when necessary. The scale of some of the plantings amazed me. In front, he planted two full-sized trees to flank the front door and its adjacent turrets, each roughly thirty feet tall. Between them I hired Maurizio to lay down a cobblestone courtyard that led to the driveway in front and directed cars to the garages to the side. A series of hedges and smaller holly trees was arranged around these roads. Just southwest of the house, a grove of forty fully grown birch trees was planted in rows. Next to the garage, four fully grown holly trees were planted. Around the outdoor pool, a bluestone patio and walkway led swimmers to and from the house. And to the east, the surrounding landscape of the tennis court was adorned with bushes and low trees. Within these major detail elements, he planted various ornamental bushes and designed different fencing and lighting schemes. Uplighting illuminated the front gate, segments of the driveway and the birch grove. Rounding out the detail was a finely manicured sod lawn, fed by an automatic sprinkler system up to a distance of fifty feet from the house. Beyond that, field grasses reclaimed the former farmland to the tree line beyond. The house was clearly approaching its end.

BUT AS THE PROJECT neared its end, my headaches only seemed to grow. They ranged from the simple—material orders that arrived incorrectly, to the more complex—architects who couldn't make up their minds. In fact, the architects were becoming more hesitant about making final decisions. The delayed decision on the exterior door schedule and the conflict over whether to paint them was the first, but others followed. Peter was becoming less reliable for quick answers. I had to plan for longer lead times on my questions.

Other headaches came from simple mistakes. One day, I was working on some wall panels in the entry foyer when the cabinet installer called out to me from the study, "Hey Andy, can you come in here? I think there's something you'll wanna see." The tone was calm so I walked casually into the room, expecting a simple question. But instead, I looked in horror at the recessed lights in the newly installed cherry coffered ceiling. Water was pouring through them!

I bolted for the master bathroom, which was directly overhead. There I found Freddie Carlucci and his two sons chatting while they filled the Jacuzzi tub with water for the first time.

"The tub's leaking," I screamed in a panic.

Freddie turned off the faucet while he and his sons launched into their own version of the Three Stooges. "Did you tighten the unions on the pump?"

"I thought you did."

"I didn't, I thought you did."

The scene would have been comic if I hadn't reminded them of the cherry ceiling that was now dripping below. Their faces turned ashen as we all ran downstairs. I didn't need to say a word. They understood the financial gravity of the situation. Ladders were stood to reach the twelve foot height and the three plumbers used anything they could find—towels, rags, even their own shirts—to dry the precious ceiling. In the end, no permanent damage was done.

Another mistake involved the wet bar countertop. Lucy personally drove to the marble yard to hand pick the material. It was precut to fit the sink dimensions that I had phoned in and was installed. But when Lucy saw it, she became enraged. "It's unacceptable," she told the stone yard foreman over the phone. "This isn't the color I chose. I expect you to remake it as I contracted you to do." He agreed to make a new one, while I figured out how to remove the old one. Unfortunately, the mastic had set and it would not come out in one piece. So, I handed the laborer a sledgehammer, and told him to take the top out in pieces. He hacked away, mortified at the thousand dollars worth of smashed marble that was poured into the dumpster.

I made my own mistakes as well. My most panicked moment happened with the front door, a magnificent and expensive piece of custom carpentry— three doors, the center one being three feet wide and each finely detailed in mahogany. Designed by Robert, the raised panels in the side doors were positioned on a diagonal slant towards the middle door and the top rail formed a continuous arch across the set of three. The center door's middle panels had a seam running down the center where the grains were split, slanting in from either side.

But the center door had not been cut for the mortise lock it was to receive. I had hired a locksmith to cut the many mortises at the Winslow house—hollowing out the edge of the door so that the lockset could slide inside as opposed to a barrel lockset that slides through the face. But I already owned the jig set and decided to do the mortise myself. With great care, I lined up the jigs and began to bore out large quantities of wood from the massive door's edge. When I was finished, I sighed in relief. The hard part was done. There in front of me, the edge of the mahogany door was prepared to receive a six inch tall, one inch thick and three inch deep steel box that housed the workings of the lockset. Now, the easy part was to drill several holes in the front and back face for the handles. I lined up the template and drilled the first hole, one and a quarter inches wide. Just as my drill pierced through the wood, I realized that I had placed the template on the wrong side.

Panic set in! Sheer panic! I became completely irrational, pleading to myself, "No, I didn't just do that! Please just give me the last ten seconds back! Why can't I have the last ten seconds back?" I was shaking. This was a custom made door and I had just ruined it. I packed up my tools, telling no one what I had done, and called it a day.

I hired a metalsmith to make a brass plate but it didn't look right. The solution came from my cabinet-maker, Terry Kuhn, who sent one of his best installers with a series of mahogany samples. Matching the grain on the door to one of the samples, he cut a perfect circular patch, glued it into the hole, and sanded it in. The mistake virtually disappeared and a bottle of champagne was sent to Terry the next day.

IN THESE FINISHING STAGES OF THE JOB, Lucy and Bill were a steady presence, very much involved in the progress of the job. Lucy chose colors for paint, fabrics for walls and other details as Maura had. But unlike Maura, Lucy had no entourage. She made all her decisions herself in consultation with the tradesmen, Bill and me. Sometimes her decisions were consistent with those of the architects and sometimes they clashed. But always, her decisions were firmly made and they were final.

Bill's concerns became increasingly focused on cost control. "Andy, are there places where Robert's making decisions that are unnecessarily costly?" he asked one afternoon from his office speaker phone.

"Well," I hesitated. I didn't want to undercut Peter and Robert.

"What is it, Andy? Tell me, I want to know."

Well, the flooring details tell me to put oak floor in your master bedroom suite. And then I'm to put carpet over it."

"Is that expensive?"

"It's about fifteen hundred square feet. That will cost you several thousands of dollars, especially after we put it in the pattern they've called out."

"Does that make the house better?"

"It'll make the floor deader, but there's already a wooden ceiling underneath it. I think the architects see it as a nod to consistency and architectural integrity. In an old house, they would never have a plywood sub-floor under the carpeting so I don't think they want to do it here."

"Well, this isn't an old house. Am I doing anything irreversible if I stop this now?"

"No, you can always put the wood in later."

"Okay, skip the oak."

And so it went. Sometimes the architect's plans would win and sometimes they would lose. But a tide was turning. The architects were being phased out while Bill and Lucy's opinions were phasing in. Some decisions were minor details to which Peter and Robert had little objection. Lucy, for example, decided to finish one of the rooms in the basement as a game room. She asked me to help design it. Together, we laid out the room, designing paneled wainscoting and other treatments for making the room consistent with other elements in the house. I described the room to Peter who dismissed the project as architecturally unimportant.

A decision that was more contentious involved the interior light fixtures. Bill had flatly rejected Robert's proposal to custom design them. But, ignoring Bill's decision, Peter faxed drawings anyway.

"What do you want me to do with these?" I asked Bill.

"They did what? They sent you drawings anyway? These guys...this is why most of the architects I know make such poor profits. What kind of a way to run a business is this?" He sighed, "Okay. Well, what do you think of them?"

"They're interesting, very dramatic."

"What do you think I should do?"

"Well, I could make some mockups out of cheap materials—cardboard and balsa wood—and you can decide for yourself."

"Okay, since they made the drawings, we might as well hear them out. I can't believe these guys!"

In the end, the Shaws accepted one of the designs and rejected all the others, preferring instead to purchase fixtures.

Over lunch, I told the crew of the decision on the lighting fixtures. They had seen the mock-ups and gave varying reviews on their merit. When I mentioned Robert's persistence, Benjamin, as always, had his opinion. "They can't let go of it. It's never the client's house. It's always a statement of themselves."

"Well, they need to face the reality that they're paid to do a job," said Frank.

"Well, they're not in this just for the money," I added. "They're making art. And I'm glad of it. Could any of us have come up with this place?"

"Well, no," Frank conceded. "But at some point they've got to let go and give the owner what he wants."

"It's a change in the relationships," Benjamin said. "There are three relationships going on here: one between the owner and the architect; one between the house and the architect, and one between the house and the owner."

"Where do we fit in?" asked Frank sarcastically.

"Well, we don't really. Sure, a shitty contractor can ruin a house like this. But a good contractor helps the architect and the owner realize their dream. They do it by managing those three relationships. At the beginning of the process, the architect takes the owners' abstract ideas and turns them into drawings. The owners can't articulate anything without the architect who gives them voice. Together they're making the design of the house, but it's through the architect. The architect is teaching the owners how to say what they wanna say and the owners are completely dependent on the architect to make the plans, and to tell us what to do."

He was enjoying his audience, looking as though he was delivering a lecture. "As the house starts to materialize, the owners can see what they've done, where before they couldn't. The architect was their eyes, but now they can see on their own. Through the process, the owners are learning. So the relationships naturally start to change. Just like a parent letting go of a child, an architect has to let go of the owners and let them get directly involved with the house, get involved without the architect as intermediary. That's hard for anyone to do. Just like a parent is afraid that his kid will screw up his life if he makes his own decisions too early, an architect is afraid the owner will screw up the house if he lets him make decisions too early."

Frank said, "Yeah, and then there's always that little thing called money.

If the owners don't take control when they want to, the architects will spend 'em dry. I think architects sometimes look at the owner as unimportant to what they really wanna do, which is make a monument to themselves.'"

"Well, Robert has made a nice monument here," I said. "And he's now facing the reality that Bill and Lucy are ready to finish it. We'll see how long he lasts. William was gone before the end of the Winslow job. I'll bet Robert and Peter will get the boot, too."

ROBERT WAS DISGUSTED with the store bought fixtures and didn't hide his opinion before refusing to discuss it again. Peter was more pragmatic, accepting the financial concerns of the Shaws. We talked about the conflicts over designs. I sympathized with their position and asked if he felt frustrated.

"Yeah," he sighed. "Sometimes I feel like we can't dot the I's and cross the T's. I like to take out that frustration at home by doing work on my own house, much to my wife's chagrin."

"Well, I'm surprised to say that I've realized that it would be bad to have the same person designing and building. It came to me when I was helping design the basement room with Lucy. I felt conflicted. I wanted to help her come up with the room that she wanted. But I also found myself resisting ideas that were going to be a pain in the ass."

Peter laughed. "Are you saying that I give you tasks that are a pain in the ass?"

"Well maybe," I was laughing too. "And maybe that's important. If you leave the design work to the person who has to build it, he'll come up with designs that're easier to build, but not necessarily the most bold or the most creative. And as the job reaches its later stages, as this one is, those designs'll be more and more focused on ease of building."

"I'll take that as a compliment, I guess."

"I think it is," I answered. "Do you ever drive by a house and say to yourself, a contractor designed that house?"

"Yeah, all the time."

"And how do you know?"

"Because they're ugly."

"Well maybe." I laughed. "But I think you know because they don't reveal what motivates the architect—the desire to create something beautiful, something that is higher than themselves. They represent what the builder wants, what motivates him. If it is the joy of building, it may look interesting for its structural features, but not its architectural features. And if it is being built for simply making money, it has neither."

"I like that. Now tell me, what was motivating you on this room? What am I going to see when I next visit?"

"Good question! You'll see a room that is a combination of Lucy's desire to make a fun room, my desire to give it to her at a modest price and the inescapable influence of every design feature you've drummed into my head about what a room in this house is supposed to look like!"

"Inescapable. I like that. You've learned wisely, grass-hopper."

ONE AFTERNOON, I PAUSED to count the number of subcontractors I had supervised on this job. The number exceeded sixty. For design work, there were architects, landscape architects, structural engineers, and mechanical engineers. The trades included: carpenters (finish and rough), electricians, plumbers, HVAC contractors, security system installers, built-in stereo installers, telephone company, exterior masons, interior masons, structural steel constructors and welders, cabinet makers, wood flooring contractors, roofers, coppersmiths, insulation contractors, plasterers, tilers, painters, wallpaper hangers, upholsterers (for fabric walls), mirror and glass installers, sauna installers, lightning rod installers, concrete crew, excavation, oil tank installers, landscapers, water well drillers, water filtration system providers, lawn sprinkler installers, generator and transfer switch installers, crane operators, tennis court installers, indoor and outdoor pool builders, garage door fabricators, fencing contractors, portable toilet company, waste disposal and lunch truck. And finally, there were suppliers of concrete, marble, wood windows (2 different companies), steel windows, interior doors, exterior doors, custom front door, stereo equipment, structural steel, wood trusses, specialty lumber (Gregory), standard lumber and materials (Ridgefield Supply), indoor gym equipment, kitchen and laundry appliances, tiles, stone (flagstone, cobble stone, gravel and stone dust), rebar, nails, and lighting fixtures.

Each subcontract marked the passage of time. Each reflected the stage of the process in which their skills fit. But as time passed, the one constant, the carpenters were now finding that their time was also coming to an end. I was sad to see them go and they were sad to leave their creation. Even Riley expressed some hesitancy when it came time to leave weeks earlier. "The project was just getting fun," were his parting words. But I was relieved to see him go. Riley was part of a past that I wanted to put behind me. I was thankful for the lessons that I had learned from the Colorado guys, but the final lesson was about when to part ways. And I was ready for that to happen.

I sent the rest of the crew off in teams to Riley's project, now well underway, keeping just as many carpenters as I needed to help me finish the remaining rooms. When the time came, I sent the last ones away, leaving just a laborer with me to manage the remaining subcontractors and tie up loose ends—hanging towel bars, paintings and other accessories on the house.

THE FINAL MONTH passed quickly. My laborer and I took charge of all activity both inside and outside the home. A sign at the front door asked that all entrants remove their shoes. The finished floors had a shine like glass, reflecting glare from windows, doors and light fixtures. The security team ran tests on the motion detectors and lasers that were set about the house. The HVAC crew tested the heating and air conditioning systems.

The electricians installed the last outlet and switch covers, and took care of a few odd items that procrastination had left till last. One particularly awkward item was the underwater lighting of the indoor pool. The electrical foreman put it off as long as he could, and in the meantime, the pool had been filled with water. The unfortunate soul who got this job had to screw them into place while submerged.

Freddie Carlucci and his sons put the final touches on the appliances in the kitchen. Gas was fed to the stove and water was fed to the refrigerator's ice maker. Working in the basement to run the water line, Freddie made his presence known on the first floor when I watched a ten inch long drill bit blast through the finished floor of the main hallway. It was a clean hole. But Freddie had miscalculated the location of the refrigerator, piercing the floor ten feet too far to the north. Having no idea that he just marred one of the more dramatic features of the house, he continued to snake a water hose into the hallway. I watched, shaking my head. It was too close to the end, and Freddie had made too many comical errors for me to really get angry. To fix the error, we bartered over a solution. Freddie agreed to install the wine refrigerators for me while I set about repairing the damaged floor.

Following the cabinet-makers' example on the front door repair, I found a sample of oak to match the grain in the damaged piece. I cut a plug, installed it flush, and to make absolutely sure of a match, I painted the grain to blend it in and applied urethane over it. I spent two hours on the repair, pleased with my correction.

THE LAST DAYS were about punch lists and repairs. Most I took care of myself—a window that wouldn't open, a painting that needed to be hung. Others required a subcontractor's return. The cabinet-makers replaced a door that had warped. The painters fixed a ding in the plaster after it was hit by the appliance delivery crew. Val fixed a piece of marble in the master bath that had been hit by the painters. Like a surgeon, he picked up the tiny chips that had been broken loose, glued them into place and when dry, filled and sanded the rough cracks until the entire surface was smooth and shiny again. Maurizio Donatella fixed one of the slate hearths after the flooring crew chipped it with their sander. Another marble hearth was stained with grape juice and, to my amazement, he removed the stain with a poultice. These finishing steps and repairs were fatiguing. We were all tired and ready to put this job behind us. Every new mistake, every new repair was met with an agonized sigh.

As the house approached completion, it revealed itself in continually new ways. And for these last days, the house belonged to my laborer and me. As we set about our tasks, we would tell each other about new revelations. "Have you seen the master bedroom porch in the late afternoon? The light shines right into the bedroom."

"Have you noticed the echo in the indoor pool room? The sound vibrates off the redwood trusses."

We also had strong opinions about what should be happening within. "I'd put a chandelier there." "I wouldn't have chosen that dark fabric for the dining room walls."

One night, Sharon and I returned to the house at nine o'clock, turning on every light we could find. Then we stood in the field, admiring the illuminated house from this new perspective. It was a glorious sight, one that I had never seen before. I had been on this job for more than a year and a half and it had never looked so grand, so stately. I had never felt so proud.

I invited the whole crew to come and tour the final product that they had built. Shoeless of course, they walked in silent awe at their creation.

I invited my family to visit. Sharon barbecued at my house and we took them on a personal tour, Sharon knowing the house very well by now. As my brother stepped into the front entry room—again, having first taken off his shoes—he called out in a deep baritone, "Rosebud." Before we had covered two-thirds of the tour, my mother, feeling too tired from the distance traveled, had to stop and wait for us in the study.

WHEN THE DAY to turn the house over to the Shaws finally arrived, I spent the morning getting ready for the final inspection from Charles DiMaggio. One hour prior to his arrival, I was on my knees shaving some wood off a sticking door with my utility knife. I shaved off a small piece, tried the door, found it still to be sticking and shaved off a little more. I repeated the process four times until finally, I slipped. The utility knife slid into my left knee, just above the knee-cap. The full half-inch of blade penetrated my leg. I knew it was going to bleed. I also knew that I did not want to stain the finished floor. So I went outside and sat on the front steps to inspect the wound, putting my shirt under it to protect the fieldstone.

I called into the house, "Freddie, you have any band-aids?"

"Sure, I'll be right down," came his reply from the second floor.

I had no time for this, I thought. I bent my knee to inspect the wound and it peeled open, a deep red stream beginning to flow. This would require stitches, I thought. It would also require a stronger constitution than I could muster. I felt my head start to spin. Fearing that a full fall onto the fieldstone steps would cause more damage, I laid down. The next thing I knew, Freddie was over me, waving smelling salts under my nose. I sat up slowly, looked down at the wound, felt my head begin to spin and lay back down again. I passed out three times before I could finally stomach a view of the wound which, without my help, was being tended to by Freddie.

My first comment while coming out of my stupor was, "Smelling salts? Who uses smelling salts anymore?"

"Don't complain," Freddie said. "They woke *your* ass up."

With bandaged knee and a doctor's appointment for later in the afternoon, I met with Charles. We walked through the rounds of the house. I knew the routine and had preceded him in this process by checking every outlet and light-switch, trying every thermostat, toilet, sink and shower and assuring myself that everything was in operation.

"Well, Sonny, I think you passed. Congratulations. Come by my office this afternoon for the certificate," Charles closed his notebook. "You know, you should be proud of yourself. I have to admit, I had my doubts about you when I first met ya. I thought you were just another one of those smart-ass kids who think they know everything and have no respect for anyone else's opinion. I'd say I was wrong."

"Thanks, Charles. Sorry if I came across that way. I didn't know I had."

"Hey, don't let this go to your head or nothin'. All I'm telling you is that you turned out *not* to be an asshole." He broke into a laugh and slapped me on the shoulder. "You're a good kid. Don't let anyone tell you otherwise."

That afternoon I had three stitches in my knee and a certificate of occupancy in my hand; issued to: "Andy Hoffman/S&S Custom Builders and William and Lucy Shaw."

It was official. I had built the Shaw house.

I prepared a package to be given to the Shaws that evening. It included: the Certificate of Occupancy; three keys that opened all the doors to the house; an album of construction photos taken during the entire project; and a description of all the systems in the house, how they were built and how they operated. And with little fanfare or ceremony, Jack and I handed everything over to a grateful Bill and Lucy. The house was theirs.

EPILOGUE

FTER THE SHAW HOUSE, I built one other house for Jack; a seven thousand square foot country home on a fifteen acre parcel overlooking a white water river. And in this job, our relationship reached a climax in its level of closeness, a closeness that I had not thought possible after our confrontation over the Winslow house bonus. That closeness became clear to me in a single moment.

I met with Jack to give him an update on progress. He had assumed no oversight on this job and in every sense it was mine. And so I expected a very short meeting. He just listened as I laid out everything that he would have been telling me just four years earlier. His pleasure at my control of the job was palpable, his contentment clearly displayed on his face. As he walked me to the door, he grasped my hand and looked me in the eye, "Stuff, I'm proud of what you've become." The words and his grip created a warmth and power that I had never known could exist in a handshake. But then he did what I would never have expected. He released my hand, wrapped both his arms around me, enveloped me in his massive frame and said, "Andy, I love you like a son." I have no idea how long that hug lasted, nor do I completely remember walking out the door.

That event brought about one of the final steps in my apprenticeship to builder; I had become Jack's equal; I had become the builder that he already was. He would never have just given me that right or status. I could only earn it by taking it when I was ready and, importantly, when he was ready. It was the only way that I was going to earn his final and highest praise, what he was most cautious about giving, what was most precious to him, his complete trust. I could see no one else who had gained that level of closeness with Jack, not his own son Neil and certainly not any of the others who worked for him. And yet it was a closeness I needed to learn to understand before I could accept it.

Jack shared himself with me in the only way he knew how. It was the same way that he dealt with the rest of his world, as a business; a business where he separated everyone into those who were with him and those who were against him. And in this world, very few existed in the former category. He trusted very few people, both in his professional life and in his private life. For him there was no distinction. Once I accepted and understood that, I could move beyond the hurt of the Winslow bonus fight, stop strangling my affection for him and free myself to give him the level of trust that I was most cautious to give, the role of a father figure in my life. And with that mutual recognition, that mutual acceptance of who each was and who we each had become, we forged a bond that I will not soon match.

This was my last job with Jack. I enjoyed building it and did it well. But in terms of the challenge, its scale and complexity were nowhere close to the Shaw house and the task of building it felt more methodical, more routine. I was shocked into this realization one day when a carpenter pushed back on a level of detail I was demanding. "What do you think you're building here? A work of art?"

I quickly asserted my authority and told him, "I'm building the house I want to build, and you have to decide whether you want to be a part of it."

But his question had stopped me, brought me back into the reality that this was not the Shaw house. My expectations for detail might have been misplaced. I realized that I needed more of a challenge. While others may have been satisfied to do this for the rest of their lives, I knew that I would not. I wanted more. Ultimately, I spent just under five years building houses for Jack, and he accepted my departure supportively, even writing a recommendation for my next step.

As I write this, I am twenty years older and look back often on those years and houses, constantly coming to new realizations for what they meant for me and my life. Sharon and I broke up. Our lives had turned in different directions. She went to culinary school and, last I heard, was a caterer. I am now a college professor, having earned a doctoral degree, and I build young minds with books and lectures where I once built houses with wood and nails. How I got here is another story; the pursuit of my next calling. But no matter where my life takes me, building will always be a part of me.

I reconnect with that part of myself each year in an annual pilgrimage to the world I left behind, visiting the Shaws and Winslows, and some old subcontractors. I drive by Alfred Rogers' house in Nantucket and strain to see over the low brush that conceals it. I see bits and pieces of the house in TV and magazine interviews that he has done. Pictures of the Japanese garden at the Winslow house were published in a book on Japanese design, which I proudly show to friends along with the hundreds of photographs that I have taken myself. It is a source of frustration that I cannot show them the real thing.

The Winslow house has since been sold. The fifteen-acre lot has been subdivided and five new homes line the once private driveway. One summer day, I introduced myself to the new owner, appearing at the door with the announcement, "I built this house." At first cautious, the woman gradually warmed to me, showing me around, describing what she liked and what she planned to change. I felt regret at the house taking on new form. But it showed me that it was still alive, ever growing and evolving. I hope she doesn't find the time capsule. It's too soon to be discovered. And when I visit the Shaws, they express continued joy with their home. It is settling into the Connecticut countryside, aging and improving with a beautiful grace.

Yet, no matter how much the Winslow house changes with development or the Shaw house changes with age, they are, in some way, still mine. The paint fades and weathers, the wood moves, the plaster cracks, but the connection endures. Repairs and changes make it less familiar, revealing the hand of another carpenter, another designer. But I continue to admire the many features that were guided by my hand: the continuous wood grain in the cedar closet drawers, the tiger eye in the entry fireplace, the perfect alignment of the window sills, the butterfly in the stone veneer, the waves in the shingles, and even the painstaking centering of the electrical outlets.

The houses conjure up other visions as well, but they are from another time and another place. As I walk through the hallways, I also see what the owners will never see. I see each house's growth and the people who nurtured it. When I look at the master bedroom in the Winslow house, I see all the competing designs that were considered before this one finally prevailed. When I look at the main stair balustrade in the Shaw house, I see Dick using a power sander with the sandpaper upside down, jokingly sabotaged by Benjamin. When I look at the redwood ceiling over the pool, I see one of Arthur's only mistakes, his furious cursing after he cut a two-inch diameter bolt pocket in the wrong place on a very expensive piece of wood and had to make a plug to fill it. When I look at the teak guest room shower, I remember how often I had to remind Mike to minimize his cuts since each one would crystalize the wood's oils into a kind of sand that would dull his blade. He never believed me until he finally burned out his blade. These memories, these grand accomplishments of a time gone by, come flooding back to me with the same power of satisfaction and pride that I felt when Jack and I celebrated their completion and handed over the keys.

These pilgrimages would be unthinkable without a visit to Jack. He was always glad to see me, and I him. In many ways, he remained a source of support, advice and wisdom as I moved on to other pursuits. To my great disappointment, his business struggled after I left. And through that struggle, I could see one more lesson of what had been drummed into me for so long. The business is a ruthless one and that ruthlessness finally caught up with him. It was as if he were predicting his own future when he first warned me about the dangers of the business, "If you get one crooked subcontractor, one asshole, he'll put you in the red so deep and so fast, it'll take you years to dig yourself out." In his case, it was one crooked employee that brought about his demise.

Jack eventually fired Riley and replaced him with a new supervisor named Carlos. Behind Jack's back, Carlos tried to convince the client that Jack was stealing from him and that he should fire Jack and hire him directly. It was a silly attempt, really. For Carlos, the only possible result of such a deception was to be fired. The one unmistakable lesson I learned from this business was that trust was everything and there was no way that the client was going to hire someone who was being so clearly untrustworthy. But this also sowed the seeds of doubt about Jack's ability to hire trustworthy people, and when this job was finished there were no more referrals to large scale homes. Jack's hard-earned reputation was no more. His company focused on small projects while he drifted into other endeavors.

Perhaps to regain past glory, or perhaps to regain an employee he could trust, he often tried to hire me back. While I always declined, I derived a strong sense of security from his constant attempts. He never knew that I relied on his presence and interest as an optional doorway back into this world of construction, this world that had given me such joy. But in July

1996, that doorway was abruptly closed. While living in Chicago, I was awakened very late one night by the phone. Sleepily, I answered as a woman screamed hysterically and incoherently on the other end. I was about to hang up, believing it was a crank call, when she gathered her composure and voiced the words, "Andy, this is Jane. Jack's dead!" I stood frozen, shocked awake by the bluntness and brutality of the announcement.

Jack was riding his motorcycle with friends when he raced ahead on a winding road and crashed into a guard-rail. This motorcycle was his pride and joy. It was a Harley-Davidson Sportster, customized to his own design. He actually made a twin of this bike and gave the other to his son, Willie. They both resembled Jack in every way. They were clean, both in style and polish. And they were powerful and loud, commanding attention with bored-out cylinders, racing carburetors and straight pipes that would shoot flames when the throttle was opened up. When I visited, we would take rides together. The only concession he made to his advancing age was that he now wore a helmet.

But despite this concession to safety, the pain of his death was compounded by a cruel irony. He violated one of his own cardinal rules, one that he taught me when I bought my first Harley. "Andy, listen to what I'm gonna tell ya," he warned me. "If the bike's gonna go down, let it happen. It's not that important. And always, always, make sure it goes down before you!" Instead of heeding his own words, he tried to save the bike, only to go down first, getting pinned between the sliding bike and the stationary guard-rail. This time, he chose not to wear a helmet. He was fifty-three years old.

Jack's death was a devastating blow. He was a part of who I was. With his death, I felt a loss of so much that helped form me and a loss of what yet could be. I made arrangements to fly back for the funeral and called Lucy Shaw to see if she planned to attend.

"Yes, of course I'll be there. Where will you be staying?"

"I'll find a hotel."

"Nonsense," she said. "You'll stay with us. We'll be in the city when you arrive. I'll leave a key under the mat."

I'll never forget my drive down the long dark driveway, approaching the colossus of a house and reaching under the mat to let myself in. Once inside, I instinctively began my ritual walk-through, assessing how the rooms had worn from life. I could not resist. Once done, I leaned back on the sofa, turned on the TV and realized that they had built what they wanted. "A country house, a house you could live in and put your feet up in." I stretched out and rested my feet on the coffee table. This would be the first and only time I have slept in the house.

As I got comfortable, the pain of Jack's death hit me with a greater force than I had previously felt. I looked around at what we had created. For every degree of pleasure I derived from the house at this moment, I hurt that much more because the man who helped make it all possible for me was now gone. I mourned him that night. I was the man that he helped form, alone in the house that he had helped me build. I wanted him so badly to be there with me and to share in the joy of seeing what this creation had become. We built it together in S&S Custom Builders, a company that died with Jack. And for this, and for all that Jack had meant to me, I wept.

Jack's body was in a closed casket, a condition in his will should his appearance be marred in any way. That was just like Jack, always wanting everything neat and clean. Many of our subcontractors were there, as were his sons. Eric was philosophical, having since reconciled with Jack. We talked comfortably as he pointed towards the casket and acknowledged, "I have a lot to thank that man in there for." Neil, sadly, never reconciled with his father. He looked horribly pained, almost contorted, as he arrived with a baby girl that he had never introduced to his father or to Jane. It was tragic that he should have to bear that burden. Willie remained affectionate towards his father. Against the protests of his own wife, he announced that he would rebuild Jack's motorcycle so that the twin bikes would still exist.

Jack's death closed a chapter in my life. But this chapter is a foundation upon which the others are built. Jack lives on within me, just as I one day hope to live on within others. What I learned most from him was that, in the end, for my career to be a calling, it will not be what I designed, but will be the collective of what I experienced. It will not be aimed towards a fixed end of stability and certainty, but a continuous pursuit of growth and awareness. That growth will not be for others to critique and review but for me to judge and deem satisfactory. I now know that my very first decision to become a carpenter in Nantucket was but the first step in a journey I did not know I was taking. And that is what makes it so wonderful. For all its seeming irrationality, it was my announcement to myself and to others that my life was my own. Jack helped me to see that.

When I started this journey, I merely wanted to be a carpenter. But I surpassed my wildest dreams and became a builder, a distinction I did not even know existed when I started. And this realization led me to one overriding and inescapable truth, that a life well lived must be a creative endeavor. Whatever form that creativity takes—whether it's carpentry, building, teaching, raising a family, or writing a book—the challenge of looking within ourselves to find that creative element makes us who we are. But chances are, if we are genuinely open to the possibilities of a calling, we will find that that satisfaction will come from someplace far different from where we expected to find it.

So now, as I close this book, I find myself standing inside a one-hundred-and-twenty-year-old Victorian house that I have bought and am renovating. It's my first house. I have reunited with my tools, which spent the last twenty years in my sister's basement. I strap on my tool belt that feels just as familiar as it ever did. No time seems to have passed. I reach down and find the hammer, utility knife, tape measure and nail sets just where they are supposed to be. I withdraw them and it is still second nature. A pencil once again lies behind my ear and I have a new note pad that lists the things I need to do and the materials I need to buy. I've organized the subcontractors to move through the house in orderly succession. And in anticipation of their arrival, I prepare to build new walls according to my renovation plans. I lay some two-by-fours on saw horses and pick up my circular saw. It feels comfortable in my hand, the blade gliding surely through the wood. The scream of the saw quickens my heart and the smell of sawdust filling the air returns me to days gone by. I am still a builder; and I am still in love.

GLOSSARY

Anchor bolt	A bolt embedded in a concrete wall for attaching the building frame.
Back cut	To cut on an angle, away from the side that is visible to the viewer.
Balloon frame	A wooden building frame in which the wall studs run the entire height from the first floor sill plate to the top plate at the eave.
Barrel lockset	A door lockset that is installed by boring a hole through the face of the door.
Bearing wall	A wall that structurally supports the roof or floors.
Blind nailing	A method of attaching planks to the subfloor with toe nails driven through the edge so that they are completely concealed by the adjoining plank.
Blocking	Also called cats, these are short pieces of wood attached between joists, studs or rafters to stabilize the structure, inhibit the passage of fire, or provide a nailing surface for finish materials.
Board foot	A measurement of lumber that is 12 inches wide by 12 inches long by 1 inch tall—the equivalent of 144 cubic inches.

Builder's level	A tripod mounted device that looks like a telescope and is used for sighting level lines across the jobsite.
Cant strip	A strip of material, often an asphalt composite, with a sloping face used to ease the transition from a vertical to a horizontal surface.
Carrying beam	A horizontal beam that supports other beams.
Caulk	A water or silicone based sealant.
Chop saw	Also called a miter saw, this is a power saw mounted on a hinge which is used for cutting precise angles in wood.
Circular saw	This is the most common hand held power saw.
Collar tie	A piece of wood connecting two opposing rafters to resist the downward pressures for them to spread.
Coping saw	A handsaw with a very thin and narrow blade, used for cutting detailed shapes in wood molding and trim.
Coffered ceiling	A coffer is a sunken panel in a ceiling, dome, soffit or vault, often bordered with trim for ornamental purposes. A coffered ceiling has many such panels in a box-like geometric pattern.
Dogs	Small pieces of steel used for temporarily attaching adjacent concrete forms.

Dormer	A structure protruding through the plane of a sloping roof, usually with a window and its own smaller roof.
Eave	The horizontal edge at the low side of a sloping roof.
Elevation	A drawing that views a building from any of its sides.
Face nail	A nail driven through the side of one piece of wood into another such that it remains visible.
Fascia board	The trim that covers the exposed horizontal edge of an eave.
Flitch plate	A flat piece of steel, usually between a quarter and a half inch thick, that is sandwiched between the framing lumber of a header for spanning greater distances.
Footing	The widened part of a foundation that spreads a load from the building across a broader area of soil. This is poured first and the wall is poured on top of it.
French door	A symmetrical pair of doors hinged at the jambs of a single frame and meeting at the center of the opening.
Gable end	The triangular wall beneath the end of a gable roof.

Hammer drill	A power drill that both spins and impacts the bit. It is used for drilling into concrete.
Header	A wooden beam that carries the load across a window or door span. Usually made of two (for two-by-four walls) or three pieces (for two-by-six walls) of framing lumber nailed side by side with a piece of plywood for filler.
Jamb	Either of the wooden sides of a door frame opening, into which the door closes.
Joist	One of a horizontal group of closely spaced boards (usually two-by-ten or two-by-twelve spaced every twelve or sixteen inches) used to support a floor deck.
Level	Perfectly horizontal.
Lolly column	A cylindrical steel column used in basements for supporting carrying beams. They can be hollow or filled with concrete.
Mastic	A viscous adhesive substance used for adhering marble, tile or other materials to a subsurface.
Mortice lockset	A door lockset that is installed by boring a cavity in the edge of the door.

Mullions	Vertical or horizontal strips of wood between individual pieces of glass in a window.
Plumb	Perfectly vertical.
Punch list	A list of small tasks that must be finished as the house nears completion.
Purlin	A beam that spans across the slope of a roof to support the roof decking.
R-value	The numerical measure of resistance to the flow of heat in insulation. The higher the R-value, the greater the insulation value.
Rafter	One of a sloped group of closely spaced boards (usually two-by-ten or two-by-twelve spaced every twelve or sixteen inches) used to support a sloped roof.
Rake board	The trim that covers the exposed sloped edges of a roof at the gable end.
Rebar	Short for reinforcing bar, a piece of steel that varies from quarter inch to one inch in diameter that is embedded in concrete to provide tensile strength.
Screed	A flat piece of steel on the end of a long pole that is used for finishing concrete floors.

Scribe	To trace a line.
Sheetrock	An interior facing panel comprised of a gypsum core sandwiched between paper faces. It comes in thicknesses from quarter inch to three-quarter inch and sheet sizes of four by eight feet or four by twelve feet. It can also be made as water resistant (blueboard) and fire resistant.
Sill plate	The plate of wood that lies on top of the concrete foundation wall and marks the perimeter of the house. Or, the bottom plate of wood on a framed wall or the bottom of a window frame.
Soffit	The undersurface of a horizontal element in a building. This could be an exterior soffit, as in the horizontal overhang of the roof. Or, this could be an interior soffit, as in the horizontal surface of a boxed frame over kitchen cabinets or a bathroom sink.
Stick frame	A wooden building frame in which the wall studs run the height of each successive floor.
Story pole	A strip of wood marked with the exact course heights for shingle siding.
Stud	One of a vertical group of closely spaced boards (usually two-by-four or two-by-six spaced every twelve or sixteen inches) used to create a wall.

Table saw	A power saw mounted on a table that is used for cutting wood length wise (ripping)
Toe nail	Fastening with nails driven on an angle.
Tongue and groove	An interlocking edge detail for joining planks, in which a tongue like protrusion on one board fits into a rectangular slot on the one next to it.
Top plate	The top plate of wood on a framed wall.
Tray ceiling	A tray ceiling that has four sloped sides and a flat top.
Truss	Any of a variety of structural frames, usually based on the geometric rigidity of a triangle, made up of straight members, for the purpose of functioning as a beam or cantilever to carry the roof or floor.

green
press
INITIATIVE

Huron River Press is committed to preserving ancient forests and natural resources. We elected to print this title on 30% postconsumer recycled paper, processed chlorine-free. As a result, we have saved:

15 Trees (40' tall and 6-8" diameter)
5 Million BTUs of Total Energy
1,412 Pounds of Greenhouse Gases
6,799 Gallons of Wastewater
413 Pounds of Solid Waste

Huron River Press made this paper choice because our printer, Thomson-Shore, Inc., is a member of Green Press Initiative, a nonprofit program dedicated to supporting authors, publishers, and suppliers in their efforts to reduce their use of fiber obtained from endangered forests.

For more information, visit www.greenpressinitiative.org

Environmental impact estimates were made using the Environmental Defense Paper Calculator. For more information visit: www.edf.org/papercalculator